The Opposite of Everyone

ALSO BY JOSHILYN JACKSON

gods in Alabama

Between, Georgia

The Girl Who Stopped Swimming

Backseat Saints

A Grown-Up Kind of Pretty

Someone Else's Love Story

The Opposite of Everyone

Joshilyn Jackson

HARPER LUXE

An Imprint of HarperCollins*Publishers*

FIRST HARPERLUXE EDITION

ISBN: 978-0-06-244030-3

HarperLuxe™ is a trademark of HarperCollins Publishers.

Library of Congress Cataloging-in-Publication Data is available upon request.

16 17 18 19 20 ID / RRD 10 9 8 7 6 5 4 3 2 1

With gratitude for good teachers. Here are some of mine:
Ruth Ann Replogle
Dr. Yolanda Reed
Chuck Preston
Astrid Santana
Dr. David Gushee

Heartily know,
When half-gods go,
The gods arrive.

—RALPH WALDO EMERSON, "Give All to Love"

And as elephants parade holding each elephant's tail,
but if one wanders the circus won't find the park,
I call it cruel and maybe the root of all cruelty
to know what occurs but not recognize the fact.

And so I appeal to a voice, to something shadowy,
a remote important region in all who talk:
though we could fool each other, we should consider—
lest the parade of our mutual life get lost in the dark.

—WILLIAM STAFFORD,
"A Ritual to Read to Each Other"

The Opposite of Everyone

Chapter 1

I was born blue.

If my mother hadn't pushed me out quick as a cat, I would have been born dead and even bluer; her cord was wrapped tight around my neck. She looked at my little blue lips, my blue toes and baby fingers, and she named me after Kali. Kali Jai.

My mother was in the middle of a six-month stint in juvie for shoplifting and possession when I was born. She had thirty-six hours with me in the hospital before the state took her to finish out her sentence. My grandparents—stiff, unhappy couple that they were—got temporary custody.

Kai told them my name, but my prune-mouthed gramma filled out the paperwork. Gramma would later claim to have misheard, saying, *What I put on that birth certificate sounds like whatever that was you said, but in American.* My mother didn't know until she was released back into her parents' custody. By then, everyone in town was calling me Paula Jane.

You were originally named for the mother goddess who brings hope and springtime, Kai told me often, when I was growing up. My lullabies were praise hymns—"Kali, Jai Kalika!"—sung in my mother's smoky alto, and Kali starred in many of my bedtime tales. I'd fall asleep imagining a goddess made of sun and flowers, gold and green, and beautiful.

When I was five, I found a picture of Kali in one of my mother's sketchbooks. Kai was drawing a series of gods in colored pencil. I recognized some of them as characters from her stories. Hard to miss Ganesha, a big-bellied fellow with an elephant's head, dancing with his trunk curled high. And I knew Hanuman, the monkey god, leaping over the ocean with a bouquet of mountains in his hands. Then I saw my own name. Kali.

"Hope and springtime" was jet blue and savage, her skin a stark contrast to the burning city serving as her backdrop. She waved silver scimitars and torches in her many arms, standing barefoot on a dead man's chest. Her skirt was made of human heads and hands, and her flame-red tongue was impossibly long, unfurled to swing between her naked breasts. My mother found me staring at this image, my fingers tracing the familiar letters of my own name beneath it.

Am I bad? I asked her.

No, baby, no. Of course not. She sat down on the floor beside me and pulled me into her lap, sketchbook and all. *You can't think of Kali in such a Western way.* She spoke with all the authority vested in her by her flea-market prayer beads and her lotus-flower tramp stamp. She explained that in the Eastern Hemisphere—a half of the world that she had neither seen nor deeply studied—*Kali* meant "change."

Kali destroys only to renew, to restore justice. Kali brings fresh starts, she said. She leaned her head down over me to whisper. Her hair was long and dark, and it fell around us in a tent, smelling like campfire smoke and orange peel. *Your name literally means "Hail to the Mother," over in India.*

But I was born in Alabama. My mother invoked Kali on the black and bloody soil of the American South, and she didn't get renewal, hope, or springtime. She got me.

And wouldn't she be proud of me right now, if she were here? And if she were speaking to me. I was parked in front of Zach Birdwine's house in the East Atlanta Village, stalking him, determined to force a fresh start of some kind or another. I was better at the burning part, quite frankly. I certainly wasn't here to crawl up in his lap and ask him, sweetly, *Am I bad?*

It wasn't the kind of question I asked anymore; I was a divorce lawyer, and as such, I knew to never ask the question if I didn't want the answer. Granted, this answer was changeable, depending on who told my story. Most clients would protest that I was the epitome of goodness, thank you, while their exes wouldn't answer with anything printable. My friends and business partners liked me fine, but my own mother had changed her answer long ago.

To be fair, the first time I asked her, I had yet to ruin her life.

And Birdwine? When he quit me at the end of August, he'd made it plain that I was worse than bad. I was evil and he was all three monkeys. He had a paw on each ear and each eye and two clapped over his mouth. Maybe more than two over the mouth; he said he couldn't talk to me.

I hadn't seen that as a problem. Birdwine and I weren't the kind who went around having swampy feelings, much less yammering about them. If he needed to talk, well, wasn't that what AA was for? He'd known I wasn't anybody's priestess or therapist years before we rolled into the same bed. But one day he decided—almost randomly, it seemed to me—that he was done with me.

Well, fine. But I wasn't done with him.

All ye gods and little fishes, stalking Zach Birdwine was dull work, though. I didn't know how crazy people managed it, squatting in the closet of whatever movie star had caught their fancy, fondling undergarments, sniffing shoes, and waiting, waiting, waiting. I'd been here so long, I'd had to go refill my gas tank to keep the car warm. All apologies to Mother Earth, but I couldn't properly stalk Birdwine with no heater here in February. Not unless I wanted to turn blue again.

I'd worked on a motion I was drafting until my laptop battery ran down. I'd eaten the tacos I'd gotten from the taquería across the street and all the Tic Tacs I had picked up at the gas station. I'd paid all my bills online via my iPhone, finished the book I was reading, and practically worn out my touch screen playing the sudoku app.

Now I sat stewing, staring back and forth between Birdwine's junky bungalow and the road, willing his old Ford to come belching down the street. Maybe it already had. Maybe he'd seen my Lexus and kept right on driving. I thought of it as an anonymous kind of car, and in my neighborhood, it was. But here, on this edge of the village, gentrification was a failing work in progress.

My car stuck out like a sleek, black thumb, parked between some barista-slash-musician's little Civic and ancient Mrs. Carpenter's crumbling heap of Buick.

Still, he had to come home sometime. He lived here, and the second bedroom was his office. So far, he'd ignored two voicemails, three emails, six texts, and a pricey muffin basket with lemon curd and local honey. Now he got me on his doorstep until he either faced me or abandoned his dog and all his worldly belongings.

The funny part was that Birdwine himself could well be sitting in his own car with a sack of tacos and a sudoku puzzle, stalking someone else. He was a private investigator; stakeouts were his bread and butter.

Perhaps the waiting is less onerous when one is being paid for it, I thought, and then realized that I should be paid, actually. Zach Birdwine was my ex, sure, but I was a stalker-by-proxy, acting on behalf of Daphne Skopes. As soon as I got my laptop charged, I'd log these hours and add them to the huge bill she'd already run up with my partner Nick. He'd looped me in because this case had started rotten and was quickly going rancid.

It had begun when Daphne Skopes came home from a girls' weekend in Turks and Caicos to find her husband had changed the locks and canceled her credit cards. He'd drained their joint accounts, as well.

To be fair, the other "girl" on the getaway had a Y chromosome, a silky mustache, and a place in Daphne's bed. Her husband was not feeling reasonable, and his last settlement offer had been the title to her car. Period. No alimony, no part of the retirement accounts, no cash, and neither their house in town nor their Savannah beach house.

Bryan Skopes was trying to starve his wife, who had no real assets, into accepting any bone he cared to throw her. His role was to alternately bluster and look martyred, while his lawyer practiced obfuscation and delay. Between them they had stretched every step of these proceedings past all reason. They had botched discovery, sending partial documents or unreadably poor copies. They had filed endless motions for continuance. They had rescheduled every mediation at the last minute. Nick hadn't even been able to get his motion for fees before a judge yet. Months had passed, the bill was deep into five figures, and our firm had yet to see a dime.

I'd watched Bryan Skopes puff and rage with gusto, then let his eyes dampen in a wounded but manly fashion. He was fully committed, going for the Oscar, but I didn't buy his story. When we met, there had been a pulse, a moment when he ran a stealthy gaze over my body. It left a faint patina of some filth, sexual in nature, like a slime against my skin. I kept my face impassive, but inside, I'd started smiling. I'd seen his small, soft rotten patch. His weakness was women, and if I could prove it, the wronged husband act would ricochet and hurt his case. He was crafty as hell, though; Nick's investigator had produced no evidence of extramarital activities. I needed Birdwine.

My stomach rumbled and I checked my watch. The tacos had been hours ago. If Birdwine was on a case—or if he was on a bender—he could be gone for days. So be it. I could walk down to the mom-n-pop on the corner and get a protein bar. I'd grab a rawhide chew for Birdwine's big-ass mastiff, too, while I was at it. Looper had a dog door to get in and out, and an automatic feeder dropped his dinner every afternoon, but he'd appreciate the thought. I'd sit here all night, if I had to. I had less than three weeks before the Skopes deposition, and I needed Birdwine on it, ASAP. If only he were speaking to me, I could hire him to find himself for me.

I heard a knuckle-rap on the glass right by my head, and I jumped. I peered out to see Birdwine's old brown leather bomber jacket and his Levi's. I hit the button to crack the window. Birdwine was a natural mesomorph, built thick with a big, square head like Looper's. He was tall, too, so he had to step back and bend down to see me.

I put one hand over my heart. "I didn't see you coming."

He shrugged as best he could, bent over. "I'm good at sneaky. It's in the job description."

He looked fit and clear-eyed. Wherever he had been all day, it hadn't been a bar.

"I need to talk to you."

"You don't say," he said, very dry.

"I'm serious, Birdwine. Come on. Ten minutes."

"Well, I'd invite you in, except I hate you," he said, but he smiled when he said it. It was his real smile, too, showing me the gap between his two front teeth.

It made me smile back, though I didn't like the way he brought his hand up to press three fingers against his temple. I'd worked with Birdwine for almost nine years now, and I knew his signs. He'd been in AA for a decade, but it hadn't taken. Not completely, anyway. Two or three times a year he'd drop down a boozy hole, vanishing for days.

I'd learned early to see a binge coming in his body language, in his speech, in the very air vibrating around him. His disappearing acts had never yet blown a case for me, and if they ever did, it would be on me. I knew his limits. I risked hiring him anyway, because when he was sober? No one could touch him. If there was a speck of dirt, Birdwine could find it, and I believed

Bryan Skopes was hiding a whole tillable field of loamy sex-grime.

I said, "Climb in here, then. Promise it won't take long."

I rolled up my window and hit the unlock button for the doors. While Birdwine walked around to the passenger side, I tossed my briefcase in the back so he could sit. A blast of winter wind pushed all the heat out of the car, leaving me shivering as Birdwine folded his big body and jammed it in beside me. He started messing with the seat controls, scrolling backward, and his face looked like he was readying himself for a root canal.

I had a file on Skopes tucked in my door's side pocket, and I passed it over to him. His eyebrows puzzled up. He flipped through a couple of pages before turning to me. He had heavy-lidded eyes, large and very dark, the kind that always looked a little sleepy. Now he slow-blinked them, not quite an eye roll, but it spoke volumes.

"This is about a job?"

"Yes," I said. "What else?"

He started chuckling then. "I don't know, Paula. Look at these emails." He shifted his big body forward and fished his phone out of his back pocket. He tapped the screen and scrolled through his trash folder. "Here we go. This one is titled 'Birdwine, we have to meet.'

And here is one titled 'I NEED you to call me.' 'Need' is in all caps, by the way."

"Oh. I see what you mean," I said. I hadn't thought about the context when I'd typed those phrases. I'd written the truth, without thinking how it might read to an ex-lover. "You thought I wanted a relationship postmortem?"

"Yeah. What was I supposed to think?" he said.

Ironic, really. He'd ended it because we "couldn't talk," but this week he'd ignored every attempt at contact, thinking I wanted to sit down on floor cushions and light up friendship-scented incense and process our breakup over a cup of organic oolong. This from the guy who played his cards so close that when he'd ditched me, I was caught off guard; I hadn't known we were officially a couple.

I'd thought we were one-stop shopping. We worked together often, and once, after a bad night, we'd fallen into bed together. I liked the way his big hands caught in my long tumble of shaggy black hair, liked his deep rumble of a voice. He was good, rough trade, with a hairline scar cutting through one eyebrow and a long nose that had been broken more than once. I liked its complicated, crooked path.

Once we started, we kept coming back to it. I was built tall and athletic, but his body was huge—a thick-armed, beastly thing. He could toss me to the bed like I was made of air and ribbons. It was unfamiliar and exciting, to be bent and twisted into shapes, lifted, hurled around. The sex was often my favorite kind, blunt and urgent, but then it could turn languorous, too. We'd stretch time until the sex felt almost sleepy, right up until the end. Then it wasn't, and we'd tip each other into animal oblivion.

For months, we wore each other out nearly every afternoon. At his place, mostly. He didn't like my loft. It was all open concept, with a back wall made entirely of windows facing Atlanta's ever-rising skyline. He was the kind of guy who went right to a corner seat at any restaurant. He couldn't eat if his back was to the door. My place felt way too exposed, and the only interior walls were around the two bathrooms and the laundry. My cat had the run of it, and that creeped Birdwine out. He didn't like to look up and see Henry perched on the dresser like a fluffy white ghost, watching us and purring to himself. Birdwine was a dog guy.

So we'd come here. We'd close the door on Looper and have what I thought was convenience sex. Finest kind, yeah, but we didn't snuggle up after for sharing time. We had the broad strokes of each other's histories already anyway, from working together for so long. Our post-sex pillow talk was about the Braves' chances or the angles of a current case or where my bra had gone.

I was surprised when he ended it, then shocked when he also turned down every job I offered. Then he stopped taking my calls altogether. I'd backed off, giving him room to cool down. He hadn't cooled yet, going on six months later. So here we were.

I said, "I'm not a thirteen-year-old girl with a crack in my heart, Birdwine. We had a thing. It stopped working for you. Fine. I still respect the hell out of your work. I still want to hire you. Why throw the baby out with the bathwater?"

"In your metaphor, this is the baby?" He tapped the Skopes file. I nodded and he said, "I forgot what a hopeless romantic you are." His tone was still light, but one hand came up to scrub at his eyes: another bad sign. "Why didn't you title the email, 'Job for you' or 'Can you find this guy,' or hell, just the guy's DOB and Social."

I was wondering the same damn thing. It wasn't like me; I was fine-tuned for connotation. But I matched his light tone and said only, "Well, next time you avoid me for months, I'll know how to proceed."

He chuckled. "I'm still avoiding you, Paula. There has been no break in my avoidance. You're the one slumming it in my neighborhood." He paused, then added, very drolly, "Hey, look! This is becoming a relationship postmortem, after all. Neat."

"So take the job, and I'll get out of your hair." He didn't answer, but I couldn't let it go. Birdwine wasn't replaceable. Finally I said, "What if I double your rate?"

That got his attention. Birdwine lived pretty strapped. He put a long, level gaze on me and said, "Will you stop with the muffins and the urgent, breathy letters?"

"Absolutely," I said.

"Actually, send muffins anytime you want. I got no problem with muffins. But you need to stay on your side of town. Have one of your minions email me the files, and use a reasonable title, like 'Here is a case for you.' I'll send you my results back in an email titled 'Here are my results.' How does that sound?"

Shitty and untenable in the long term, actually, but I said, "If that's what it takes to get you back on my team," which was the truth. Just not the whole truth.

I couldn't work with Birdwine at a distance. Not indefinitely. I needed to see him on the regular; his binges happened at random intervals, but the signs of an impending one were cumulative. Today, right now, he could be months from breaking. The eye-rubbing, the little taps at his temple, these could simply be the stress of this unpleasant conversation. He could go in the house and not eye-rub or tap or drink himself into ugly oblivion for weeks and weeks. On the other hand, if the signs repeated and intensified, they were harbingers of an imminent disappearance that could leave me stranded at my deposition.

"Damn, but you're pushy, lady. I'd forgotten that, too," he said, and now he was laughing outright. "Okay. All right. Let's get this clear—I'm not on your team. I'm doing a job for you because you're paying me a stupid amount of money."

"Good enough," I said. It was a foot back in his doorway, and once I had a foot in, well, he was right. I was pretty damn pushy.

"I take it you need a fast turnaround?" Birdwine asked.

His hand, resting flat on the folder, almost covered it. Outside of his physical presence, it was easy to forget how large the gods had framed him: big hands, big feet, long thick thigh bones, massive wrists.

"I have to depo this guy on the twenty-fourth. Right now, I have zero leverage."

"How low can I go?" Birdwine asked, limbo style.

"Low as you like," I said. "This is a straight-up BANK case."

BANK was my acronym, and it stood for "both assholes, no kids." BANKs were the best. They were lucrative, and I could fight as dirty as I liked without helpless teenagers or toddlers wandering into the crossfire. When there were kids, or if the client was a dear and tender soul, I had to move carefully, try to minimize the damage.

"Excellent," Birdwine said. He liked low roads just fine, but he shared my soft spot for little pawns caught sideways in divorce. It was another reason we worked so well together. "What am I looking for?"

"Sex," I said, with certainty.

Before I met Bryan Skopes, I knew just by looking at his file that he had more than earned the *A* in BANK. Sure, he was in the Rotary Club, and he served on the finance committee at his church. He made sure his aging father was well cared for. He no doubt thought of himself as a "good person." Most people do.

But his first wife got no alimony and her child support was a pittance, though she was raising the two daughters he rarely saw. His second wife was fifteen years his junior. She'd worked for him as a receptionist, which further weighted the relationship. I didn't see a "good person." I saw a narcissist with a sex-and-power complex fueled by a genuine disdain for women.

Meeting Skopes in the flesh had both confirmed and lowered my opinion. The stealthy look I'd clocked him running over me—it wasn't like a hungry man with empty pockets gazing at a buffet with no hope of more than a whiff. This had been the eye-flick of a sated gourmand, one who was getting well fed on the regular. That glance had been insulting, but not for having sex in it. It was insulting because he clearly felt entitled to it. He thought he had the upper hand in the negotiations, and that power differential turned him on more than my body. It made the righteous in his indignation ring false.

Our client was an asshole, too, no question. But even assholes deserve fair representation, especially when up against an equal and opposing asshole. In this case, I'd lucked into the lesser of two evils. Daphne was still evil, just lesser. Sure, Bryan Skopes thought of women as commodities, and sure, he had bought Daphne. But to be fair, she'd consented. I couldn't respect her; I didn't like her; it didn't matter. So she had sold herself—well, I was her lawyer. My job was to make Skopes finish paying for her.

"You mean a mistress?" Birdwine asked.

I shook my head. "Don't waste time hunting for a romantic meeting of true minds. Look lower—this guy has got the secret nasty oozing out his pores."

This was how we worked together; I found the weak spots, then I pointed Birdwine straight at them and shot him. Together we had many more hits than misses.

If I was right, and if Birdwine could catch him, Skopes would have to dial down the accusing, wounded tone and bring something much more substantial than a car title to the table.

"I'm on it. We done?" Birdwine asked.

"Yeah. Thanks, Birdwine," I said.

"Please, call me Zachary." He gave me the close-lipped version of his smile, bland and insincere.

"Heh, I see what you did there." When he first started working for me, he'd told me only his ex-wife called him by his first name, and she'd remarried ten minutes after their divorce was final. These days she was living down in Florida, too busy squeezing out babies and pretending he was dead to call him anything. "I'll stay out of your way." I didn't add, *for now*.

He got out. I drove off to get some dinner, my worries about *Skopes v. Skopes* already fading. If Birdwine stayed sober, then this problem was already solved.

I wasn't sure he would stay sober, though. I became less sure as days passed with no word. Still, I stayed cool. Skopes and his lawyer, Jeremy Anderson, had been playing the delay game for months now. I could delay right back until Birdwine came through or until I found another way to break Skopes.

On February fourteenth, I stayed late researching a tricky precedent. By the time I finished, it was past eleven. I closed my computer down and got out my checkbook. I wrote *Cash* on the line that said *Pay to the order of.* My mother's legal name was Karen Vauss, but I had no idea what name Kai was floating in her current incarnation. I signed the check and ripped it from the book.

I put it in an envelope from my personal stationery— plush cream-colored paper with *Paula Vauss* and the address of my midtown loft engraved in dark burnt brown. I scrawled Kai's PO box number in Austin on the front and sealed it.

I sent her a check on the fifteenth of every month, both a ritual and my only form of communication with my mother for a decade and a half now.

It was my way of asking, *Are we square yet?*

Cashing it was her answer: *You still owe me.*

I paused before I threw it in my outbox, even though I had plans to meet up with a guy I knew. We were going to hook up at precisely 12:01, once Valentine's Day was safely over. Still, I lingered. I could let Verona send my paper proxy out with the rest of the mail, let it ask its monthly question, right on schedule. Or I could run it through the shredder.

I toyed with this choice every month. What would Kai do, if it simply didn't come? Silence might settle in between us, and I'd know I'd finally paid enough for nailing her gypsy feet down, stealing almost a decade of her freedom. Silence sounded close enough to peace for me to let it count. Either that, or she'd show up on my doorstep, demanding to cut a pound of flesh out of my body.

Not for the first time, I wondered what would happen if I got more aggressive. What if I mailed Kai a note instead? I pulled a legal pad toward me, then sat staring at it. Minutes passed, and the paper stayed word free. I needed to go home and change and feed Henry before my date. By now he would be marching up and down the stairs from the great room to the lofted bedroom, impatient for his wet food, but still I sat there, staring down at the blank page.

Finally I closed my eyes and felt my hand begin to move the pen against the paper. I wrote out the essential question, blind: *What will it take to make us square?*

When I looked at the words, I could see they were too blunt, too bald. Worse, they admitted culpability. I scratched them out and wrote instead: *You named your kid for Kali, so what the fuck did you expect? You got exactly what you asked for.*

That sounded more like me, but it wasn't at all mend-y. Well, making amends was not my forte; any fortes I had lay in the entirely opposite direction.

I could break things in a thousand ways—anything from surgical dismantling as meticulous as bomb squad work to wrecking ball–style mass destruction. If I broke a thing, it stayed broke. If I broke one of my things, I lived with pieces or replaced it. I tore the page off and crumpled it up. I shot it at the wastebasket in the corner, and I nailed it for a cool three points. Screw it. I put the check in my outbox and, as always, setting it in motion was a relief. Kai was paid, so for a week or two, I could push her from my mind. Soon enough, she'd creep back in, making me feel faintly itchy until I wrote out her next check.

As I stood to go, I heard the ding of an email landing in my inbox. It was from Birdwine, titled just as he had promised: "Here are my results." Safe bet he wasn't asking me to be his valentine. What else was new? I sat back down and opened it. The body of the email said only, *Yep, you called it.* There were two attachments.

I opened the first and found a hefty, hefty bill. Heftier than I had expected. The next attachment was a PowerPoint file. I started clicking through the slides.

There was Bryan Skopes, seen from above, but still recognizable. He was good-looking in a blunt-faced, former frat boy way, but with too much scotch and too many fried oysters gathering in the paunches under his eyes and around his waist. He stood in a thicket of evergreen azaleas with a hollow heart. The bushes made a room that was well screened on all sides, but roofless.

The photos had been taken from above, and as far as I could tell, Birdwine had panthered his way very high up into a tree that overhung the thicket. He could have broken his neck, but he got the money shots: Bryan Skopes was not alone. A friend with magenta hair knelt in front of him, her face jammed between his legs. As the images progressed, his spine flexed back and his round, florid face tipped up. His mouth fell open, slack. His eyes were closed, or he might have made eye contact with Birdwine. I grinned at the thought; wouldn't that have been so disconcerting?

Near the end, I came to a slide that made me stop clicking forward through this common, sordid story. In this shot, the girl was still on her knees, but she was looking up at Skopes. Her face was round and smooth, fat-cheeked as a baby's, and the skin under her eyes was unlined and faintly pink. I felt a lemony trickle of something sour and sharp enter my blood. She was so young. Fifteen, maybe.

In the next slide, she was standing while Skopes packed himself away. In the next, their hands were touching, palm to palm as he passed her the money. The sour trickle in my blood became sharper and more acidic. So I was right twice: Skopes was cheating, and he liked his sex with an ugly power differential. This poor kid was so young and fresh she didn't know to get paid first. *Another month of street living will fix that,* I thought, and for once, being right didn't make me feel good.

I looked at her baby cheeks, her downturned mouth, and it was as if I knew her. Hell, I could have become her.

I knew girls who had become her, back when I was in foster care. Sometimes I still dreamed that I had fallen off the world with them. I would tip into sleep and find myself walking right off Earth's secret, jagged edge. I would hurtle past the world turtle, past Joya who tumbled limp and silent, past Candace who reached for me with needy-greedy eyes. Past everything, into an endless nothing. Not even stars.

I could have ended up exactly like this girl in Birdwine's slides, with her hennaed hair and her cheeks still full of baby fat. I could have spent my days crouched and shivering on my knees for some asshole standing in azaleas, and all at once, going after Bryan Skopes felt personal. I was no longer working only on behalf of Daphne. She was my client, which meant I'd bring my A game, sure—but I wasn't fond. Daphne was standard trophy wife material. Her main interests were grooming and toning so she could be attractive at cocktail receptions. She was blank and selfish and more than a little boring.

I had no doubt that Daphne had driven past plenty of girls like this magenta-haired creature. They were common enough in Atlanta. This kid was one of a thousand strung-out runaways all over the city, unwilling or unready to be salvaged, getting by in whatever way she could.

I felt certain Daphne had never once thought to buy a girl like this a sandwich or offer a ride to a shelter. But I also knew my client had never taken a kid like this into the bushes, used her like a Kleenex, and then handed her a wad of greasy money. I felt myself shifting from professional advocate to my own self, playing for my own stakes. If I had my way entirely, Skopes would go to prison and learn firsthand how hard life could be on the knees.

It wasn't feasible, and not only because it was against my client's interests. This girl he'd used was smoke, already gone. Maybe Birdwine could find her, given time and money, but she wasn't going to testify or press charges. I knew her kind.

So what I had left was hitting Bryan Skopes hard in the money sack, in his misapplied belief in his own good personhood, and most of all, in his gloating love of power over women. I could make him bend over for Daphne and for me. The very idea made my spine feel longer. I could feel myself growing taller. I ran my tongue over my teeth, hungry for next week's scheduled depo. How much had Skopes given to that girl? I wished I could see the money clearly. A couple of twenties? A fifty? I didn't know the going rate, but this I did know: Skopes was going to pay more than he'd ever thought for that one-off in the bushes.

I closed the PowerPoint and forwarded a copy to my partner Nick with a note: *Can we get Daphne in here this week? I need to prep her.*

I went to PayPal to send Birdwine the full amount of the bill from my own account, instantly, plus a sizable bonus. It would be a paperwork ass-pain to get reimbursed, but I wanted the speed to resonate with him. Usually his invoices had to go through Verona.

In the message box I typed, *Thanks for the dirty pictures—better than a box of chocolates,* but then I erased it. I barely had him back working for me. It was too soon to try for our old combative-flirty banter. I tried, *See why I can't do without you, Birdwine?* but that read too personal. After a moment's thought, I changed it to *See why I can't do without you, Zachary?*

Still too personal; he'd been very clear, in the car. I sent it blank, then started a fresh email with a different case file attached. I typed in, *This guy's discovery is BS. He's hiding money. My bet? In something artsy-fartsy like sculpture or wine. Find it? Regular rates.* I hit send and waited.

Two minutes later, the reply came back: *On it.*

That was that. Birdwine and I were back in business. Still mostly on his terms, sure, but I was shifting him. We were heading in the right direction.

Even better, in a week—about the same time it would take for Kai's check to clear—I would meet with Bryan Skopes. He thought that he'd get everything he asked for. Well, maybe so. My mother had named me for Kali, after all. He would get what he was asking for, all right. It would be my pleasure to give it to him.

Victory called up a secret face that lived under my copper skin, my pale and tilted eyes, my fat-lipped mouth. Right now, that face wanted all its teeth to show. I felt flat and sharp-eyed, with a tongue that longed to loll out and taste the metal in the air. This face was ready to eat everything. It didn't belong at Cartwright, Doyle & Vauss.

My partners, Nick Cartwright and Catherine Willoughby Doyle, were old Atlanta aristocracy, genteel rainmakers, plugged into the social scene. They were cousins who looked more like siblings: lanky, blond, elegant. Wealthy couples with complex estates came to our firm when it was time for a quiet, civilized divorce. The kind of marriages we dissolved were thick with trust funds, fraught with prenups and questions about who should get which houses. We were expensive, but we earned it, slicing up complicated financial pies, and people who couldn't afford our skill sets didn't need them. When these polite uncouplings soured, as they often did, well, that was why my name was on the letterhead. I was the blunt instrument at the back of the closet.

I met Nick in law school. We found we worked together well, in bed and out of it. I was bold and aggressive, he was meticulous and a born negotiator. In mock trials, he played carrot, I played stick. He brought me into his father's well-established firm, and when his dad retired, Catherine and I became full partners. My skill set complemented theirs, and as a former foster kid of murky racial origin who did criminal pro bono cases twice a year, I singlehandedly made the firm look progressive and all kinds of multicultural. They liked me especially on days like this; I had decimated Skopes.

After the depo, they were in a postwin pleasure haze. Catherine sighed contented sighs and Nick looked at me fondly, as if I were his own zoo tiger. They invited me to celebrate, but I declined. I couldn't keep my savage face screwed down while they decorously popped a bottle of expensive bubbly. Nick had crystal glasses to chime and ting together during wordy toasts, and right now, my flexing hands might shatter them.

I said I was going to cut out early, and Catherine beamed approval, telling me to toddle off and have a lovely evening, I had earned it.

At home, I paused in the entry, trying to kick my heels off with Henry yelling his weird, overloud meow and scraping his side-fang along my ankle to claim me. If I was home, Henry felt certain it was suppertime, no matter what the clock said.

"Damn straight, buddy," I told him. "I'm going to open you a can of tuna. Real deal. Solid albacore."

Henry ran ahead of me, across the wide room toward the kitchen. The maid had come that day, so my whole loft smelled like orange oil and vinegar, and my feet slid smoothly across the glossy hardwoods. I dropped my iPhone into the bay and saw she'd left my mail in a stack on the kitchen counter. I ignored it and hit my victory playlist. The Kongos came on, and I cranked it, grinning. The volume didn't bother Henry. Like many white cats, he was wholly deaf.

Victory made my blood run fast, vibrating in my body as I danced barefoot to the pantry. Ye gods and little fishes, how I loved this high. I'd held it in back at the office, but now I wanted to pick up Henry, leap around with him until he was thoroughly alarmed. The musician I was seeing on and off had an out-of-town gig, but this British guy I used to date had texted me. I would text him back, tell him to swing by and help me make a dent in my best bourbon. We'd put this day to bed, hard and proper. I deserved to climb onto this joy, ride its bucking rhythms until I was wrung out and pleased and creamy through and through.

"Asshole never saw it coming, Henry," I told my cat, pausing my dance just long enough to scoop the tuna onto a plate.

When Skopes first came in today, I'd smiled for him. I'd crossed my legs and swung my foot, calling his attention to a skirt that was cut too high to ever see a courtroom. I had on sleek black stilettos, their blood-red soles promising all kinds of carnage. His gaze bypassed their warning to crawl predictably over the bare skin of my legs.

The conference room table was clotted with bodies: Nick and Daphne, Skopes's lawyer, a court reporter. To me, they had all been gray shapes at the table, irrelevant and insubstantial. The only true color was the opposing red of Skopes's power tie, the only light the faint glow of my laptop. It was booted up and open at the table's foot, facing in to show Skopes and his lawyer my soothing screen saver—tropical fish drifting in and out of a reef.

I spoke first, chanting the case number to begin the ritual that kicked off every depo. The court reporter swore Skopes in, and I asked him to state his name, his address, his birthdate for the record, giving him bored eyes. Letting his lawyer, Jeremy Anderson, give me bored eyes back.

As we completed the formalities, I moved the cordless mouse I'd placed beside my stacked papers. On my laptop, the lazy fish screen saver vanished, revealing an image from Birdwine's slideshow. Skopes stood in the bower of azaleas with his head tipped back and his eyes closed, his mouth yawped open and slack. It was color replacing color, light replacing light. Skopes didn't notice.

"Are you much of a gardener, Mr. Skopes?" I asked.

"A gardener?" he said, and made a scoffing noise. "I *have* a gardener."

"Interesting. Does he tend azaleas?" I asked.

At the head of the table, the court reporter's hands paused for a hairline fracture of a second. He'd noticed the slides. Then he gave a shrug so infinitesimal it was practically internal. His hands resumed their rhythmic bobbing on the steno with the world-weariness common to his breed. Daphne Skopes and Nick stared blandly at him, as if shorthand typing was a fascinating sight, just as I had prepped them to do.

"I don't know the names of flowers," Skopes said. These were not the kinds of questions he expected. He had good instincts, and they were telling him that something was amiss.

"Please get to the point, or move off gardening questions," his lawyer said.

"Sure," I said to Anderson. Then, purely to keep a rhythm, I asked Skopes, "Where did you go to college?"

"Vanderbilt," Skopes said.

"And did you join a fraternity at Vanderbilt?"

The slideshow finally caught Anderson's attention. He made a faint, choked noise.

"Do you not want me to answer that?" Skopes asked, turning to his lawyer. He saw Anderson's face. Followed his line of vision.

The room got very quiet.

The slide changed.

"Did you join a fraternity at Vanderbilt?" I repeated, as if nothing were happening. As if Skopes's ugliest self weren't on display here, in front of the wife he had bought for similar purposes, but with more socially acceptable currency.

"You absolute bitch," said Bryan Skopes in a flat voice.

I wasn't sure if he meant me, or Daphne, or the girl his eyes were on. The very young one, with magenta hair and baby cheeks. The one on her knees.

The picture changed again. He was staring at it, at himself, trying to see a way around all that this was going to cost him.

"You absolute bitch," Skopes repeated, his voice still toneless, but now his face was washed with red.

I kept my own face blank, perused the papers in front of me. "I'm not familiar with a fraternity called You Absolute Bitch. Would that be Psi Alpha Beta?"

Skopes stood up. His forehead was beginning to look sweaty. I could see him measuring how these photos might play to a much larger audience. To his Rotary Club. His church. His father. The neglected daughters he believed he loved, just as he believed that he was a good person. These pictures told a truer story, and for this moment, he was the one tasting helplessness. He was flayed open, all his inner ugliness exposed to the air.

"Give her what she wants," he said. Anderson tried to speak, but Skopes cut him off. "Just give her what she wants."

My favorite words.

Skopes thought he was saying them to his lawyer, or perhaps even to Daphne. He was wrong. Those words belonged to me.

After today, it would devolve into paperwork. Nick and I would do a long billable dance with Jeremy Anderson, slicing up the fat financial pie. That was nice and all, but my meat was in this moment. This perfect, unrepeated moment when Skopes was exposed. When all the stories that he told himself were washed away, and he saw himself, true.

Now I paused to set the dish of tuna on the floor. Henry wolfed at it. I grabbed the phone to text the Brit, and there, sticking out of the stack of mail, was the corner of a thick cream-colored envelope. I pulled it out, and saw my name and my return address engraved in burnt brown. Kai's PO box in Texas was written in my spider-scrawl. It was the very one I'd tossed into my outbox in the last hour of Valentine's Day. Now it had three red words in my mother's handwriting, slanting across the front.

Return to Sender.

All thought stopped. All breath. My victory went bang out of my head. All my plans for the night went, too. My cat and my own hungers—gone. I couldn't even hear the music.

Some time passed. Maybe half a minute, maybe a few seconds. I couldn't tell.

This close, I could hear Henry making a low, over-loud grumble in his chest that he felt as only a vibration.

I heard him smacking up tuna. I turned the envelope over and saw the flap was sealed with Scotch tape. I hadn't sent it that way.

My hands felt swollen and clumsy. They trembled so violently that I could barely get it open.

Inside, I found my check. She'd written *VOID* in the same red pen across the front.

Finally, a different answer. But why now? I'd sent a check every month for almost sixteen years, repeating its endless question. I'd sent tiny checks while I worked my way through junior college up in Indiana. One week, I sent five dollars, and it wiped out my account. They got a little bigger when I got a full ride to Notre Dame and then Emory Law, larger still after I graduated and established my career. One hundred and eighty-some-odd checks had made their way from me to Kai over the years, one by one, each asking, *Are we even?*

Her answer was to cash them. Without fail, even though my mother moved often and on the fly. Once or twice a year I'd get a change of address card, impersonal and cheery, shifting her mail from one PO box to a new one in another city. She always made sure to collect my check and cash it, though.

The voided check trembled in my fingers. I turned it in my hands, and saw more words on the back in my mother's left-leaning hand:

No, thank you. I have enough money to last me the rest of my life.

That was a joke. The cancer got everywhere before I noticed, so "the rest" will be quite short. Weeks, if I am lucky. I am going on a journey, Kali. I am going back to my beginning; death is not the end. You will be the end. We will meet again, and there will be new stories. You know how Karma works.

It was more than a note. It was an epitaph. Or a poem. Or a threat. That was all I knew at first read.

I read it again, and saw what it did not contain. There was no absolution.

In fact, the whole thing seemed designed to make me angry. I hated cryptic missives, and mystic-ness, and condescension. Of course I damn well knew how karma worked, but I did not believe in it. I didn't believe in reincarnation, either, or fate, or that time was any kind of wheel, and she knew it.

If I took all that crap away, I understood what she was saying. That my debt transcended even death. Hers and mine. We could both die and rot to dust, and my dust would still owe hers.

What I couldn't understand was this: a thousand miles away from me, in Texas, my mother was dying.

This was information that I couldn't process.

"My mother's dying," I told the cat, trying out the words. They were ashy and fine in my mouth, but I tasted truth in them.

Hearing it out loud, I still felt nothing. I felt so much nothing, swelling black and dense inside of me, that I couldn't even blink. My eyes dried and itched. Time stretched into something endless.

A solid week had passed while my check worked its way to Texas and back. Kai might already be dead.

At that thought, a raw ease came into my shoulders, and at the same time, I had the gap-tooth, ugly feel of something missing, the urge to jam my tongue into the hole. My insides jangled at the dissonance. If she was dead, I didn't belong to anyone but Henry.

The note took up the whole back of the check, but I noticed more tiny letters, running sideways up the margin. My numb fingers turned the little paper, and my dry eyes read. Eight more words were squeezed against the edge, clearly the last thing she'd written to me. Perhaps the last thing she'd write to me, ever:

(Obviously I don't want you to come here)

My mother was dying, and she didn't want me at her bedside.

"I'm fine with that," I told her, or maybe I was telling Henry.

I was oddly glad then that my cat was deaf and couldn't hear me saying this true and ugly thing. From far away I heard my own voice laughing because that was so stupid. Did I think a hearing cat would have understood the English? I laughed, and Kai was still dying, telling me not to come, and then I stopped laughing, because my body had stopped breathing.

Her absence coiled itself around my chest, my neck. It was pinching all my airways closed. I felt my ribs folding, squeezing inward to crush at my heart. My arm went numb, and I thought, very calm, *I'm having a heart attack.*

I lurched to grab my phone. My thick-fingered hand fumbled it and I watched it fall away. I noted with dry interest the spiderweb created as the screen cracked. I wasn't scared. I was something worse than scared. I was blue and turning bluer. I was drowning in dry air.

Then I was on my knees, scrabbling to retrieve my broken phone. I got the number pad to come up, and for the second time in my life, I found myself dialing 911. To dial it again now was such black irony, and I had no faith that this call could save me.

I could feel my mother's cord rewrapping my throat, leaching the living color from my skin. I slipped down sideways to the floor. My heart flopped and skipped. My arms and now my legs were losing all sensation.

I could barely hear the woman on my phone asking, "What is your emergency?"

I wanted to tell her I was having a heart attack. I wanted to ask for an ambulance. But I couldn't answer. Not that question. The last time I'd answered it, I'd begun the long, long process of killing my own mother. A process which was only ending now.

The voice inside my phone was talking louder now, calm and firm. "Hello? Can you speak? What's the nature of your emergency?"

I had no air to answer. I didn't even try. I pushed the phone away. It slid across the sleek wood floor, the disembodied voice inside still calling out. I turned away, turned toward the blackness, and there was karma, after all. I let everything that I deserved come at me. I let it come, at last.

Chapter 2

I measure the years of my childhood by my mother's boyfriends: Joe, a murky blond fellow in my baby memories of Alabama. Then Eddie. Tick. Anthony. Hervé. Dwayne. Rhonda. Marvin. Each knows a different Kai with a different last name and a different history, but she always keeps her story straight.

I pick up who I am on the fly, eavesdropping. Eddie the yoga teacher believes my father was a Tibetan monk who lifted up his saffron robes and broke all his vows for Kai, just once. My copper-colored skin is a shade too dark for Tick the skinhead, and though I have Kai's light green eyes, they are set disturbingly aslant. My mother is long and pale—very beautiful, if you're into the Irish thing. Tick is. Enough to pretend that he believes my dad was an Italian count she met while hitchhiking through Europe. Kai tells Anthony my dad was a blackanese yoga teacher, and shows him a picture of Eddie. Kai had me so young that Hervé asks if I'm her little sister. We go with it, and I get used to saying Kai instead of Mama.

Man after man rests his head in her lap and listens, rapt, as she spins us a new history. We are never from Alabama. Her parents are never their sour and earnest selves, one managing a hardware store, one hounding the bereaved with an endless stream of church-lady casseroles. We are better than the truth. Kai makes us better, changing us to orphans fleeing tragedy or runaways escaping a dark past.

Even my bedtime stories are spectacular: Old South folklore dipped in Hindu poetry and god tales. It is an odder alliance than a Reese's Peanut Butter Cup—*Oh no! You got your slutty blue god in my Bre'r rabbit! No, you got your racist rabbit in my sex god*—but she makes it true. On campfire nights, she blends in chunks of the Stephen King and Edgar Allan Poe books that she's read to tatters.

As I get older, I try to parse my history, to separate what she says from what I see. Impossible. My story is a Frankenstein's monster made of stolen parts, many too small to be sourced, the original morals melded or cut away entirely. Every year or so, she reincarnates, whole, and makes me a fresh self, too. The only constant in my childhood is us. We cling together through our every incarnation.

Now, somewhere out in Texas, she is dead. *Weeks, if I am lucky,* her note said. Kai has always been quite lucky—but five months have passed. By now there is no new Kai to be invented, no voice to tell me all the lives she lived while we were estranged. There is only silence and absence.

Small wonder, then, that yet another panic attack hit me when I saw my mother's eyes. They were looking right at me, just outside my office building.

At first, all I saw was a white guy, tall and very young, politely opening the door for me. I looked up to say thank you, and our eyes met. His were spring green, crescent shaped, thickly lashed. My mother's eyes, set deep in the face of a stranger.

They were so like hers. Identical. I had a hideous vision of this boy burrowing his way into the ground like a long, pale worm. I saw his eyeless face pushing itself down deep under the loam to find her missing body. I heard the Lego click as he pressed her stolen eyes into his gaping sockets.

My heartbeat jacked. I breathed in sharply and smelled campfire popcorn, patchouli, and hashish. I swayed and put one hand on the frame, dizzy, and then, dammit, dammit, it was happening again. It was as if Kai's ghost had been waiting to ambush me in my office building's sleek and modern lobby, and I'd sucked a wisp of her right up my nose.

The kid's upsetting eyes widened, concerned, and he grasped my arm as if I were his papery frail auntie. He marched me to one of the ice-white benches near the elevator bay and plopped me down onto the upholstery. I leaned my elbows on my knees and lowered my head, trying to get air into my screwed-shut lungs.

This kid was nothing to do with me. He was a stranger in my office building's lobby who happened to have a pair of spring-green eyes, but my stupid heart kept thundering around my chest cavity. I could feel it throbbing in my lips and ears and fingers.

It pissed me off. Granted, a person is allowed an episode or two when her mother dies, even if her mother had the parenting skills of your average feral cat. The firemen who responded to my silent 911 call had been very understanding. I didn't begrudge myself the three more panic attacks I had in February and March—but they should have tapered off in April. They should have stopped altogether before the summer came. Instead, they'd escalated, becoming more frequent and more easily triggered. Now here I was, panicking in

July, when I should have already finished up whatever stage four was and hit acceptance.

"Are you okay?" the boy asked. He was a long, narrow object with a prominent Adam's apple and a mop of honey-brown curls.

"I'm fine," I said.

I breathed in through my nose, counting slowly to four; when the attacks kept happening, I'd Googled what to do. I held the air in for the recommended two count. Just this weekend I'd gone booth surfing at an arts fest, and I'd lost my crap when I saw a rack of bright, Kai-style silk wrap skirts billowing in the wind. Not three days later, these crescent-shaped eyes had me freaking out like it was my new hobby.

Being pissed about it wasn't helping me calm down. I began the slow four-count exhale, one hand pressing my heart as if I was trying to reset it to its regular, calm beating.

The kid fished in the pocket of his over-shiny khaki pants and came out with a mini Hershey bar, the paper wrapper crinkled and its corners blunted by age. He held it out to me. I blinked at it.

"I always carry them. It's a habit," he said. "My mom was diabetic."

"I don't have diabetes," I said, snappier than I would have liked. I was thirty-five, and this kid was somewhere in his early twenties. That hardly put me into sickly mother territory. Then I wished I hadn't said it at all, because what was the follow-up? *It's not diabetes—I'm just having a psychotic episode.* I took the candy from his soft, white paw and said, "I skipped lunch."

It wasn't the whole truth, but it was true. I unwrapped the Hershey bar and crammed it in my mouth. It was unpleasantly warm from the kid's pocket.

"Thank you. I'm fine now," I said, trying not to drool the melting chocolate down my front. My throat was so clamped I could barely get air down it, much less this waxy candy. He nodded, but he didn't leave. The kid's accent was light, but he was definitely southern; there was no stopping him from doing chivalry.

According to Google, I was supposed to go lie down someplace quiet, do the breathing thing, and imagine sunrise or a beach. I didn't have time right now; an A-list client was quitting us. Nick had sent a frantic text a good half hour ago, asking me why the hell I wasn't in the meeting.

I'd forgotten. I'd gone haring off instead to the DeKalb County Jail, chasing yet another pro bono criminal case. The potential client was female, very young, and guilty mostly of falling in love with a felon. Now she wouldn't testify against him, and the DA was going to nail her to the wall. I'd been helping girls like this, two a year, ever since I'd passed the bar. Now I'd done five since February, back to back, neglecting my own practice. They were practically the only things I had been doing. There was no way I could take this new case on, but I'd texted the potential client's name to Birdwine anyway, asking him to dig up info on my own dime.

I'd availed myself of plenty of free therapy back when I was in school at Notre Dame and Emory, so I didn't need to peruse the stack of old *Psychology Today*s at my dentist's office to know why I was doing it. These girls were living incarnations of my mother. Too bad understanding the roots of my compulsion didn't stop me from having it, or from taking an early lunch hour and driving off to meet with yet another one. I'd forgotten my promise to sit in on Nick's meeting. I'd parked by the jail, checked my phone, and seen the string of panicked texts he'd sent me while I was in transit.

I'd roared back toward midtown, tearing a hole in Atlanta traffic and almost murdering a tottery pedestrian, yelling at my phone to dial Nick. He'd answered, leaving the client in Catherine's soothing hands long enough to give me a fraught, unhappy update.

Last quarter had been low, mostly thanks to me, since Nick and Catherine were billing as reliably as ever. This client we were losing was a BANK case. If the BANK walked, this quarter would dip even lower. I didn't have time for another pro bono, much less a haunting or a breakdown or any other flavor of dead-mother BS.

Now the kid sank down beside me on the bench, waiting for me to either need an ambulance or be fine. His cheap pants and generic navy sports coat were out of place in our upscale lobby, but his body language was right. His spine was hunched, his brow was furrowed, and he worried a blue folder back and forth between his hands. Our small midtown building housed mostly dentists, therapists, and lawyers, so everyone who came here looked about this happy. Maybe his diabetic mom had good insurance, the kind that let him pay midtown prices to fix his cavities or his depression.

I tried another Google-approved deep breath, mentally consigning the kid to the void, along with pro bono cases and all damnable silk skirts. I had to focus. I needed to butter and bedazzle our BANK client back into our stable. I had to explain the missed meeting without admitting I'd wasted yet another billable hour driving toward yet another destitute criminal. Then, assuming I got to six P.M. without running into a henna tattoo or a beaded headband and freaking out, I'd go home. I'd scrub this day off my hide in a boiling shower. Maybe work some sudoku with Henry trying to lie down across my puzzle book.

Those images worked for me better than the recommended beaches. The worst of it seemed over. My heart was banging away, but I could no longer feel it in my eyeballs, and the dizziness was gone. I even got the candy to go down, though it left my mouth feeling dingy and coated.

I stood up, and the kid rose, too, turning to face me. His eyes dropped in that young man's way that seemed almost inadvertent, sneaking a fast glance down my body. He immediately straightened his spine, making himself taller than me, and when his disconcerting eyes came back to my face, damned if he didn't smile at me all hopeful. It was adorable, how fast he moved me out of the diabetic-mother category once I was on my feet. I had to smile back, though I'd pretty much been dead from the neck down for the last five months. Even if I had been on my game, this kid wasn't in my league. He was cute, but he was practically a fetus. Also, it was a sucker bet that my suit was worth more than his car.

He knew it, too. He turned pink all the way to his ear tips and grinned, busted. Then he ducked his head and lifted one shoulder in a "worth a shot" shrug I couldn't help but find engaging.

"Thanks for your help," I said. "I'm fine now."

"My pleasure," he said.

I headed for the elevator bay, and he followed in my wake. My heart was still jangling, but I was on the back side of it, and I had to get upstairs. The BANK client, Oakleigh Winkley, was fat with money, but she wasn't fat with much else. The more money fat, the less fat clients have of any other kind. In particular, I would never say, *Here comes Oakleigh Winkley, fat with patience.*

I pressed the call button and the kid reached out and pressed it, too, three or four times.

"Oh, sorry. It's just, it makes the elevator come faster, if you press it more," he said, so earnest it took me a second to realize he was being funny. He didn't talk like someone from Atlanta proper, though his southern accent was faint enough to peg him as suburban, not rural. "Hey, do you work here?" he asked, scanning the directory between the elevators. "Do you know where I can find Cartwright, Doyle, and Vauss?"

He said my last name wrong, as if it rhymed with house instead of loss.

"I own a good piece of it. You must be here to see one of my partners." I'd already missed my only meeting today, unless I counted Birdwine. So there was that small mercy. The kid's botched flirt had been charming, but I didn't want to sit down and stare into his Kai-style crescent eyes across my desk.

"Oh, cool," he said. "I'm Julian Bouchard?"

He said it like a question, as if he was wondering if I'd heard of him. I shook my head—I hadn't—and was about to extend a hand and introduce myself when the elevator dinged and the doors slid open.

He stepped back, saying, "After you," like a proper baby gentleman.

I got on and pressed the button, telling him, "We're up on seven."

Julian ducked his head in that engaging doglike way again and turned to face the closing doors. "Thank you."

He looked too young to be married, much less divorcing, very much less able to pay our rates. His loafers had a man-made upper. We kicked kids like this gently down the food chain to cheaper lawyers, ones who specialized in dividing up hand-me-down furniture and debt.

The elevator dinged our floor, and as the doors slid open, I saw I'd caught our BANK, just barely. Oakleigh was in mid-storm-out. She clocked our human presence, but didn't look up from her phone long enough to recognize me. She jabbed at the screen, her color very high, waiting for the breathing shapes in the elevator to get out of her way.

The very thought of dealing with this much pissed-off princess made me press my palm against my jangling heart again. I was filled with a sudden longing to let the doors slide closed between us before she saw me. I could ride back down to six. There was an office full of shrinks one floor down, the good kind that could write prescriptions. Surely there was a pill that could stop little pieces of dead mother from manifesting during work hours.

Julian waited for me to step out first, like a mannerly, pale duckling, fully imprinted and waiting to follow.

"This is my client," I said to him, quick and sotto voce. "Head left, and we're at the end."

He opened his mouth to say something, but I was already stepping out, blocking Oakleigh's path and readying a sharky smile. She tried to sidestep, still engrossed with her phone. I matched her, and her gaze finally fixed on me long enough to realize who I was.

"Hello, Mrs. Winkley," I said. She flicked her hand, maybe waving hello, maybe shooing me aside. She angled right and I matched her again, staying between her and the door. Behind me, Julian slipped out and headed toward our offices. "I understand we need to schedule a meeting?"

At last she spoke. "Do you? Because I understand that we should have met an hour ago. I don't have time now. I'm not that interested in being shunted off on you, anyway."

I remembered Oakleigh's voice as high-pitched and kittenish. Not right now. She looked a little sweaty, a little pink, and her practiced lilt was bordering on screechy. In this morning's deposition, Oakleigh had lost her crap. Nick's panicked text had actually read, "she lops he crake," but I was fluent in autofill. On the phone, he'd told me in a terse whisper that when Oakleigh's fit was at its zenith, the husband muttered something Nick did not quite catch. Oakleigh understood it, though. She physically attacked her husband, leaping up and beating him about the head and shoulders with her outsize Hermès bag. The camera was rolling, and the husband cowered perfectly. His lawyer tried to look shocked and appalled instead of so thrilled he was practically having an orgasm. He was now threatening to take the case in front of a jury if negotiations didn't turn his way.

Most of our divorces settled in mediation. If mediation failed, we went before a judge. But in Georgia, either party could choose to let a jury decide who got the dogs and who got the silver spoons. It was risky, but a viable strategy, especially if the client was a long-suffering saint with a spouse who sinned spectacularly on YouTube.

Juries could be punishing, much more so than judges, and they came in with a host of biases. Now that there was video of our client beating her husband into jam with a handbag that cost more than the average Atlanta juror's monthly income, a jury trial was a real threat.

Nick did a lot of things beautifully, including tennis, oral sex, and mediation, but he did not do juries. Neither did Catherine. My name attached to a case could often make opposing counsel feel re-interested in fair. They'd go right back to mediation. And if it didn't? Fine with me.

Divorce by jury was all about which lawyer could spin a better tale, and I'd grown up with a woman who could make a heap of stolen parts sound truer than the truth. She could shade a story I'd heard a thousand times until all at once the meaning inverted and it became its own opposite. I was her kid. I operated inside the ethics of my profession, but I could spin like nobody's business.

That made *Winkley v. Winkley* the exact type of case my partners tossed to me. I had not been there to catch it. Again. Dammit. I could feel a familiar post-freakout headache rising up behind my left eye.

"You're not being shunted, Mrs. Winkley." I spoke in my lowest register. I'd met Oakleigh only twice, but I knew her type well. She reminded me of a milky-colored Arab pony one of Kai's old boyfriends had owned. She was a flirty, saucy piece of business, but if you turned your back, she'd sink her teeth deep into the meat of your shoulder. Oakleigh and the pony both responded better to an alto.

"Evans. I'm taking back my maiden name," she snapped, tossing her head. "And now you've let my elevator get away." She reached around me and pressed the call button.

I said, "Since we have a minute, you may as well explain what made you—" I caught myself about to say *lose your shit* to an already door-bound client. Damn Julian Bouchard and his familiar eyes. I edited on the fly. "—made you so unhappy at this morning's meeting?"

Oakleigh twitched one shoulder in a furious, small shrug. "Clark robbed me." She must have seen confusion flash on my face, because she said, "Clark? My husband?"

I hadn't met the husband, and I wasn't 100 percent sure who was repping him. Nick had said from the beginning that I should be sitting in on *Winkley v. Winkley*.

"He came to the house yesterday to get some clothes," Oakleigh went on. "I was there, but I stayed downstairs while he packed. He left with a suit bag, and that's all. But this morning, I was in the dressing room, and it didn't look like he'd taken any suits. I started looking around, and you know what he really packed?" Her eyes squinched up, small and mean, and her lips made an ugly, angry bow. I would have to train this face out of her repertoire. No juror should ever see it. "Everything from the upstairs safe. We kept ten thousand in cash there, and some bearer bonds, and my Cartier watch. That was an engagement present, so it's purely mine. Then at the deposition he looked right at me and said, 'What watch?' Smiling like a viper. I swear I can see his old nose when he makes that smile, and I invented his new one. It was my present to him, and he took my watch, so I should get that nose back. I should get to tear it right off his smug face."

She stomped her foot. She was wearing this season's clompy Balmain booties. They cost about nine hundred dollars, each, which meant one of her shoes was a fair trade for both of mine.

At least I had her in a conversation now. "Ms. Evans, if this goes to a jury, you need a lawyer who can put this morning's depo tape into a context."

She seemed to be listening, but all at once she sidestepped and went past me, saying, "Thank you. I'd best go find me one."

A second later, the elevator dinged, arriving. She'd seen the call light go out and done a perfect end run.

I shouldered forward to stop the doors from closing behind her. Her heels had a good two inches on mine, but I was tall, and she was tiny. I got a pretty good loom in.

I said, "There are a ton of lawyers in this town who can get you a fair settlement. But between you and me? I don't think you're interested in that. We're past fair, here, aren't we? He took us past fair when he stole your watch." I racked my brain for any bit of info from her file that I could use. Her husband owned his own company, I thought. Consulting? I couldn't remember, so I kept it vague. "You don't want alimony trickling in for a few years. You want to take that company he's so proud of, and hack it up, and set the bits on fire. Make him watch while we sell the burning pieces for a chunk of capital."

Oakleigh's eyes seemed to focus on me for the first time, so I kept going. "You want to raze his fields and salt his earth so nothing ever grows there again. You want to drag him through thorns until he's throwing all your rightful money at you with a shovel just to make it stop."

I'd given variations of this speech before. It was my standard BANK case speech, and I was good at it; I gave it all I had.

"You want his sins unearthed and dragged scream- ing into sunshine. You want your own small sins explained, so it's clear you were driven to them. By him." Oakleigh had stilled, and her neck had lengthened, her shoulders curling toward me as I spoke. I leaned in toward her another inch, let her feel how much taller I was. "That's what I do. It's what I do best, in fact. And all the things you want? Your husband wants them, too. He wants to go to a Denny's one day and have you be his waitress. That's what he's telling his lawyer, right now. This morning, you gave him ammunition. What else does he have on you?" Her long lashes swept down, so thick they had to be extensions. When she looked back up, I smiled as coldly as I could. "You want me. Between him and you. Between you and his lawyer. Who's he got?"

"Dean Macon?" she said. "Everyone says he's really good."

"I'm better," I said. "I've eaten Macon from the ground up, more than once." This was true on several levels, back before I'd traded in my libido for panic attacks.

I had her. I knew I had her, but before I could close, the elevator began making a loud, obnoxious beeping noise, complaining that I had held it for too long. The spell I'd cast on Oakleigh broke.

"Let's schedule a meeting, Oakleigh," I said, too loud and too late.

"I'll think about it." She waved a hand at the blaring doors. "Ugh, that sound!"

I pulled my card out of my bag and held it toward her, trying to recapture her. "You're going to want this."

I didn't step back. Oakleigh compressed her plumped lips, as if I was handing her a dead bug. I stood my ground, though, ready to let the elevator shriek until we both went deaf and died of old age.

Finally she snatched the card and stuffed it in her handbag. I smiled and stepped back. The doors closed, framing our BANK as she was going, going, gone.

The smile fell off my face, and I turned and leaned against the wall. They were such rare things. Our last true BANK had been *Skopes v. Skopes,* which felt so far away from where I was now that it was practically mythology. I was sick down in the pit of me, and it was more than the panic-attack hangover. I hated losing, and I hated letting down my partners, especially Nick. Oakleigh's brand of ugly put him off his feed, and he counted on me to handle cases like this.

I pushed off the wall, checking my watch, though I wasn't sure why. There was nothing left on today's calendar but Birdwine. If the gods had any mercy, he would have brought me nine good reasons to take a pass on this pro bono.

When I opened our door, I saw Julian standing by the coffee table, looking ill at ease. Verona was away from her desk, but Julian wasn't alone. Birdwine had arrived a little early. He sprawled on the sofa with both arms stretched along the back and his long legs stretched under the glass coffee table, taking up enough room for two of him.

He sat up and grinned as I came in, showing me the gap between his front teeth. I'd always liked that gap. When he first started working for me again, I'd gotten mostly the close-lipped smile he gave strangers. But now? I saw this one on the regular. Something about me screwing my life to the wall had made him comfortable. It wasn't schadenfreude, though. It was more like one fuckup relaxing in the presence of another.

I smiled back, and then I said to Julian, "I'm sorry. It looks like our receptionist stepped away. Someone should come help you in a sec, okay?"

He shifted his weight from one foot to the other. "Oh, sorry. I'm not in a hurry." He seemed to preface a lot of his sentences with an *Oh* and an apology, like a verbal tic.

"You can sit down if you like," I said.

He swallowed, eyeing the sofa. "I didn't realize it would be so, um, fancy."

"You want to come on back?" I asked Birdwine. He stood to follow me. I told Julian, "Please help yourself to coffee."

As Birdwine came around the low table, Julian flushed again and said, "I don't think I should. I mean, I'm not a real client. I'm here for something personal."

That was odd. He did seem too young and broke to be a client, but the only creatures who came to see Nick for something "personal" were thirty-something brunettes with Pilates abs and red lipstick. Catherine, a full partner with a husband and three kids, barely had a private life.

"I think we can spare a coffee. Maybe even sugar, if you keep it to one packet," I said, mock stern.

Julian smiled and turned toward the coffee station. As he and Birdwine crossed paths, Birdwine said, "Are you really interested in this one, Paula? I can dig more, but—"

When Birdwine said my name, Julian whirled back, stepping toward me, and they banged together. Julian fumbled his folder, and all the papers spilled out in a scatter.

Julian didn't seem to notice. He pushed past Birdwine and came at me, fast. For the second time he grasped my elbow, putting his face too close to my face. "You're Paula? Paula Vauss?"

"Vauss," I said, automatically correcting his pro-nunciation. His grip on my elbow was so tight it almost hurt. He'd gone pale, and I felt something bad, almost electric, prickling in the air between us.

Birdwine felt it, too. He ignored the dropped papers and stepped toward us, purposeful. I gave him a little headshake. Birdwine would break this bendy straw of a boy in two. I felt a threat, but it wasn't this bewildered kid. It felt like it was rising up around us both, envel-oping us.

Birdwine took my hint, backing off, but only by a step. Julian blinked in slow motion, like he was waking up. He stared down at the papers spread across the floor.

"Oh, sorry." He let go of my elbow. He dropped to his knees, ineffectually swabbing at the mess. He scooped a couple back into the folder, but his crescent-shaped eyes stayed fixed on me. Two hectic spots of bright color burned in his cheeks, and that bad current was still running back and forth between us. "Is there another Paula Vauss?" he asked me.

"I'm sure there must be several, somewhere," I said.

I dropped to my knees by him, helping him gather his things. I wanted this kid gone. I didn't want what-ever fresh, electric hell he'd brought in with him, tucked into his pocket with his waxy mini candies.

Julian said, "But you're Paula Vauss, the lawyer. The one born in Alabama? And you went to Emory Law?"

"What the hell?" Birdwine said.

I froze. "Did you have me investigated?" I said, outright belligerent now.

Julian stared at me with such intensity, and the more he stared, the more upsetting I found his eyes. They were so perfectly the color of my mother's.

He said, "I thought that you'd look different. You know?"

I didn't know. I shook my head.

"What's going on here, kid?" Birdwine asked.

Julian talked over him, saying, "I thought that you would look a different way."

He scrabbled through his scattered papers, then picked one up and held it out to me.

I took it. It was a birth certificate issued in Georgia, but not from a town I knew. The lines had been filled in by hand, and it was a copy, so it was very hard to read. It certified the live birth of a male child, six pounds, nine ounces. The first name started with a G. Maybe Garrett? The last name was easier to read, maybe because it was so damn familiar. The last name was *Vauss.*

My lungs tightened a notch, and my gaze jumped around on the page, hunting for the mother's name.

Karen Vauss.

"Paula?" Birdwine said, from somewhere very high above us.

The certificate was twenty-three years old. So this kid had been born when I was twelve. When I was in foster care. My heart stuttered, straining forward like an impatient horse hoping for the cue to canter. If this pale, unlikely boy was truly Kai's, then he'd been born while she was incarcerated, just like me.

That gives us at least one thing in common, I thought, and had to jam my mouth shut to keep a crazy laugh from getting loose.

It was possible. Kai had called me while she served her time, but I never got to visit. If this boy was Kai's— the whole ragged story of my childhood teetered on the edge of reinvention, waiting to retell itself. If this boy was Kai's, I'd cost her so much more than I'd ever known. The ocean roar was starting up again in my ears, and this was going to be a bad one. This one was going to make my earlier freakout look like the gentle fluttering of tummy butterflies.

"You're hunting for . . ." I couldn't bring myself to say *your mother.* It was only a letter away from *our. Our mother.* I didn't want to think those words. "You're hunting Kai." My voice came out so thick and slow.

He blinked. "Is that what she goes by? I hired a guy, a private detective, to find my birth mother. He hasn't found her yet. He did find you."

There are a lot of Vausses in the world, I thought. *There are a lot of Karens.* But my lungs, twisting themselves closed, did not seem to be listening, and my vision was getting furry at the edges.

The line for the father's name was blank. That line was blank on my birth certificate, too. My body shuddered and my teeth banged against each other in a chatter. I tried to make out the letters of the child's first name. Not Garrett. That was definitely an *h* at the end. Garreth? Either way, a yuppie name. *Nothing Kai would choose,* a calm, inner voice said, while my body gulped for tiny sips of air.

Then the letters resolved themselves. It wasn't two *r*'s. It was a single cursive *n*. The boy child had been named Ganesh. What southern woman names a baby after Ganesha, a Hindu god with an elephant head? Who names a kid after the lord of luck and fortune?

But I knew who. The same mother who would name a kid for Kali. I threw the certificate away from me and lurched up to my feet. The earth spun, trying to tip me sideways.

Birdwine caught me around my waist, and the solid wall of him was the only thing that kept me standing.

"Paula!" he said again.

Ganesha was often in Kai's stories as a feasting god, an eating god. One who could never be filled up.

Julian was standing now, too, coming at me, his mouth open, saying, "Do you know where I can find her?" and I could see that his green eyes were terribly hopeful and endlessly, endlessly hungry.

"You thought I'd look like you, is what you meant," I said. The laugh got out. I could hear me laughing crazy from very far away. "When you pictured a sister, she was white." The little Nazi had the grace to blush bright red.

"Sister?" Birdwine said. We both ignored him, even though his right arm was the only thing keeping me from puddling to the floor.

Julian said, "Oh, sorry, no. Well, yes. But I mean, it's fine. I don't care if you're—" He floundered, not sure what I was, and I didn't feel like helping him. I didn't feel like anything, except for maybe throwing up or screaming. I couldn't breathe, and my heart slammed into my ribs over and over, like it was trying to get out. Julian ended with "—you're good."

The darkness grew, coming in from either side, like those elevator doors closing. I saw Julian's red face framed in the narrow opening between the black, his lips shaping that *Oh,* that *sorry,* and now I could see so much more that was familiar in his jawline, his broad forehead, his narrow build, his long-fingered hands. I saw my mother, manifesting in his shapes and colors. Was this what her note meant? Had she somehow sent him, to show me the true tally of my debt to her? I couldn't breathe. I couldn't breathe at all.

Julian stepped toward me, and Birdwine physically moved me behind him, pushing me roughly down into a chair without turning, his eyes fixed on Julian. He seemed to swell into a wall between us, rising up to his full height.

"This would be a great time for you to go," he said, calm and deadly serious. There was a fraught pause, and then he took a single step toward Julian, big as a bear, every line of his body meaning business. Julian's eyes flashed wide, and his mouth popped open. Birdwine took one more step, his arms rising, and Julian turned and fled, abandoning his papers.

I put my head down, hands braced on my knees.

Birdwine did not give chase. He turned to me instead.

"Are you—" he said, but stopped mid-question, as if he was uncertain how to end it.

"I can't be seen like this," I gasped out, sick and shaking so hard I couldn't try to stand. "Nick and Catherine already think I— Oh, shit, help me, Birdwine."

He was already moving, swinging me up like this was a year ago, back when he was my lover and I was made of air and ribbons. He carried me fast down the hall toward my office.

I let him. I even closed my eyes and let myself sink into it, cursing my stupidity.

Kai had been gone only five months, and already I'd forgotten the most essential—maybe the only empirical—truth about her: My mother never *stayed* anything. Not even dead.

Chapter 3

I am a mouse in a red saddle, the girth pulled so tight around my chest that I cannot breathe. This is what I know: Ganesh has come. I am Ganesha's little mouse, and as the huge god plops onto my back, my lungs compress, and I am flattened into something paper thin and airless.

The stricture around my chest eases, and I am not the mouse. I am me. I am eleven, and Ganesha is only a dear and funny fellow from my bedtime stories. I lie weeping in a bed soaked in the antiseptic reek of roach spray. Kai has doused the mattress so they don't come and touch me with their whispery, plastic feet while I am sleeping.

We used to live in Asheville with Hervé, who had horses and an inheritance that let him say he was a folk musician. Kai kept him as her boyfriend for more than two years, a personal best. Then they started fighting more and more, and he called me a little shit when I spilled juice into his sitar.

The next time he took a fishing weekend, Kai told me to grab my stuff and load it in the old Mazda Hervé let her use. It was not my first hasty evacuation, but it was the first one I was actively against. I stared at her, big-eyed and balky, while she shoved her underpants into a duffel.

I wasn't crazy about Hervé, but I liked his horses plenty, and I loved the hippie co-op school his money paid for. Before Asheville, we'd homeschooled. It was easier than reenrolling me as we changed names and cities, pausing only in the places where we lived with Eddie, then Tick, then Anthony. Kai loved teaching—I was working ahead of grade in English and science— but I was a class of one. I'd pick up day-pass friends at parks or fall in with a tribe of campground kids, good for a weekend.

At the co-op in Asheville, I had friends I got to keep. I felt at home there from day one, sitting in a multi-age classroom so mottled with colors that my copper hide was just another bead in a mosaic. My purple thrift-store pants were rendered regular when placed between a sari and a snaggy home-knit rainbow tunic. There was a girl named Meadow and a boy named River, not related. My essay on marsupials was taped up in the middle of the honor wall, and I'd collected nineteen Reading Challenge stickers. Only my friend Poppy was ahead of me, with twenty.

Kai saw me, frozen in the bedroom doorway, and said, "Thirty minutes and we hit the road. Anything that's not in the car gets left behind."

I knew from experience she meant it. I ran and started throwing all my favorite books in the trunk, claiming space, while Kai thoughtfully and thoroughly robbed Hervé. Kai drove the Mazda to Greenville, where a guy she knew gave us cash for it, even without the title. We took a Greyhound to Lexington, where we bought ourselves an old VW bus with a mattress in the back that gave us lice. We threw the mattress by the road and got a futon, slowly camping our way south to Georgia.

We met Dwayne right when the weather started turning cold.

Now we're living with him in a sagging farmhouse deep in Paulding County. Kudzu heaps are laced around us, shielding us. From the highway, the house isn't visible at all. Neither is the path that runs through the woods behind us, winding through the clearings where Dwayne's pot plants are growing.

I have become the me my mother has invented to match the her she's made for Dwayne. The word *mama* is an odd shape in my mouth after spending two years as Kai's orphaned baby sister. This new daughter-self pinches at me from the bottom up, like I'm wedged into my own old shoes. I don't belong in this place. Paulding County people are either black or white, and they don't mix. The only Asians I've seen are three middle-aged ladies who work at Viet-Nails. If they have kids, they keep them elsewhere.

We could be here awhile, though. Dwayne is not a palate cleanser. He's a genuine boyfriend, with broad shoulders, curly hair, and square white teeth set evenly, like Chiclets. He's easygoing, and he makes Kai laugh. Worst of all, he's nice to me. No matter how mad and mean I get, no matter how I goad him, he laughs and calls me Bossy Pony, tugging on my bangs like they're a forelock. That goes a long way with my mother.

I miss the big bay gelding quietly. I miss my school out loud. So loud and so consistently that Dwayne decides to fix it. He sells fake IDs as well as pot and stereo systems of dubious origin, and he gets me registered for the local public middle school. My name there is Pauleen Kopalski; I don't look like a Kopalski, and I can't remember how to spell it.

At this new school, the white kids drop half their consonants, the black kids drop their helping verbs, and I don't speak like any of them. I don't get their references. They all stare openly at me, practically nose-picking as they ogle my pale and tilted eyes, my copper skin, my shaggy black hair. It's not because I'm pretty, either. At eleven, I am breastless and storky-legged, doughy in the middle. I have a huge outbreak of stress pimples on my forehead.

My second week there, a couple of seventh-grade white girls trap me in the bathroom.

"What are you, anyways?" the first one asks me. I don't answer. I look down, wait for them to get bored and go away. "Are you black?"

The other answers for me. "She doesn't seem that black."

I try to step sideways for the exit, and they jostle me back. They use their shoulders. When I try to bolt sideways, the first one catches me and shoves me, her hands sinking in my squashy belly.

"I know one thing, she's a Fatty-Fatty Ass-Fat," she tells her friend.

Her friend repeats it, laughing. "Fatty-Fatty Ass-Fat! That's what we can call her."

The push and the injustice leave me breathless. These girls own the third-best lunch table, and one of them has a boyfriend. The meanest wears a pair of real Guess jeans, and she has pretty hair and hardly any ass at all, just a narrow slice where her slim legs meet.

They step in closer, crowding me into the corner by the stalls. The meanest had an egg for breakfast, hours ago; I can smell the salt and rot of it behind her teeth.

I feel something—someone—new, rising to my surface. It is not a Paula I have been before, but I find it inside me anyway, both new and already mine.

I've been a lot of things, but until Asheville, I've been them all in tandem with my mother. We've been tambourine players and yoga teachers and Ren Faire workers. We were vegans with Eddie, then spent the next winter squatting in Tick's deer blind. We've read palms and tarot on the street near Anthony's tiny New Orleans apartment. At the Asheville hippie school, away from her, I was somehow all those incarnations—an amalgamated girl who felt like me.

This is different.

"Are you some kind of ching-chong thing?" the meanest says, making more red rise up beneath my copper skin.

In fight or flight, Kai has always chosen for us, and my mother is made out of wings.

I don't think that I am like her—not in this way. My ears are cocked inward to hear a rushing sound like churning water, a violent, foamy washing away to something bedrock and essential.

"Let me by," I tell the meanest. I've decided it's the last thing I will tell her.

When she says, "Not until you tell us what you are," and shoves me back against the stall, my hand is already a fist. I rear it back and punch it toward her belly, and it feels good. I like when it connects. I like to see her fold and puke onto her shoes. I like the way her friend's face blanches right before she runs to get a teacher.

These two girls are white honor students who've been in this county since first grade. I am new, and racially confusing, and I didn't do well on the Monday fractions quiz. I'm the one who gets suspended.

Now I lie in my stinking, bug-sprayed bed, thrashing and snotting, and I'm not sure where the fight-y girl has gone. I'm not even sure that she was more than panic and adrenaline. I weep and kick like a ruined infant until Kai comes and pulls my head into her lap. She runs her fingers gentle through my hair.

My body stays in a stiff curl, unyielding. "I hate it here." It's not the first time I've said this. My face is slick from weeping.

"You can't get into fights," Kai says.

I didn't mean to. They started it and pushed at me and pushed me. I only punched a girl who deeply needed punching. "I hate that school."

Kai keeps petting my hair with soothe-y fingers. "You haven't given it much of a chance. Dwayne did some things to get you in, babe. It's what you said you wanted."

"I hate it there," I say. "And they hate me."

I'm on that whole clique's radar, now. Next week, I'll have fifty watery-eyed rednecks blinking their pink-rimmed lids at me, waiting for a chance to smash me into paste. *Maybe I'll be that fight-y girl again,* I think. It scares me. I like it, and that scares me, too.

"Baby, you can't call attention to yourself this way. We can't have DFCS sniffing around here. You can't get in fights or disappear from school." When I don't answer, she adds, "Keep your head down, okay? Try to find a friend or two. It will get better once you settle in."

"Is she okay?" Dwayne asks her, from the doorway.

"She's fine," Kai tells him.

"Poor kid. Middle school is hell," he says. He leans in and sets two dollars down on my roach spray–smelling blanket. "If you want, you can bike up to the Dandy Mart. Get yourself a Coke and Pop Rocks. Would that make you feel better?"

"Maybe in a little. Give us a sec," Kai says. She waits until he leaves before she lies down beside me. Her voice is soft from sweetness, not from whisper. "I'm going to tell you something that happened a long time ago. A very long time ago, but it's happening right now." That's how Kai begins her bedtime stories. It's her way of saying *once upon a time.*

As she speaks, she curls in even closer. I am enveloped in the familiar smell of pot smoke and fresh orange peel. I still to listen. I think she's going to tell the story where Kali fights the Red Seed Demon. Every time, Kai tells it just a little different, but it is my favorite; in every version, Kali wins.

Instead, she tells me a Ganesha story.

A long time ago, right now, Ganesha has a saddle mouse. That mouse carries the feasting god, carries his big belly, his heavy elephant's head, and all the lunches that Ganesha tucks inside himself for later. The mouse wears a little red saddle and a silver bit. He carries Ganesha to the market, to the temple, to weddings and funerals, to sickbeds and to celebrations. Now he's carrying Ganesha home from a feast. The god lolls on his little mouse's saddle, holding his round stomach, so full of feast that he is groaning.

At the crossroads, Ganesha's mouse meets a rat scuttling home with a small bag of rice bound to his back. The rat eyes Ganesha's mouse, strapped into the saddle, staggering under all that god.

The rat says, "You poor thing! How can you carry the weight?"

And the mouse says, "What weight?"

I wait, but that's the end. My eyebrows knit together. I've heard a hundred iterations of this story, too. In most, they don't meet a rat. They meet a cobra, who scares the mouse into bucking Ganesha off—it's slapstick, and very funny. I have not heard this version before.

I hate it, instantly. I will never come to like it any better. I hate it because I understand it. She is telling me to settle into this life. To accept it, as I have accepted every other role she's handed me.

But in Asheville, I started making a Paula of my own. Asheville Paula was competitive and smart. She liked horses and lining up her reading stickers in a careful row. Paulding County Paula is only starting, but I already know I'm not going to be good at accepting things, especially a life that smells like roach poison. I already know what it feels like to hit a girl hard enough to make her give her breakfast egg back. The story Paulding County Paula wants is Kali shredding Red Seed Demons, winning against all the odds. Instead, I'm being told to lose so endlessly that losing becomes normal. To duck my head down and become Fatty-Fatty Ass-Fat for my whole life here. After a little while, Kai's story tells me, I won't even notice it.

I couldn't do it. I don't think I even tried.

It's not easy to imagine the Paula Vauss I'd be today, if we had stayed in Asheville. It's close to impossible to picture the woman I'd be now if I had listened to that story, tried to learn the finer points of eating shit. Maybe I would have fallen off the world. Maybe I'd simply be a sweet and gentle soul.

Maybe I would have grown up with a brother.

Now I wondered, when Kai told me the story of Ganesha's little mouse, did she know she was pregnant? Did Ganesh—no, Julian—exist yet? Perhaps he was a single cell, busily becoming two. He'd kept on growing, though. Now he was a full-grown godling, sitting on my chest, caving all my ribs in.

Birdwine came back from the lobby, closing my office door behind him. He'd gathered up Julian's abandoned papers while I lay here picturing elephant-headed gods and demon wars instead of Google's recommended beaches. Not very soothing, really. No wonder I was still flat on my butter-soft leather sofa with my chest constricted and my bare feet propped up on a stack of decorative pillows.

"Did anyone see you?" I asked.

"Verona was back at her desk. I acted like this was my stuff, like I'd dropped it," he said, holding up Julian's folder. "How're you doing?"

I wasn't sure. I stared over my toes at the built-in shelves, assessing. Strange that I remembered that old nickname given to me by the mean girls in the bathroom. I hadn't wasted hate or even thought on them for years. I never went back to that school or saw them again. I never had to learn to bear that weight.

Just above my toes, on the third shelf down, I saw my own familiar cream-colored envelope, addressed to Kai's PO box in Austin. I hadn't wanted it in my loft, but I hadn't thrown it out or shredded it. I'd brought it here, the voided check with her note on the back still nestled inside it. The red words on the outside, *Return to Sender,* matched my pedicure.

The envelope was the only flotsam on shelves that had been meticulously staged by our decorator to reflect what she called "Lawyer Luxe." I'd left this thing propped against the leather-bound books, a macabre souvenir from a funeral after-party I had never thrown. For the first time, this struck me as weird. No, past weird. Downright crazy. I'd set it there and then grown myself a great big blind spot all around it.

I tried a deeper breath and found my lungs were mostly working. Birdwine took the chair closest to my head, his face set to careful neutral with a twist of wry. My shoes sat side by side on the coffee table in front him, my suit jacket draped beside them. Birdwine shoved them toward the center to make room for Julian Bouchard's blue folder, restuffed and primly closed.

"Are you, what, conscious?" Birdwine asked.

"I didn't faint," I said, testy.

"I know," Birdwine said.

"I'm not a *fainter*," I said.

My chest was tight, but my heart still seemed to be inside it, attached to everything that mattered and doing its job, so I sat up. Mistake. I was instantly dizzy, and Birdwine teleported to the sofa's edge beside me, easing me back down flat with his hands on my shoulders.

I looked down at his hands, then said, "Did you unhook my bra?"

"Yeah, but it wasn't to help you breathe or anything," Birdwine said, very serious. "I was copping a feel."

"Oh. Fine then," I said. I hadn't even felt him unhook it as he carried me. Very smooth. His hands stayed on my shoulders, and I was barefoot with my bra hanging open under my white silk shell. After a second, it got weird. He was working with me again, but he was careful to keep a lot of air between our bodies. He let go of me and went back to the chair.

"Did Julian come back?" I asked, hoping that he wouldn't say, *Yep. He's waiting in the lobby with his mouth stretched open wide like a hungry baby robin.*

"I didn't see him," Birdwine said.

Good. I needed to lie here quietly, in a room entirely innocent of surprise brothers, and get my head around it.

Eventually, I would have to face him. Give him his folder back. I would have to look into those familiar eyes set in a baby-cheeked face, as smooth and pale as Percy Bysshe Shelley's, and apologize. That fuzzy-headed boy-child had come to me with his hand out, hoping I could tuck a lovely mother in it, close his fingers soft around her. I didn't have that. I didn't even have her ashes in a jug up on my mantel. All I had for him was this envelope.

She's dead by now, I could tell him. *I have this note. You want to bury it or burn it?*

"I ran him off," Birdwine added, rueful.

"You think?" I said, half smiling. Birdwine had stepped in to fight for me when I was down. Then he'd caught me up and carried me. Some of the hard, clear lines he'd kept between us felt bent at crazy angles.

I wasn't sure where it was safe to step. I tried a cautious "Thank you." It sounded stilted, maybe because I felt so raw it was as if all my skin had been peeled off and put back on inside out. I tried again. "Thanks for having my back."

He said, "*De nada*. I feel bad I scared the kid. But in the moment, I was sincerely expressing my true feelings."

"What all did he bring?" I asked, glancing at the folder.

"I didn't study his file, Paula," Birdwine said, and now *he* sounded stilted. "I wouldn't go snooping in your personal business." One line redrawn, but then he quirked his eyebrow and softened it by adding, "Not unless somebody hired me to."

"Ha ha," I said. "I wasn't accusing you. I'm just saying, when an ex-cop, a trained investigator, gathers up a sheaf of papers, he might notice things. You can't turn your eyes off, Birdwine. You can't make your brain not think." I scootched down and got my feet up a little higher on the stack of throw pillows. Pressed together, my feet hid the returned envelope entirely. "Did you see anything, purely in passing, that makes you think the kid's legit?"

Birdwine shook his head. "Legit your brother? You tell me. Did you notice your mom having a baby a couple decades back?"

I shook my head. "She was in prison the year he was born. If she had any babies, she didn't think to mention it."

"I see," Birdwine said, and the nice part was, he did. He'd heard Kai stories over the years. Enough to get she hadn't been June Cleaver. He touched the top of the folder. "Purely in passing"—he paused to clear his throat—"*purely* in passing, I saw adoption records. So he is looking for his birth mother."

"And it's Kai," I said, more statement than question.

Birdwine spread his hands, like an apology. "I didn't see anything to shut the idea down."

If I really felt uncertain, I had an easy way to check. My best friend was a geneticist. William was on paternity leave for another month, but I could go by his lab with Julian. We'd give them blood or hair or spit into a cup.

The problem was, I didn't feel uncertain. It wasn't only the timeline, or the birth certificate with *Karen Vauss* on it, or the fact that his birth name was Ganesh. Sure, when I added those up, the answer came out brother. But it was more than that. I could see my mother in the lines of him.

Julian was my half brother, and I had changed the course of his whole life. That meant I couldn't pass him a couple of sweetened-up Kai stories with a hot drink and a cookie, pat his head like he was Cindy Lou Who, and send him toddling back to his adoptive family. I owed him more than that.

His existence shifted history. His birth, his loss, remade my mother, and recolored all her choices. Every story I had told myself about her—about us—had a different meaning and a different moral. I hadn't cost her twenty-two months of freedom and a boyfriend. I'd cost her a child.

Birdwine wasn't done yet. "I'll tell you what really bothers me. I saw stuff printed on Worthy Investigations letterhead. Tim Worth is a vulture who shouldn't have a PI license. When he gets a missing person's case, he digs up everything he can in a day or two—and it's usually a lot. He's very good. But then he hands out the info in little drips, billing all the while. He's had this kid on a string since last November." He caught my questioning glance and chuckled, busted. "I noticed—purely in passing—that the letterhead was dated."

What awful timing, I thought. For all of us. On January fifteenth, I'd mailed the last check Kai had ever cashed. A good investigator could have found Kai for Julian last year. Julian could have bypassed me entirely and met Kai before she died. Probably before she even knew that she was sick.

Birdwine started talking again, rolling his hands the way he did when he was laying out a hypothetical.

"So the kid's about to slip Worth's hook, and Worth gives him you as a stopgap. Hoping to get another month's bill in. Ten to one Worth's known exactly where your mother is since the day after he took the case."

"My mother isn't anywhere," I said. I relaxed my ankles and let my feet drop apart. The envelope appeared between them, coy and closed. I pressed my big toes back together, playing footy-peekaboo with a war telegram. Playing baby games with a paper body in a paper bag. Birdwine looked at me askance, and I suddenly thought, *What the hell?* I tried it out. "I think Kai's dead." It sounded weird, even to me.

"Oh, I'm sorry to—Wait, what?" He'd reacted to the inherent sadness, but he floundered as the phrasing struck him. "What do you mean, you *think* she's dead?"

I waved a hand at the envelope. "She sent me a note last winter. It's right there, if you want to read it."

He got up and went to get it. As he scanned it, I could see his mouth was filling up with questions. They rolled around, as unwieldy as if he'd stuffed his cheeks with marbles. The first one that got out was "You didn't go to see her?"

"Nope," I said. "Turn it, there's another sentence in the margin."

Birdwine spun the check and squinted at it.

(Obviously I don't want you to come here)

He looked back up at me, his heavy-lidded eyes gone even sadder. "Jesus, that's harsh. You think she meant it?"

"If not, she could have told me. My address and phone number were printed on every check. Meanwhile, I haven't had a phone number for her for more than a decade. I don't even know what name she was using. For eight months, I mailed her checks to a PO box in Austin. Before that I mailed them to other PO boxes in other states. I didn't move or change jobs. She knows where I am, if she wants me." I stopped, and Birdwine raised his eyebrows at me. He'd heard it, too, the way I'd used the present tense, resurrecting my mother via grammar. "Knew. Wanted," I corrected. "She's dead enough."

"You don't sound sure," he said.

"No. I'm sure. Her note says, *Weeks, if I am lucky.* So. The first two months were hard, I'm not going to lie. Every day, I wondered if my mother was off planet yet, or reincarnated as a lab rat or a meat cow—something suitably pejorative." Or somewhere in pain, still dying inch by inch, still not wanting me to come. "Now, I don't think about it."

Or when I did, I mostly felt a terrible relief. Truly terrible, like a person who's been told they no longer have to carry the weight of their own gangrenous and rotting left arm. It smells, it hurts, it's literally killing you—but it's still the only left arm that you'll ever have.

"I would have found her for you," Birdwine said.

"I know," I said, acknowledging it as a kindness. "But then what? Fly to Texas and let her kick me in the teeth in person? She'd kicked them plenty hard enough from a thousand miles away." And yet, in this brave new world that held a lost Ganesha, how much could I blame her? I wasn't sure yet.

Birdwine still had the check turned sideways. He scanned the line again: *(Obviously I don't want you to come here).*

"Damn," he said at last, and put the check back in the envelope.

"Yeah, it's hard to take in," I said. "But I had years. Long before she died, she'd reinvented herself as a person who never had a daughter."

"No," Birdwine said instantly, flat and certain. He put the envelope back on the shelf, leaning it against the books in the exact spot it had been in before. My feet, boosted on the pillows, blocked my view of it again. "A parent can't just do that."

"Kai can. Look at what happened today, Birdwine. I've apparently got a brother, and she never even hinted he existed."

Or had she? The Kai who came home from prison was a different person. I thought it was because the terms of her parole pinned her to Atlanta for eight more years. She was legally bound to a history that had soured for her. I'd cost her almost two years of her life, her freedom for eight more, and Dwayne. But those things had only camouflaged the larger loss. Postprison Kai drank more, sang less, told fewer stories. She was no longer the Kai who'd cuddle up to me and whisper. She didn't even fall in love much, dating stolid Marvin, who helped with rent and slept over every Tuesday. But sometimes, on afternoons when she was sad and drinking wine, she would still tell a Ganesha tale. *Long ago, right now, baby Ganesha and his mother are playing in the river.*

Birdwine waved a hand between us, shooing away the topic altogether, and came back to his chair. "I'm sorry for your loss."

"*De nada.*" I opened my feet to reveal the envelope. *Now you see me.* I closed them. *Now you don't.* "You're the first person I've told, actually," I said, still surprised I'd said it to him. Maybe it was a matter of positioning. I was prone on the sofa and Birdwine's chair was in the shrink spot, by my head.

"You mean, that she's gone?" I nodded, and Bird-wine's eyebrows went up. "But it's been months."

"Yup."

Birdwine leaned forward in his chair toward me. "You didn't tell *anyone*?"

He sounded skeptical, and he came down hard on the last word. Maybe we should have had that relationship postmortem last winter, because he was asking me if *anyone* included my best friend, William. It usually didn't. Back when Birdwine quit me because we "couldn't talk," I'd said that neither one of us was big on sharing. He'd laughed, a bitter sound, and said, *You talk to William. I talk at my meetings. But you don't know me, Paula, and you don't want to. If you did, you wouldn't like me much. We might as well go ahead and call it.*

I shrugged as best I could, prone. "I only told you. Just now." Which was true. But the whole truth was, William and his wife were at home with their newborn son, after a pregnancy that had been touch and go from the beginning. I wasn't going to heave big scoops of My Dead Mother or I'm Having Panic Attacks onto William's plate. It was full, and Kai would still be dead when he emerged from brand-new-baby fog. "I'm pretty much on my own with this, Birdwine."

Birdwine looked like he was ruminating. I let him, and a small silence grew between us. I thought about rehooking my bra, but my chest still felt tight. Instead, I reached under my shirt and began working myself out of it while staying flat. I'd done it plenty before with Birdwine in the room. Back then, I'd done it under more cheerful circumstances. Hell, back then, I'd done it under Birdwine.

Maybe he was thinking the same thing, because he looked away.

"Sorry, this thing feels miserable. How'd you know to unhook it?" I asked him, trying to make the scene feel a little less *Flashdance*.

"My sister gets like you did, when she's under stress," Birdwine said. "She sheds anything binding and gets her feet up higher than her head."

I pulled my bra out through an armhole and flung it over my jacket. It was a sleek, white, simple thing, meant to be invisible under silk.

"I didn't know that, about your sister," I said.

"There's a lot you don't know. We Birdwines play our cards close," Birdwine said, and then he did look back at me, right into my eyes. "We're great at poker."

I had a cat-stretch kind of feeling in my belly then. One I hadn't felt in quite a while. I propped myself up on my elbows, gratified to find the room didn't swing around me and the nausea didn't come back. I was all at once aware of how thin my silk shell was, how bare

I was under it. Something about silk, it could feel more naked than naked. It would be nice, really nice, to get up and out of here. Grab Birdwine and take him someplace quiet before he got all his lines back into order. Not think about my surprise brother and all the ways he reshaped my past and grayed the future into something murky. Let the world spin on, unsupervised.

I remembered exactly how sweet and rough Birdwine could be. I remembered the way he would throw my body toward the bed, catch it on the way down, one big hand cradling my head to save it from the headboard. Birdwine was looking back at me, but I couldn't get a read. He did play a good hand of poker, as I well recalled.

There was a quick double tap on the door—purely perfunctory—and then it swung wide open, and there was Nick. Worse, he had a client in tow. She was a bobbed, preppy forty-something in a prudish floral headband. I didn't know her, which meant that she was new, or worse, a potential he was trying to land.

Nick was talking as he came in, but he stopped dead in the doorway and went silent when he saw me. The client's momentum ran her into his shoulder. I jerked my feet down, scattering stacked pillows.

Nick's mouth unhinged as he took in the scene. There I was, scrambling to sit up with bare legs, bare feet, and my bra on the table, very white against my black jacket. Half the couch's little cushions were now scattered on the floor, and I could smell the faint electric crackle that had risen in me right there at the end, sexing up the air.

"Good God, Paula," Nick said, nostrils flaring.

Over his shoulder, the client's eyes had gone as round and wide as a bush baby's. Ten to one she was some kind of dedicated Anglican. My luck.

"You're driving down the wrong track," I said to Nick, straight up, but his face and his assumptions didn't change. He should know better. I'd never leave my door unlocked and roll a man around in here like an amateur. Not during business hours.

He was too pre-angry to think it through, especially today, when I'd no-showed at his meeting and we'd lost the client. Now Prudence Headband looked ready to rabbit out in Oakleigh's footsteps. She put her hand over her mouth and her wedding set alone, heavy with diamonds, told me this was a client Nick would very much want.

Birdwine rose to his feet and came between us.

"Hey, Nick. Ma'am. Please excuse us. Paula's had some awful news. Her mother died."

His words hit the room like a second shockwave; I saw the client's face trying to readjust itself, wobbling toward sympathy, but finally settling on puzzlement. Grief did not a bra on the coffee table explain, and Birdwine, thick and muscular in his workman's boots and untucked, rumpled shirt, didn't hit this woman's demographic.

"Oh. I didn't know," Nick said. His voice had gone solicitous, but his gaze on me was chilly. He did know how long Kai and I had been estranged.

"Yes. It was quite a shock," Birdwine said to Nick. I drooped sadly, letting my body language back his story. "I'm Zach Birdwine, Paula's investigator. Please excuse my casual dress. I was on a stakeout until ten minutes ago." He smiled his more formal, closed-mouth smile, stepping forward as he introduced himself to Headband. She relaxed a bit, shaking Birdwine's hand and mumbling her name and some condolences in my direction.

Nick looked down to straighten the lapel of his jacket, which was beautifully tailored and did not need any straightening. Clearly a dead-mother story of dubious origin wouldn't poof him out of his justifiable temper.

"I'm not handling it well, Nick," I said. "I'm sorry." I meant it, and on more than one level.

"And I'm sorry for your loss. We'll definitely talk later." Nick gave me a reckoning stare, unmollified.

"Yes, we should sit down together," I said. "Maybe Monday? Right now I should go home and see to things."

Not much he could do with a client in the room. By now she'd bought what Birdwine was selling and was giving me a look full of genuine sympathy.

"Of course," he said. "Don't worry. Catherine and I can get along fine without you." The tone was proper, but he leveled his eyes at me, making the words into a threat. I looked back, and there was a lot of history between us. I'm not sure what he saw in my face, but his mouth softened and he added, "Go home. I believe your calendar is clear. You have a lot on your plate, sounds like, and you need to make some decisions about what you want." He meant long term, but it sailed right over the client's headband, as it was meant to.

She said to Nick, sotto voce, "Do you need to drive her? Or call someone? She shouldn't be alone."

"I'm taking her home, ma'am. I'll call her people," Birdwine said.

My people, that was a nice touch. My people consisted of friends with a brand-new baby, my pissed-off partners, a sudden brother, and an envelope. Still, that Old South phrase conjured up a vision of concerned aunties with casseroles, clucking neighbors bearing Bundt cake. It put Headband at ease to see the details of death being properly handled by a tall person with a Y chromosome and workingman's boots. She could bustle right on back to her divorce.

Nick led her off, leaving my door pointedly ajar. He needn't have bothered. Whatever bit of sex had started rumbling around in me was gone, reburying itself in the deep hole it had died in months ago. As for Birdwine, I wasn't sure he'd even caught the vibe. His gaze on me was thoughtful, nothing more.

I stood up and put my jacket on, stuffing my bra into the pocket, then dropped my heels to the floor and slipped them on, too. I picked up Julian's blue folder. I needed to return it to him, sooner rather than later, and I didn't know when I'd come back to my office. After a second's thought, I got Kai's envelope off the shelf as well.

As I took it down, I had a sudden, strong urge to tell Birdwine Kai's story about Ganesha's little mouse. *This happened a long time ago. It's happening now.* I turned the envelope over in my hands, once, twice, and then I understood. I wanted to tell Birdwine because I was living it. I'd been Kai's mouse, saddled up and bridled, this whole time. When my check came back, I'd felt such relief, to be told that I could finally set her down. So relieved I failed to notice that I hadn't actually done it. I was still carrying her, and the weight of her was breaking me.

What weight?

Kai and I stopped speaking the day I went away to college. She finished her parole and evacuated Atlanta before I moved back for law school, and yet I'd kept her corpse's paper effigy sitting on a shelf for five months now. I was neglecting my business and letting my partners down. I was doing endless pro bono hours for young, nonviolent female criminals with bad boyfriends, as if I were the patron saint of dumb-ass girls. I couldn't remember the last time I got laid, and I had panic attacks over bits of ghost I saw rising in silk skirts and green eyes.

And now Julian existed.

What weight?

I turned to Birdwine. "I don't know what to do next."

Those were not words I said a lot. I'm not sure I'd said those words in that order since I was old enough to vote.

"I do," Birdwine said. He stood up. "Go to Worthy Investigations and beat Julian's case file out of Tim. Julian's paid for the information in it a thousand times by now."

He said it as if assuming I was going to help Julian, and that surprised me. Except for the very few inside my tightest inner circle, most people would put down money that my next move would be to lock my office door and screw Birdwine on the sofa. Or they might wager I'd go ambush Oakleigh Winkley, re-sign her as a client, and take her husband to the cleaners. Either one of those paths fit my reputation. Me helping Julian? It seemed like such a sucker bet that no one, right down to my barista, would be inclined take it.

I hadn't known Birdwine saw that far into me. While we shared a bed, or perhaps even before that, in the years when we'd been colleagues, he must have paid attention in his stealthy, watchful way.

I'd seen him as a professional asset, a buddy, and then a convenient bedmate. It was true to say I'd deemed him highly valuable, in all three capacities. After he quit me, I had certainly expended a great deal of irritating effort to get him back into my resource pool. But the whole truth was, I'd also seen him as too damaged to take seriously. A fuckup. Not my equal. And I wouldn't have been sleeping with him if I saw him any other way.

I couldn't predict his choices the way he'd just predicted mine; I'd been surprised when he'd stepped up for me in the lobby. It made me feel ashamed, especially since I couldn't see much difference between us. Not these days. Maybe that was why I moved in closer and talked to him the way I only ever talked to William or my cat.

"In Kai's old campfire stories, there were twenty-eight hells that roiled around in space south of the Earth. Very south, down at the bottom of the universe. Sometimes one broke loose from the pack, and it always made a beeline for Earth. I think I have at least four of those hells up my ass right now, Birdwine," I said. My voice was low and shaking. I was scared and tired and I didn't try to hide it. It felt like a relief, not to hide it. "I want to do right by this kid, but how can I? He's looking for his mother."

"Not just his mother. He did come here to meet you," Birdwine said.

I made a scoffing noise. "So I can offer him an about-to-be-unemployed half sister with a bitch reputation and a fast-developing panic disorder."

"When you put it that way . . ." Birdwine said, chuckling. "So find Kai."

"She's dead," I said, sharp.

"I know, Paula," Birdwine said, in a tone used for humoring lunatics. "I can tell by all the wheezing and shaking that you're perfectly happy to leave it at that." That made me smile. "Find out when she died and where she's buried. You'll feel better, and the kid's a citizen. He'll like having a place to plant Thank You for Giving Me Life daisies." I nodded. That sounded like the least that Julian would want. Birdwine went on, "So, to bright-side it, it looks to me like Nick thinks you need some time off. I say we hit Worthy Investigations in the morning."

That word, *we*, washed over me. In my own way, I had asked him for help twice now. This was Birdwine saying yes. He was offering something like a friendship, and all ye gods and little fishes, I could use a friend right now. His offer was a living thing between us, so new and pink and blinking that it made me nervous. I nodded, accepting it, and all at once Birdwine seemed as uncomfortable as I was.

"Pass me a legal pad," he said. "The kid's contact info is in the file, but give me a little time before you set a meet. I'll take his Social down and do a quick background for you—just in case." I got him one from my desk, and he spent a moment bent over the blue folder, jotting a few things down. Then he headed for the door, pausing in the doorway to look back. "Want me to pick you up tomorrow?"

I shook my head no. "Your car smells like a gym sock. I'll get you. Nine o'clock?"

"Ten," he said. "What are we, savages?" He closed the door behind him.

The workday was hours from being over. I should go find Nick and try to get right with him, or at least give the afternoon's hours to a live file, doing something billable. I stood as if wavering, but I knew I was only delaying the inevitable. The double panic attack had left me too wrung out to concentrate on breaking up the fat estates of angry strangers.

So I gathered up my laptop, the note from Kai inside my returned envelope, and the blue file that Julian had abandoned, and I went home. I wanted to find out everything I could about my brand-new brother. After all, he'd just inherited the largest debt of my life.

Chapter 4

I incur my debt in Paulding County, Georgia, on a sweet spring night as my mother plays her mandolin and sings campfire songs. I am huddled and sunk into one of the ancient beanbag chairs on Dwayne's covered porch. I have one of Kai's sketchbooks open on my lap. I'm trying to copy the way she draws eyes, but it's gotten too dark. The porch light is dead, so Kai has lit candles. I can't concentrate, anyway.

I squinch my eyes to peer across the small yard, hemmed in by heaps of kudzu. It's dirt and weeds, mostly, dotted with lightning bugs. They are all looking for true love, flicking their tails on and off in the gathering dusk. It's hard to see past the candlelight, but it seems to me that someone is moving in the kudzu.

Maybe it is only a deer. They come sometimes, hoping to eat some tender baby pot plants.

Is it a deer? I can't tell if I want it to be a deer or not. I've been sick and scared down in my very pit for days now.

Kai, oblivious, is draped on the sagging back-porch sofa, her wrap skirt bunched up almost to her hips. She has her long legs draped across Dwayne's lap, which makes her play her beat-up mandolin at an odd angle. The bug zapper backs her up with its irregular percussion. She's not a great player, but her fat, lazy alto usually melts me into sleepiness. Not tonight.

Dwayne leans over her legs, digging in the ashtray to find the second half of a joint. He lights it with his Zippo, then holds it for Kai. She pauses the song long enough to pull in smoke and hold it.

"There's a hole in the middle of the sea," Kai chokes out on the exhale, smoke streaming, and Dwayne laughs. He joins her when her breath is back. "There's a frog on the bump on the log in the hole in the middle of the sea . . ."

She acts like this is just another chapter in our endlessly mutable story, Kai towing me as she moves from man to man. I never fought or even questioned it, because of the truth at the root of our shared life: Kai doesn't love me like she loves the boyfriends.

Boyfriend love is the light on a bug's back end, flicking on and off across a lawn. It begins with lies and kissing. It devolves into fighting and boredom. It ends with hasty packing and sometimes robbery. It is easily replaced by fresher love.

Me and Kai were always more than that. Me and Kai have been a single unit, made out of only us. I liked it fine, until Asheville. I had a life there, separate from hers, the way she had a separate life with Hervé. When Hervé called me a little shit, my heart sank because I knew his days were numbered. Within a month, it had cost him his girlfriend, his pill stash, his old Mazda, and all the cash in the house.

Here, Kai has us, and she also has Dwayne. I have us, and a school where I am Fatty-Fatty Ass-Fat. I get that we've burned Asheville, but I can't stay here, in this place. I told her so. I tried, at least, but all she did was tell me a Ganesha tale. Now I am sick with waiting. My body is a twisted ball of rubber bands, each pulled tight and straining against the others. The deer that might not be a deer moves in the kudzu, and he has friends now. I sense them more than see them, a gathering of motion in the darkened woods around us.

"There's a—" Kai pauses, mid-song. "I forget what's on the frog."

"Wart!" says Dwayne, cheerful and definitive and dead wrong.

Kai shakes her head no at him and looks to me. "What's on the frog?"

It's a fly. But I stay silent, hunched up, sitting as stiff as a person can sit in a saggy beanbag chair. I peer into the darkness, seeking movement in the kudzu. Wind or deer or my deliverance?

"Wart! Wart! Warrrrrr!" Dwayne barks, wolf style, losing the final *t* on the end howl. He's been drinking room-temp beer all afternoon, and he didn't eat any of the hot dogs.

"Okay, weirdo," Kai says, laughing, and starts up again, giving a wart the fly's rightful place in the order of things. She leans her head back as she sings, and her deadfall of dark hair spills over the tall arm of the sofa. I stop studying the kudzu to look at her. Her body is a ribbon made of elegant muscle, small breasted, with a richly curved back end. Her bare legs stretch and flex across Dwayne's lap, the skin as pale and smooth as porcelain.

I slump lower. I am shaggy-headed and squashy. *Fatty-Fatty Ass-Fat.* I take my globby stomach in my hands and squeeze. Kai sees me doing it as she finishes the verse. She sets the mandolin aside and smiles and sighs at the same time.

"Quit worrying at your puppy tummy. I had one exactly like it when I was your age. Very soon, you're going to use that tum to make yourself some cute little boobies and a girl butt. You'll like that puppy fat, as soon as it moves to the right places." I scowl and let go of my gut, wrapping my arms around it instead. She's clued in I'm unhappy, but she has the reason wrong. She didn't listen. "Oh, the puppy's mad because I talked about it getting boobies!" Kai says. She stands and holds her arms out to me. "Come here, Puppy-puppy."

Her smile is stoned and kind and warm. Maybe the weaving motion in the kudzu is only deer. With my pretty mother smiling at me, holding out her hands, I want it to be deer. Mostly.

I go to her, and she tucks me close, enveloping me in her familiar scent, but the tension wrapping my bones does not uncoil. I keep my shoulders hunched against her hug, keep my arms wrapped around my own soft middle. I told her not to send me back. I told her.

She feels the stiffness in my body and drops a kiss onto my hair. "Grumpy puppy. There's fun parts to growing older. Come inside and pick a color, and I'll paint you on some grown-up lady toes, for practice."

She starts to sing again as we stand up, but not the campfire song. "Jai Kali, Jai Kalika!" Her smoky voice, singing my old baby name, is warm and sweet against my ear.

Here in the West, Kai has told me many times, *we think of Kali as a dark goddess. But the name I gave you—Kali Jai—it literally means "Hail to the Mother."*

I let her tow me toward the door as she sings my theme song in her fat, low voice, and it occurs to me that even if I discount the blue skin and the long red tongue, the skirt of human hands and all the weaponry, it's still a strange damn name to give your baby. Hail to the Mother?

Kai is the mother. The translation of my given name is actually something close to "Yay for Kai."

I glance over my shoulder as Kai fumbles open the back door. The deer in the kudzu have wound themselves all the way around us. The movement in the leaves is now enough to draw Dwayne's attention.

"Hey, hush there a sec, babe," he says. He is too late.

They come out of the blue darkness in a swarm. I am surprised by how many of them there are, how fast they move. They are large, real men, bulky in their vests. I can't tell what is them and what is only the moving dark around them. Their long, black-clad arms are made longer by the guns they hold, and they yell in an untidy chorus, telling us to be still, to get down, to be on the ground.

My heart swells. I am frozen, both jubilant and sick with dizzy terror. I willed them to come, and they did. I willed a way out, and the way came creeping up from behind us, through the woods, past the rusty shed. They came as Kai sang, "Jai Kali, Jai Kalika!" as if my own name was the signal.

We will have to move, now. I have a vague idea that the police get to keep crime houses for themselves. Too bad on Dwayne, but River's dad took a bust for pot, and he only got six months. Dwayne's done two years before, for B and E, and before that he did some stints in juvie. Six months is nothing—but it's very long in Kai time. She's rarely single for half that, and by the time he's out, we'll be other people and long gone.

"Whoa, whoa, whoa!" Dwayne is yelling, his hands up.

"Get down," yells the closest cop.

Dwayne is sliding off the sofa to the ground, but Kai clutches me and screams something so close to my ear that the word is lost in the outsize, blasting sound of it. She jerks me backward, into the house. Outside I hear the cops yelling in protest. She locks the door, then runs for the master bedroom, pulling me along.

"Stop," I say, but she keeps pulling.

This isn't how it's supposed to go. Tick got arrested once in the Dairy Queen, and that was the end of Kai and Tick. When the cops came in, she put her hands flat on the table, one on each side of her Peanut Buster Parfait.

She said, "Keep still, they don't want us," to me, and she was right.

But now she slams the bedroom door and locks it. She runs to the bedside table and pulls the stash of Hervé's pills out of the drawer. I forgot about the pills she stole, still tucked in her bedside table. Her fingerprints are all over the Baggie.

"I don't think you should—" I say, but she's already running for the bathroom.

I stand rooted, listening to a fearsome banging, then a crash; someone has kicked down the back door. In the bathroom, I hear the toilet flushing. Kai is going to get in trouble. I run to the window. It is dark in here, but light has flooded the back porch, and I can see Dwayne has been rolled to his belly. His hands are bound in silver. I hear my black army crashing around inside the house, men moving from room to room, yelling "Clear!" in firm, decisive voices.

The toilet is flushing again, and I hear Kai cussing at it. I hear wood splintering, and I back up, away from the window, away from the locked door. I press myself against the wall. Kai runs out of the bathroom to me, wraps her arm around me.

"It's okay," she says, but it isn't.

The door is forced open. Men run at us, armed and yelling. Now hands are pulling us apart. A man shoves Kai to the ground, and this is wrong. I am being pulled back, away from my mother. I resist, dig in my heels, and I find myself lifted. I become a podgy sack of thrashing, mad potatoes.

They are doing it wrong. When I biked down to the Dandy Mart and called 911 from the pay phone, I told the operator to leave us out of it. *What is your emergency?* she asked, and I told her the emergency was Dwayne. *My mom's new boyfriend grows so much pot. Thirty-two Laraby Lane, in Paulding. He tends it, and he sells it for his job. Him, not us. My mom and me only just moved here.* These men don't seem to know that. They only know Kai ran when they said stop. As I am carried bodily from the room, I see my mother crying. She is being handcuffed, and I did this. I made this be.

I yell "No! No!" to an army that is by all rights mine, but the army doesn't listen. They don't know I was named for the blue-skinned goddess of destruction. They don't know I am the force that set them into motion. No one knows. They see only the shortest girl in sixth grade, a roly-poly, too small to be taken seriously.

"Baby?" Kai is yelling. She does not know, either. "Don't worry. Just go with them. Baby? It's okay."

I go limp and am toted off to my own roach spray–smelling bedroom. It is not okay. I called them, and now they are taking my mother. I have split the planet called Me and Kai in two, when I only ever wanted a way out of here, for both of us, together.

A lady policeman sits with me, waiting for DFCS. At eleven, I don't understand the difference between River's dad, who had pet plants named Lydia and Jilly, and Dwayne, a longtime petty criminal with a basement greenhouse full of seedlings and mature plants growing tall back in our woods.

The yard outside my window is a sea of red and blue lights. I called them, and they came and took my mother. Kai is fingerprinted and regressed back into Karen Vauss, a girl from Alabama with a juvie sheet and no visible employment history. She is charged with obstruction and destroying evidence.

I am taken to a temporary shelter. It is loud and even scarier than middle school. My hands are fists. I keep them fists, in case.

"Why did you run?" I ask Kai, crying on the phone.

"I was surprised," she says.

I wonder if that means she was *not* surprised when the cops came for Tick at Dairy Queen. Did Kai make a 911 call of her own? For one wild second I am full of hope. I could confess, and she would understand because she'd done it, too. But the words die in my throat. Tick started sweet, but he got meaner, especially toward me. If she got him busted, it was for both of us, not her alone.

DFCS contacts my grandparents, but they won't come and get me. Kai hasn't spoken to them since I was three or four, when she traded blond Joe for Eddie, a guy she'd known in high school. Eddie was mixed race: black and something Asian with a dash of Cherokee. My grandparents told Kai to dump him or get out. We got out. My only memory of them is dim and sour, anyway: Gramma staring at me as we toted bags to Eddie's car, calling after Kai, *You'll end up with another just like this one.*

Maybe Gramma meant it literally, but that didn't matter. When they arrested Kai, I had no idea where Eddie was, and though he'd been nice enough, he'd never acted like a father. I didn't give his name to my caseworker, and I guess Kai didn't, either.

I ended up in a group home in east Atlanta, while Kai pled guilty in exchange for a reduced sentence. Twenty-two months, with time served, short enough so that DFCS didn't bother to start the paperwork to terminate parental rights.

It was also more than twice the length of pregnancy. I hadn't known until today that she took my nascent baby brother with her off to prison. I'd cost Kai a life with her second child.

The day I called 911, I was a child myself, unable to predict the consequences. Dwayne and Kai were the adults, and they both regularly indulged themselves in felonies and misdemeanors. They'd both done time before, and their choices made it likely they'd do more, some day or another. Yet that intellectual understanding didn't change the way I felt, when I thought of how our lives unfolded, after. Had Kai known she was pregnant when she took that deal?

The answer was likely in Julian's folder, currently sitting closed on my onyx dining table. Through the wall of windows, I could see Atlanta's skyline reaching up toward blue, untroubled skies. It was a solid ninety degrees outside, and my open loft was hard to over-air-condition, but I could not stop shivering. I changed into a hoodie and a pair of jeans so old and faded they were as soft as pajamas. Then I went downstairs to breach the file.

It waited for me, closed and prim, beside my laptop. I took a detour into the kitchen to get myself a beer, cracked it, and then sat and flipped the folder open. On top was the birth certificate Julian had showed me at the office. I launched my laptop's calculator and checked the date of Kai's arrest against his birthdate.

Just short of forty-one weeks. That meant that on the night of the police raid, he'd been no more than a blastula, secret to everyone except his busily dividing self. Did that make him Dwayne's? Maybe, but his birth weight was under seven pounds. That was small for a late baby. Kai may well have crossed paths with some curly-headed prison guard or lawyer as she traveled through the justice system.

Here, at least, was common ground; I also had no father listed on my birth certificate. Sure, it might be that yoga dork Eddie. Kai knew him in high school, before she dropped out, and I doubt even my mother could have found a second Asian/African American/ American Indian to love in the quasi-rural Deep South. But maybe not. Eddie had readily accepted that my dad was a Tibetan monk. Sure. Because what Tibetan monk doesn't dream about his pilgrimage to Dothan, Alabama?

Come Christmas, Julian and I could mix whatever went in eggnog and play a round of Best-Guess Our Bio Dads. It wasn't a traditional way to bond, but it could work if we put in enough liquor. *To murky origins!* I'd say. *And guys who didn't want the job!* he'd warble back, and we'd clink our cups.

I turned the page, trying to get myself in hand. Julian and I had yet to have an awkward lunch, and I'd leaped nineteen steps ahead to an imaginary awful Christmas—a family-centric holiday I didn't even celebrate. Not unless my office's near-mandatory Secret Santa counted.

I started flipping through the other papers. They'd been scattered and shuffled back at my office, and now the forms pertaining to Julian's adoption were mixed in with Social Security cards, car titles, birth certificates, and mortgage information on a house in the North Atlanta suburbs. This looked to me like the Bouchard family's catch-all file for their important papers, the kind people keep in a safety-deposit box. Julian had brought the whole thing instead of copying the relevant pieces. Then he'd abandoned it on my lobby floor.

"These millennials," I told Henry, who was padding down the stairs. He'd roused himself from his sunny nap spot on my dresser to come see what I was doing.

I began sorting the forms into linked piles on the table's surface. Henry, who had a double share of that magic cat ability to exist in the least convenient space, jumped to the tabletop. He flopped down on top of the Bouchards' marriage license. I ceded the territory and gave him a chin scratch, glad to have his heartbeat in the house. I found the original petition for adoption, and under that, the official termination of Karen Vauss's parental rights. I had a hard time swallowing as I set that one aside.

I pressed the heels of my hands into my eyes. I needed to treat this like a job. Pretend this file was part of someone else's lawsuit, random papers, telling me a stranger's story.

Fine. This adoption had gone through Horizons Family Services, a private placement agency. They'd handled the complications caused by the birth mother's incarceration. Ganesh Vauss left the hospital with Michael and Anna Bouchard two days after he was born, and the biological mother was returned to prison. The actual adoption took place six months later, after the paperwork and home visits had been completed through Georgia's slow-grinding courts. At that point, a second birth certificate was created for Julian René Bouchard.

That got to me, again. The name Ganesh had been legally wiped away by a simpler one, chosen by a different woman and written on a new birth certificate. Gramma had demoted me down from Kali, and Julian's adopted mother had performed the same function, though I hoped with kinder motives.

I'd found us a second point in common. We'd briefly been fatherless godlings from the same pantheon. We were just mortal strangers now: Julian and Paula.

I traced the letters of my brother's second name, trying to imagine the preprison mother I had known giving up her baby.

Well, her back had been against the wall.

My grandparents might have taken Julian. He was a white grandchild, after all. But would Kai hand Ganesh to the same sour racists who had abandoned me to foster care? Or he could join me in the system, rolling the foster-parent dice. He'd be talking and toddling when she got out, imprinted on random strangers. He might get bad fosters, too, ones who would not hold him, who would let him cry. He wouldn't even know that she was out there, loving him, coming to reclaim him. Adoption let her choose a soft place for him. It was one road out of a thoroughly shitty wood, and she had sent him down it.

She hadn't even told me she was pregnant, but I could see that this had been a kindness. I was in that group home, and the main thing that kept me from falling off the world was my unshakable faith that Kai would rescue me. How do you promise your preteen you'll come for her, but by the way, you're giving up her brand-new baby brother?

Henry stretched, working parts of his body onto two other stacks of paper. I shoved my chair back away from the table and let him. I wished I had ten cats, enough to cover every bit of history. I was failing on every possible level to keep professional distance. I could see fresh ways that I had ruined my mother's life rising up from the white space in between the words. I should have given the whole file over to Birdwine. He could have sorted through it, extracted anything relevant, and presented me with bullet points I could digest in tiny, manageable bites. He could send it in an email titled "Here is the information."

I might do better looking at Julian's present. The farther his life moved from our shared point of origin, the less personal it became. Birdwine wanted to do a background check before I contacted the kid, but Google-stalking could hardly be considered contact. I angled my chair toward my laptop and pulled the computer toward me, grateful that a family of Smiths hadn't adopted Julian and named him John.

A quick Facebook search yielded three pages of Julian Bouchards and near variations. Midway down the first page, I saw mine. His curly hair was longer in the photo, hanging in shags around his ears. His smile pushed his eyes into half-moon shapes in that unendurably familiar way.

I clicked the link. His cover image was an eagle soaring high over a canyon, of all damn things. He had lax privacy settings, and I could see some of his posts: a picture of Yoda's face with that quote about try versus do, a tiny GIF ant carrying a huge crumb, a video of a pretty girl in Singapore playing something haunting on a hang drum. My surprise brother had romantic notions.

At the top of the page, Facebook was asking, "Do you know Julian? To see what he shares with friends, send him a friend request." I hovered my mouse icon over the button. Clicking it would definitely count as contact. Also, the term *friend request* made me feel balky. It was so immediate, almost invasive. What if the kid started in with the super-poking and the endless Facebook game requests? Besides, I'd already embarked on a new friendship today. Birdwine was the first true enlargement of my tiny circle in literally years.

That thought let me laugh at myself. *Two new friends! Careful, Paula, you might rupture something.* This was a virtual, click-based relationship, and if Julian had any savvy, he'd see past it. He'd realize what big eyes I had. *The better to stalk you with, my dear.* If he accepted, it would likely be so he could reverse-stalk me.

Well, I wished him luck with that. Like every lawyer on the planet, I had a Facebook page, but it was strictly for professional use.

Even so, I found myself sliding the mouse sideways and hitting the Send Message button instead. When the window opened, I typed, *Hey. This is*

Then I sat staring for three minutes, trying to decide between *This is your half sister* and *This is Karen Vauss's other child.* Julian Bouchard, a mysterious young human, was by blood a member of my family. Such as it was. I'd avoided marriage, never wanted kids. My mother and I had abdicated each other, and Google-stalking Kai had been impossible. She'd lived off the grid, as if the Internet did not exist.

Every now and again, I'd run across people we'd known in our long, parole-inspired stint inside Atlanta. Some of them had stories and snippets about Kai, which I took with grains or teaspoons or whole oceans' worth of salt, depending on the source. Kai was near fictional to me at this point, and she had given Julian away. He had a different mother. Anna Bouchard. I wondered what she might be like. A soft-voiced cookie baker? A brisk soccer mom? I was in no true sense a sister to him.

I decided on my name, direct and simple.

Hello, Julian. This is Paula Vauss. I apologize for my reaction to your visit. I was not aware that my mother had another child. I'm sorry to inform you that Karen Vauss and I have not been in contact for many years, and I believe that she is no longer living. I have hired a reliable PI to find what ultimately became of her. The one you hired is a con man; please do not contact him, and under no circumstances should you give him more money. I will share the results of my investigation with you ASAP.

It felt mean to tell the kid that Kai was dead in a letter—in a Facebook message, no less—but it felt even meaner to hold that information back. He must be anxious to hear from me. Especially since he'd abandoned his bank records, his Social Security card, his mother's maiden name, and a host of other sensitive bits of info into my tender, total stranger's care.

Reading back over my note, I knew the tone was too formal—downright lawyerly. It read cold, and cold was not at all what I was feeling. I was feeling nine kinds of freaked right the fuck out, actually, so maybe cold was better.

I tried to think of something kind to add, and came up with this: *I have some pictures of her and some of her belongings. I would be happy to meet with you at your convenience and share these things. I will answer any questions you might have to the best of my ability.*

There. True, but not the whole truth. Polite, but not invasive. I clicked Send, and my little missive poofed into the ether.

I sat back in my chair, wondering when he might read it. Wondering how he might respond. I needed a distraction. My loft felt cavernous, as if the vibrant purples and golds in my modern artwork could not quite fill the high white walls today. The space felt hungry for another heartbeat. One that was larger than Henry's.

I wasn't seeing anybody on the regular. I had a cadre of local exes who were often game for friendly reminiscing, but I hadn't been in the mood to return their calls. I'd had a metaphorical whole-body headache for almost half a year. Until today.

Something had reawoken in me earlier, in my office, there with Birdwine. I'd been working my way out of my bra, and I'd remembered the delicious feel of winding my body around a rough and willing male, naked and rampant. I'd felt a sweet unspooling low down in my belly, reminding me that I was made of bone and blood and warm flesh.

That energy was gone. All I really wanted now was human company. But maybe if I had some, my body would wake back up?

I got my phone and started scrolling through my contacts. Davonte picked up, but he was in Nashville, at a party, by the sound of it. Jack's number was no longer in service. I got Remi's voicemail, and then a woman answered Raj's phone. Her voice got sharp, asking, "Who is this?" I didn't know if she was wife, girlfriend, or wannabe, but I said something innocuous and hung up. Half my job came from the ugly carnage caused by cheating, and I'd never knowingly help a man break a promise to another woman.

It had only rarely been an issue. The postmodern cowboys I went for weren't big on vows. When one of them got slung up, I didn't hear from him, and if I did, I was done with him, anyway. I had a strict No Assholes policy, and I'd never met a cheater of either sex who wasn't some stripe of asshole underneath the *He doesn't understand me*s and the *We drifted apart*s and the *She won't do that thing I need in bed*s.

It narrowed my pool—the world had never once been short on assholes—but not too much. Physically, I didn't have a type. I'd dated short guys and tall guys; scrawny, thick, and ripped; red and yellow, black and white. I liked any charming fuckup who was passing through, promising good conversation, good sex, and zero complications. The world also had no shortage of fellas with commitment phobias who genuinely enjoyed the company of women—I just couldn't find one this afternoon. Not unless I wanted to go out and pick a fresh one.

I didn't. I'd given up on one-night stands in college. Too risky, and the sex was generally subpar. It could take weeks or even months to find and cultivate the kind of relationship I liked. I dropped my phone back on the table, frustrated.

With no work to keep me busy, the afternoon stretched ahead of me, unbearably long. And yet I had zero drive to go back to the office. Maybe I should have taken on that new pro bono, after all.

Henry rolled onto his back and air-paddled his paws at me, being charming but making a mess of my stacks. I picked him up and baby-cradled him, burying my face in his neck, smelling that good warm cat smell for as long as he would let me. After a minute, his affection plate got full, and he pushed at me until I let him down. I stared at the table full of papers. They stared back.

I'm not sure what I would have done had my iPhone not mercifully started ringing. I answered without even checking the screen. "Hello?"

"You call him yet?" Birdwine said, forgoing greetings.

"No," I said, defensive.

"Bullshit," he said. "Unless you emailed him instead?"

I kept silent. Facebook wasn't technically email. He was

already laughing at me. "Busted. Damn, woman, I dug as fast as I could. Here's the thing. I've been looking in the kid's financials. I've got some concerns."

Big ones, I thought, for him to call me back this fast. "About the adoptive family, or about him, personally?"

"Him. The parents were typical American middle class."

"You mean they had a lot of debt," I said, and then I picked up on the verb tense. *Were.* It made my body restless, set me pacing from the table to the sofa. "His adopted folks are dead?"

"Oh, yeah. The mom was a type-one diabetic. She developed complications when Julian was a teen. Celiac, then intestinal cancer. The dad dropped dead of a heart attack near the end of her illness. Stress got him." Bird-wine said this like it was fact, but I knew what he was doing. He was telling me the story he had read between the lines of documents and spreadsheets. I knew if I were in the room with him, his hands would be rolling in that way he had, laying out the hypothetical. "So the kid just started his senior year at Berry College when his dad bites it. He drops out. Moves home. From that point on, he's taking care of his mother. By October, she's dead, too. You want to hear the obit?"

I was lagging a few sentences behind him, trying to process as I paced back and forth across the space between the dining table and my great room sofa. Birdwine was distilling it down to something too dense for me to chew. "I don't know. Do I?"

"Nah. It's long—a full column in the *Marietta Daily Journal.* Active in her church, community, blah blah. Dies 'after a long illness.' At the end, all it says is, 'She is survived by her beloved son, Julian.'"

My heart sank. "That's it? No other kids? No spare sister or some cousins?"

"Full stop. His parents were both only children, and they're gone. Meanwhile, his old friends are off at college, his new friends are back at Berry. Kid's got nobody. He hires Tim Worth to find Kai in November."

I sighed. Julian and I were orphans, which gave us a full three awful things in common. If he took my offered meeting, I hoped he liked the Braves or David Cronenberg movies so we'd have something innocuous to talk about. Otherwise a simple lunch with him might be enough to put me back in therapy.

"I hear you oiling up your pity gland," Birdwine said. "Stand down. He's also dead broke, Paula. Worse than. Medical and hospice ate the Bouchards' retirement. Kid has three quarters of a liberal arts degree and a job at Mellow Mushroom. Whatever cash he did have went to Worth. No way can he go back to Berry. Not without a payday. He shows up at your swanky midtown office, sees your rich-people carpet, your crazy-ass shoes. I gotta wonder, what's he thinking?"

Birdwine sounded disapproving, but I took it as good news. If Julian was after money, it could make everything so easy. I owed the kid, and money was something I had. If he was an asshole, I could pay my debt off in the most literal manner and send him on his merry asshole way.

My computer dinged. I walked back to the table and saw that Julian had responded to my missive with a friend request. He was less wary than I was, or simply of a different generation, or Birdwine's suspicions were justified, and this was step one in his scheme to get his hands deep in my pocket.

"Get this," I said to Birdwine. "I sent Julian a note on Facebook not ten minutes ago. I'm already hearing back."

"See, now, that's eager. Another warning bell."

"No, it's these kids today," I told him, huffy old man style. "I don't think they ever log off anything."

"Not even to pee," he agreed. "But still."

A small chat window opened up at the bottom of the screen. I sat down and leaned in to read it.

Hello?

With the question mark, the simple greeting looked so plaintive. I remembered Julian's crescent-shaped eyes, his nervous energy. He'd been an easy blusher, his feelings showing in the wash of pink and red across his skin. I was good at reading people, and he'd smelled of hope and nerves and worry, undercut with an edge of desperation. I didn't think Julian Bouchard would turn out to be something so easy as an asshole. I hit Accept.

I'd made two friends in the space of hours, after all. Now I was on the phone with one and fielding Facebook IMs from the other. This was turning out to be a banner fucking Wednesday.

"He opened a chat," I said to Birdwine.

"You sound thrilled."

"I forget what that word means," I said. "Is *thrilled* a kind of stress vomiting?"

"Yeah, I think. Well, your guard is good and up. Go chat with your li'l hustler. We'll meet the guy who's hustling him in the morning," Birdwine said.

I started to thank him, but he'd already gone. Not a big one for *Hello, how are you*s or *Good-bye have a nice day*s, that Birdwine.

I stared at the blinking cursor under Julian's *Hello?*

The phone, still in my hand, was ringing again. I checked the screen.

It was Remi, hitting me back. My thumb moved toward the green button, but it stayed there, hovering. I wasn't sure why. My other option was the Facebook chat, and hadn't I had enough new brother for one day? I liked Remi. I liked him a lot. He had those bright black eyes you sometimes find on Cajuns and was my height, exactly, which could put us eye to eye in bed. I paused, my whole body cocked to catch any faint vibration from below.

I got nothin'. The sex that had risen in me back at the office with Birdwine had re-died, or at least was sleeping heavily now. I let Remi go to voicemail and pulled my laptop closer.

Well, hello there, I typed back to my brother.

Chapter 5

My mother and I do our time. We live in loose groups of squatty buildings that look like industrial office parks. Thirty-some-odd teenagers are housed with me, while Kai lives with several hundred inmates. My cabin holds up to six middle-school girls and a house mother named Mrs. Mack. Kai's cellblock holds forty women, watched over by armed guards. She's in prison for obstruction and destroying evidence, while I'm in a group home for the more private crime of putting her there. It's tacitly unfair that I'm in the softer, smaller version.

Especially since my mother isn't like me.

If Kai could see me now, she'd say that I'm not like me, either. I am not her tambourine girl in a beaded dress from Goodwill, or the gypsy one who'd coo, *Such a long life line,* peering at a palm over her shoulder. I can barely remember the achiever-girl I started to become in Asheville. More and more, I'm the Paula who rose up in Paulding County the first time I was asked to choose between fight or flight. In this place, I've learned—or I've decided—that I'm not a runner.

My first week here, a high school boy accidentally fell down the stairs and broke his wrist. The whole truth was, he followed me into a stairwell with some bad intentions. Week two, a girl from another cabin came to visit me, then walked into my door and blacked both eyes. The whole truth was, she muscled close and gave me a testing shove, so I smashed her face into the door jamb. I took some hits, sure. Hard ones, but I always came back swinging. The bullies have moved on, like bullies do, looking for meeker mice.

I worry more for Kai than for me. My mother's best defenses are the fade, the melt, the sneak away, the dash. Kai can see trouble from a long way off, and until the raid I engineered blindsided her, she always had us elsewhere long before it landed. Since the arrest, she's been hemmed in by bars and walls and doors, with no room to run.

I got to visit her at least, when she was in jail here in Atlanta. After her case settled, she was transferred to a women's prison in south Georgia. Her lawyer and my guardian ad litem worked it out so she could call me—we lucked into a family-friendly judge—but I can no longer read her face, her body language, look into her eyes. It's so much harder now to know how much she's lying.

"Are you safe?" I asked, on our first call after she moved.

"Of course! Don't you worry, baby. I already got myself a prison boyfriend. Rhonda." She said it light, like she was being funny, but she wasn't being funny. "Are you making any friends?"

"Not like that," I said, but I told her about Joya, a sleepy-eyed eighth grader with a comforting whiff of pot smoke in her tang. She's my friend even though she's black. Most friendships here are set by race, which should put me on my own just like in Paulding. But Joya defaults to me because her mother is in court-mandated rehab. She and I belong to someone. The other two black girls in our cabin are on the adoption track. They belong only to the state and to each other.

Now, five phone calls later, Kai and I ask easier questions.

"Are you eating enough fruit?" she says.

"Yes," I lie. "I'm eating lots of fruit."

I have the receiver pressed so tight to my ear, it will be red and sore when we hang up. I am hungry for her voice, her laugh, her stories.

I sit cross-legged on the floor of the pantry, tucked between the stacks of paper goods and the shelves of potato flakes and canned soup. I am in the large building at the center of the campus that holds the dining hall and rec room. Mrs. Mack lets me take Kai's calls from this staff phone in an alcove off the kitchen. The cord is long enough to let me drag it to the pantry and close the flimsy door.

"Fresh?" Kai asks. "That canned stuff is mostly sugar."

"Yeah, fresh," I say, though I am eye to eye with a row of outsize cans of fruit cocktail. Inside are cubes of yellow so soaked in heavy syrup that I can't tell pear from pineapple. She has to know my food here is not much different from hers there. Dumplings with shreds of chicken, tater tot casserole, spaghetti. I'm growing just fine, anyway, fruit or no fruit. My puppy fat has begun to shift, as she promised it would. I see my body getting long like hers, curving to her angles; I'm morphing myself into the shape of what I'm missing.

"Is that Mrs. Mack being nice?" Kai asks.

"I guess. I mean, she kinda sucks," I lie, but the truth under it, the one I hope Kai hears is, *No one can replace you.*

I like Mrs. Mack. She's a middle-aged black lady who calls me girlie. She calls us all girlie. *I love my girlies,* Mrs. Mack sings out every morning when she wakes us up, and I believe her. She loves us, all of us, in the same blanket, replaceable way that my mother loved her boyfriends.

"Are you sleeping good?" I ask.

"Oh, yes," my mother says.

The pattern of these calls is set. Now she'll ask me how I sleep, and how I did on my last math test, and I'll ask her what book she's reading. These little questions, the little lies we're telling, they are promises we give each other. *I will be okay if you will.* When time gets short, she'll tell me the next installment of an old bedtime tale. We're in the middle of "Baby Ganesha at the Feast" now. I'll close my eyes and let her smoky alto drift over me like warm fog. But this time, she breaks the pattern.

"Listen, I need for you to do me a favor. If you can."

I hear tension in her voice, and I sit up straighter. I say, "Okay," and it comes out halfway between agreement and a question.

I hear her swallow, and then she says, quick and quiet, "I'm doing something. I'm writing something. Like, a poem."

It's a strange collection of words to deliver with such low urgency. Kai is nineteen kinds of art-fart. She tells stories and draws beautifully, sings well, plays an okay mandolin. I'd be more surprised to hear she wasn't writing poetry in prison, but she says it as if rhyme and meter have been declared contraband. It's almost confessional, the way an inmate might say *I'm making wine inside the toilet tank,* or *I'm digging a tunnel to freedom with this stolen spoon.*

"Okay," I say again.

She goes on, still talking fast, her voice more urgent than the subject warrants. "I'm retelling the *Rama-yana.* Just the part where the demon steals Sita. You remember that? Sita is living happily with Rama in the forest. Then Ravana steals her and locks her up, and it's like prison. It's a lot like prison. Do you understand?"

"Yes," I say, and I feel my stomach curdling. She's picked this bit of the *Ramayana* because she is living it. All the organs in my abdomen have gone sour; I should be in her poem, playing the part of the demon.

Kai says, "I'm going to mail the poem to you, as soon as I get it done."

"I can't wait to read it," I lie.

"There's someone else I want to read it. Do you know who I mean?" Kai asks. A thinking pause. I don't. "I was hoping you could send it to your uncle." Still nothing. I don't have an uncle. "The one who used to call you Bossy Pony."

Is she talking about Dwayne? He's the one who called me that.

"I think so," I say. I don't say his name, because I don't know who is listening. There could be a snitchy prisoner standing near her, or a capital *S* Someone on the line. There's no expectation of privacy on a prison phone, not unless she's talking to her lawyer. "You mean the one who had all the roaches in his house."

"Yes, that's the uncle," Kai says firmly. "Could you maybe send the poem to him?"

She can't mail it to Dwayne directly. Inmates aren't allowed to contact inmates at other institutions, not unless they are immediate family. She especially is not allowed to talk to Dwayne, whose active case is linked with hers.

A silence grows on the phone between us. Dwayne was just a boyfriend, and she didn't even have him that long. Why is she writing him poems? Also, I'm scared of getting caught.

On the other hand, my mother sounds so urgent. She isn't safe, and I'm the one who made her so.

What is your emergency? the operator asked when I called 911 from the Dandy Mart, and I didn't even have one. I didn't know what one even looked like. Now I do. An emergency is Kai locked up a hundred miles away from me. An emergency is living in these cabins full of feral children.

Last night, my new roommate crept over and knelt by my bed. She slipped her hand under the covers, groping for the place between my legs. "Can I sleep by you? I'll be so nice." Candace learned this from her stepdad. Joya told me it's why she's in foster care.

I sat up and shoved her shoulders, hard enough to tip her over. "Screw off, lesbo. I don't need a prison boyfriend."

Candace is a weedy white girl who cringes when I talk to her, sidles up and sits too close when I ignore her. She's a mouth breather, snuffling from allergies, and the raw, chapped skin under her nostrils skeeves me out. She smells musty, too, as if someone filled her up with damp laundry and then forgot her.

Candace popped back up, blinking, the whites of her eyes pink and glistening with histamines. "I'll give you two dollars."

I pinched her arm, hard enough to make her suck her breath in. Hard enough to leave a mark. She crouched lower and took it like it was her due, ducking her head down. If she were a dog I'd have seen her naked belly about then. She was new, but I had a reputation. I let her go and rolled away to the wall, turning my back on her. She stayed where she was.

After a minute, the sniffling got to me. I scooted over, making room on the edge of my bed. "Don't get handsy. I want that money first thing in the morning."

She climbed in and pressed herself into my back. We slept huddled together like cold baby animals.

If I am caught forwarding Kai's messages, her sentence could be extended. I could be here longer. The state would push to terminate Kai's parental rights. If we're caught, no family-friendly judge will be friendly enough to overlook it.

Even so, I say to Kai, "I don't know his address. But I'll mail it if I can get it."

It is not a yes, but it isn't a no, either. It is *I'll try*. *I'll try* lands me firmly on the righteous side of *Maybe*.

I open the pantry door to find Candace standing close on the other side of it. She jumps back, bug-eyed. She must not have heard me hang up. I'd thought about snitchy prisoners, or someone on the line with us, but eavesdroppers on my end had not occurred to me.

"What are you doing?" I say, mean-voiced, trying to remember how much I've said out loud.

"I came across to see if there was snacks." Candace has gone about as fetal as she can while still technically standing. I push past her, and she falls in beside me, her dry, pink lips turning up at the corners. "I wasn't listening to you talk with your mom about the mail or nothing."

I spin and grab her wrist in my other hand, squeezing her hard enough to feel her bird bones grind under my fingers. She yelps, and I step in very, very close. My growth spurt has given me an inch and change on Candace, and I use it.

"You don't want to start with me. We sleep in the same room, you understand?" I say it like I hope she will start.

She swallows and her shifty gaze slips sideways, but she nods. The second she breaks, I ease my grip and smile at her, all sweet. Sugar after slaps, because slaps don't seem to last with Candace. Maybe she's too used to them? I need to be careful with her now, at least until Kai's *Ramayana* comes. At least until I decide what I should do with it.

My mother mailed that poem twenty-three years ago, and I still had it. The dark blue ink was faded, and the paper was dry and ratty at the edges, but it was still legible. I'd kept it all these years in an army surplus footlocker at the back of my walk-in closet, on the highest shelf, behind my boot boxes. It floated in other bits of wreckage from my disordered childhood: a tarnished anklet made of bells, the antique glass doorknob I stole from Hervé's house, three strings of Mardi Gras beads.

Now it was inside my briefcase. I'd dug it out right before I left to pick up Birdwine. I planned to drop by Kinkos and scan the pages. I wanted a digital copy for myself because I'd decided I should offer the original to Julian. It was rightfully his—a love poem by his mother, maybe to his father, written while he was in the womb.

"How'd your chat with the kid go?" Birdwine asked. It was the first thing he'd said since a grunty "Can we stop for coffee?" when I picked him up. I'd pointed to the cup I'd gotten him at Starbucks on the way, and he'd put his face in it.

"I don't know. Weird. Stilted. I invited him over this weekend," I told Birdwine, talking over the GPS as it ordered us into a small parking lot. I parked in front of a strip of stores that couldn't live up to the word *mall:* Chinese take-out, a tattoo joint, a quickie mart with milk and Lotto. "He's coming to the loft, but maybe I should take him out for tapas or to a steak place? Neutral territory."

"Play it by ear," Birdwine said.

As we got out, I realized I should have let Birdwine drive, after all. Gentrification had tried and failed here, and this was his car's kind of neighborhood. Across the street, Cape Cod bungalows in various stages of abandoned rehab sat in the shadows of huge Victorians that had been sliced into awkward apartments.

Birdwine pointed to a door near the end, between a nail parlor and a tiny used-book store. It was covered in signs. The top one said OFFICE SPACE FOR RENT. Under that was a sign for Krauss & Spaulding, a ground-zero firm a bare half step up from a do-it-yourself divorce kit. The Worthy Investigations sign was next, the top edge covered by a hand-lettered piece of poster board that said MASSAGE! WAXING! TAROT! WALK-INS WELCOME! That one had an enthusiastic red arrow drawn on, pointing up.

"Hooker?" I asked.

"Oh yeah," Birdwine said.

Birdwine's default setting was quiet, and he'd never been a morning guy, but this was overkill. It was as if he'd decided in cold blood to have this friendship, and now he was doggedly enduring it. If I didn't know better, I'd guess he was hungover. I did know better, though. If Birdwine had started drinking yesterday, he'd be very busy still drinking right now.

"I'm about to check you for a pulse," I said.

He rallied a little bit and said, "To be fair, I bet if you asked her to wax something, she would do that, too."

"One-stop shopping," I said, to keep it going. Up the stairs we went.

At the top was another door with multiple locks and a buzzer system. Someone—likely the hooker—had propped it open with a crumpled soda can. The narrow hallway behind it smelled like burnt Indian food.

"How did Julian end up hiring Worth? This pit should have scared him right back to the suburbs," I said.

Even before Birdwine went digging in his financials, Julian's cheap khakis had told me he couldn't afford the day rates of some high-tech midtown outfit. But I could think of a half dozen small, ethical PI firms that smelled better, both literally and metaphorically.

"I doubt he ever saw it," Birdwine said. "Worth has a slick website."

I paused to look at him approvingly. "Hey, you got a synapse firing. Are you ready to wake up and work this guy with me?"

Birdwine pulled a huge breath in through his nostrils, very loud, and shook his shoulders, like a bear rousing himself after winter.

"I got your back," he said.

A directory at the top told us Worthy Investigations had the office at the far end. We passed an unrented space on the way, the door hanging wide open. It was a single large room with some flimsy partitions set up to make cubicles. No furniture except an unwieldy wooden desk. The floor was covered in deplorable blue carpet, stained and frayed.

"This whole building feels like a murder zone," I said.

"It's very Sam Spade. Philip Marlowe. Julian probably thinks this is what a gumshoe's office should look like."

"Who says *gumshoe*?" I said, but my soft-faced surprise brother, with his Yoda slogans and his inspirational nature pictures, might.

I continued down the hall, and Birdwine followed, narrating softly in a decent attempt at Bogart. "When she strode in on her long, spectacular stems, I knew that dame was trouble."

"Damn straight," I said back, grinning.

With Birdwine roused and ready now behind me, I felt like being trouble. It was a good feeling. More than good; it was downright delicious. Ye gods, but I had missed this. I hadn't felt this alive since—well, since the Skopes depo. That was the day my check came back with Kai's note.

The door to Worthy Investigations was smoked glass. I could see lights on behind it. The detective was in.

I put my nicest smile on, the one I saved for juries. I showed it to Birdwine and blinked, sweet as a fawn. I'd bypassed my suits for a casual short skirt and a raw silk T. I'd softened my makeup, too, pale glossy lips and no hard lines around my eyes. I hadn't blown my hair out, and it swung in shaggy black loops down my back. People, white people especially, mistook me for a girl still in my twenties when I dressed down this way.

"So I'm Bad Cop?" he asked, sotto voce.

"I think so, yeah, but let's read the room," I said. Birdwine was good enough to adjust on the fly. He reached for the door, but I made a quiet tutting noise. "Ladies and Good Cops first."

Worth was sitting at a desk at the far end of a long and narrow room. He looked up as I came in, instantly making a big smile back at me. He was around fifty and in decent shape. His face was square-jawed, topped by a thatch of luxurious, prematurely white hair and a fat mustache. He looked like a dad from a 1980s sitcom, and his maroon tie and button-collar shirt leaned hard into the image.

"Are you Tim Worth?" I asked, a little hesitant.

Worth was already rising, saying, "I sure am! Please, come right on back. My girl isn't in yet, sorry, but I made coffee. Can I get you a cup?"

I was passing through his small reception area, and I didn't think there was a "my girl." The desk by the coffee station had a landline and a lamp on it. No computer, no plant, no family pictures. It looked like set dressing to me. Interesting that he'd made his imaginary assistant young and female and then used the possessive pronoun. *My girl.* I was nine steps into the room, and I was already getting a good bead on this guy. If I steamed him right, he would pop open, simple as a mollusk.

I kept my tone uncertain and said, "No, thank you."

"What can I do you for?" Worth asked, mucking up the grammar with good-old-boy charm. He was attractive enough, if you liked the type or had daddy issues. I was innocent on both counts. Then his gaze shifted past me, and his smooth smile dialed down a notch. "Oh, hello, Zachary."

"Worth," Birdwine said.

The client chairs in front of Worth's desk were low slung with sunken cushions. Worth must have read some *How to Be an Asshole* business book that had taught him about power seating. I stayed on my feet, stopping to the right of his desk, angling myself so I could see the room.

Birdwine flung himself down onto the floral loveseat in reception. It creaked audibly under him. He spread his long arms over the back and relaxed into it, at ease.

His presence made Worth wary, and he looked at me fresh, reassessing.

His brow furrowed. "Wait a second. Do I know you from somewhere?"

"I'm Paula Vauss?" I said, tilting it up into a question. "You gave my name and information to a client. Julian Bouchard?"

"Oh, the bio sister, right." He stayed standing, keeping his head higher than Birdwine's and level with mine. "Half sister, I mean. Obviously."

I felt my smile trying to widen, getting just a little sharky. "Obviously."

Worth started talking, slowly, watching me the whole time, hoping to take my pulse. "I had you on my list to call this week, actually." Sure he did. I kept my hands by my sides, my eyebrows up, letting my body language tell him I was open to him, or at least to his story. "I'm sorry the kid went ahead and contacted you." Not as sorry as he was about to be. I wrinkled my nose, cutesy-wry. I could feel Worth's gaze like a finger running all over my surface, hoping I had braille.

I let a silence happen then, to play him. I'd been off my game for months, but here my game was, waiting for me. Old muscles I'd forgotten I owned were flexing, reawakening. It was a good, stretchy feeling. I let the silence grow.

He was a manipulator, this one, and not bad. Good enough for the young or desperate or not-too-bright. But not great. If he were great, he'd have a better office space and "my girl" wouldn't be a fiction. Good not great meant I could let the silence yawp open like a baby bird's mouth, waiting for Worth to fill it.

Birdwine knew this tactic—all cops did. He picked up an old *People* magazine and started thumbing through it, pages rustling in the silence. Worth fidgeted, looked away. He cleared his throat, and then he decided to go fishing.

"That must have been quite a shock, meeting your brother. I hope that he at least was circumspect about it?" It was a solid approach, very safe. If Julian's appearance had upset me, Worth's tone of mild disapproval put us on the same team, but it wasn't harsh enough to make me defend the kid. It was almost avuncular, like a kindly tutting.

I took the cue, saying, "Not at all." I leaned toward Worth, confiding. "He showed up at my office, during work hours. He *claims* to be my half brother, but I thought"—I glanced at Birdwine, inert and easy on the sofa, absorbed in some celeb wedding or baby shots.

"I see, yes. You're a woman of means, and your long-lost brother appears out of nowhere. You're right to feel cautious," Worth said, going right where I'd sent him. "So you—hired your own investigator?" He mirrored my sloe-eyed glance at Birdwine. When I responded with nonverbal agreement, rolling my eyes as if my assessment of Birdwine matched his, he took a risk and fished a little deeper. "Your mother couldn't confirm Julian's identity?"

I dropped my lashes so he wouldn't see the flash of interest light my eyes. According to Birdwine, Worth's modus operandi was to quickly gather as much info as he could, then parcel it out in drops over long, fat, billable months. If he found Kai back in November—that must have been prediagnosis. Did he not know she was dead? If not, I had a nice trap, made and waiting for me. I put a little bait into it.

"My mother I are estranged," I said. "And I wouldn't ask her about Julian even if we were on speaking terms. She's not what I would call an honest person."

Worth came around the desk, closing the distance between us. He lowered his voice, hoping to speak below the range of Birdwine's ears. "So you hired outside help." I nodded assent and he said, in a near whisper, "Why him?"

"Mr. Birdwine did some work for my firm. But in this matter . . ." I whispered back, letting the sentence trail off, incomplete and unsatisfied.

Worth leaned in closer, touched his chest. "Well, now you've come right to Julian's source. That should have been your first move, really." He was casting himself as Daddy Worth, here to helpfully clear up a small confusion over Julian's legitimacy. I wanted to know if Julian was a con man, out to fleece me, or if he was really the brother who had been put up for adoption. Daddy Worth knew, and Birdwine didn't. I kept my eyes wide and accepted the role of Girl Who Needs Papa to Explain the Situation.

I said, "I wanted to ask you why Julian came to me. Julian doesn't seem to know where my mother is living. You found me, and, well"—I glanced at Birdwine and dropped my voice again, but not low enough. I wanted him to hear—"follow the money. It's the one thing Mr. Birdwine told me that makes sense. It couldn't have taken you long to get from me to her. I send her a check every month."

Birdwine snorted. "I said it wouldn't take a *competent* investigator long. Is your mother hiding near his ass? Is he allowed to use both hands?"

I pursed my lips as if the salty language had offended me, then looked to Worth as if to say, *Do you see what I've had to put up with?* Worth gave me a disapproving headshake, and now here we were, allies. Damn, but Birdwine could work a room.

"Well, of course I found her," Worth said, nice and loud for Birdwine's benefit. "It's simply poor timing that you came to me instead of the other way around. I followed your checks to Austin soon after I told Julian about you, but I like to be thorough. I wanted to confirm before I got Julian all riled. You've seen yourself how impetuous the boy can be."

"Confirm? You met my mother?" I said, and let my skepticism show.

"No, no. We PIs have a network. Those of us who are in good with our colleagues do, at any rate." Another gimlet glance toward Birdwine. "I had a local guy in Austin do a drive-by. He sent me confirmation, some pictures. I'd planned to contact you this week, and then bring you and Julian together in a much less stressful way."

I smiled, both for him, encouraging, and to myself, because I had this asshole now.

"Pictures?" I said. "Oh, could I . . ." I mirrored his body language, leaning in and touching my own hand to my chest. "My mother and I are estranged, as I said. We haven't been in the same state for years." I let that painful truth sit baldly in the room for just a moment, rock solid. The truth was always best. It had such a ring to it. A single good truth could support whole flocks of half-truths and misdirections. I trained sweet, lamp-lit eyes on Worth. "I'd very much like to see the pictures that your colleague took this week."

"Oh, certainly," he said. "I've got a couple printed out, if you'd like to have one?"

"Thank you. I would," I said breathily.

Worth turned to the file cabinets that stood by the wall behind him and opened the top drawer. He finger-walked his way through the B's and pulled his Julian file. He flipped through, finally pulling out a single thick sheet of photograph paper. He set the closed file down on his desk in front of him and leaned across, passing the picture to me.

It was Kai. As I looked at her, the air got heavy, as if the truth I'd set down earlier in the room had built up into a barometric pressure: I hadn't seen my mother, not in years.

In this photo, she was what? Fifty? She looked older than fifty, and very thin. Maybe from the sickness, hidden, but already spreading through her body. Maybe just because she was a smoker and a natural ectomorph. She was sitting outside, in the sunshine. It was a close-in shot, head and shoulders, with what looked like the river behind her. She still had her waterfall of dark hair, but I could see thick streaks of silver running through it. She'd grown a network of lines around her eyes and her jawline had softened. Her mouth had a set of parentheses deep-scored around it, though, as if she'd spent more time smiling than I would have guessed.

Once I breathed through the shock of seeing her, I knew why he'd picked this close-in shot. It showed only the collar of what looked like an embroidered top in thick brocade. Austin in July was ninety degrees and about as humid as Venus; this photo had been taken in November, when Julian hired him. He didn't want to risk me noticing that in this "brand new" photo, Kai was dressed for Austin's mild winter.

"Oh, look at her," I said, and moved to close. "These are from—Monday, you said?"

Worth nodded. "I got them late Monday night."

"That's amazing!" I said. I let my fond smile go wide, wider, until Worth was seeing all my teeth, and damn but it felt good to let them out. I had forgotten how much I loved to step in close, to cut sugar from my voice. "A genuine miracle. Considering my mother died last winter."

There was a long pause. Worth swallowed, and his face went red all around his white mustache. His whole face looked like Christmas morning.

"Well, now, wait. I said I got them Monday, but who knows when my guy in Austin—I mean, no. Maybe I—" He floundered into a silence.

"Hey, Worth?" Birdwine asked, still not looking up from *People*. "As a competent investigator, did you happen to suss out what Ms. Vauss here does for a living?"

I gave a self-deprecating shrug and said nothing. I didn't have to. Birdwine had launched the word *lawyer* into the room. Another ten seconds passed, and a silent torrent of other implied words came rolling in behind: *Lawsuit. Damages. Charges. Fraud.*

I reached across the desk and plucked the file up. Worth fluttered his hands after it, but didn't quite dare to try to snatch it back.

I said, "I believe this belongs to my brother, Mr. Worth, and you're done working for him." I slid the picture of Kai back inside and tucked it into my outsize shoulder bag. I started to turn away, but then paused and turned back. "One more thing. You clearly haven't lifted a finger on this case since November, and yet Julian's gotten bill after bill from you. You've bled the kid for around four hundred dollars every month. Isn't that interesting, Birdwine?"

"I'm riveted," he said. He set the magazine down and stood up, fast, filling up his half of the room. "Hey, Paula, do you feel a refund is in order?"

Worth blinked, his mouth opening and closing like a gigged fish's. He said, "Well, I could, I mean—"

I spoke over Worth. "In fact, I do, Birdwine. I'll take a check, Mr. Worth, which is nice and trusting of me, considering. Ten thousand'll cover it."

He boggled at the amount. "That's a helluva lot more th—"

"I've added in some interest," I said. I'd sized up his clothes, his office space, his fictional assistant, and I thought 10K was doable for him. Barely. It ought to cut him plenty deep. "It's what we'll call a fiscal apology. A very reasonable fiscal apology. Considering."

Worth had gone white. "I won't be extorted."

"Extorted?" I interrupted, and the last vestige of the sweet, blinking daddy's girl was gone. "This is a goddamn gift." I walked slowly around the desk toward him, the clack of my heels on his scratched hardwood timed to be a drumbeat of vicious punctuation. "If it takes you more than sixty seconds from this moment to put that check into my hand, I will revoke the offer, and I will take my brother as a client, and I will destroy you." The closer I got, the more I let my real face, the one I hid behind expensive lip gloss and good manners, out. Out and open and toothy. "This is straight-up fraud. I'll call the cops and get your ass charged and convicted, and that's mostly to set the foundation for my civil case. I will have your license, and your business, and your future. If you're lucky, the judge won't give me your nut sack, tied up in a big pink bow. But I'll be asking for it. Believe it."

There was a second of dead silence. Worth stared into my raw and naked face, and then he wordlessly opened his desk drawer and got out his checkbook. I looked to Birdwine, and I found him looking back.

Really looking, seeing everything that had come roaring joyfully out from behind my civilized demeanor. The air sparked between us. My teeth caught my own bottom lip, so badly did I need something to bite. We were together in this moment, him and me, held in the music of this victory, the song caused by the scratch of Worth's pen against the paper check.

It was hard to drag my gaze away, but when I did, I saw Worth was writing my name in the line by *Pay to the order of.* I rapped my knuckles hard against the desk.

"Do you think I need a cut of my brother's tender little pennies?"

Worth paused, then voided the check and started writing a new one, properly, to Julian.

Birdwine's gaze had not shifted. I could feel it on me. When I looked back, he was grinning. I was not pretty in victory, but Birdwine liked it. Birdwine had always liked me this way, and how had I forgotten?

Birdwine liked it plenty. I felt his gaze on my skin, and it had gone as hot as Worth's had gone cold.

Worth ripped the check out of the book and held it wordlessly toward me.

I took it, and in lieu of good-bye, I said, "He's going to take this to the bank on Monday. There's not a god above the earth or under it who can help you if it bounces."

His eyes twitched in their sockets as he ran some calculations in his head. Finally, he gave a faint, propitiating headshake, and I knew it wouldn't bounce. I could see how much it hurt, though, and that hurt made the air taste sweet against my tongue.

I walked out, and Birdwine followed, closing the door gently behind us. The old, familiar rush from the win was roaring through me. I'd missed this high, missed feeling there was no soft place on my entire body. I was made of bone and teeth and iron blood.

I backtracked down the filthy hall, and when I came to the empty office, it was the toothy, rock-hard me that paused, that turned back to face Birdwine. I was hungry for a vulnerable pulse point, for any soft place I could set my teeth. I looked at him, and I didn't see one. Birdwine wasn't scared of me or soft at all. His face had set in an expression I had not seen since he quit me. We'd been working together again on my pro bonos, but he hadn't looked at me like this. Not once, though he knew I was quite often up for some nostalgia with my exes.

I put my hands flat on his chest. I could feel his heart, thumping fast, a huge reverberation in the broad span of his chest. My hands pushed him toward the open door, and he went through, as though my push had sent him. But it hadn't. Birdwine was a mountain, not some small, soft thing that I could move. My push sent him because he wanted to be sent. I kicked the door shut behind us, and then we were alone. I reached for him, and found him already reaching, too. He picked me straight up off the floor, right out of my shoes.

I swarmed up him as he dragged me, wrapping my legs around him, my skirt riding up onto my hips. I grabbed deep fistfuls of his hair. He brought my naked face up to his face. Eye to eye, I breathed his breath in for a single blinding-hot second, and then our eyes were closed and our mouths were open to each other. His hands were on my hips now, grinding me into him, and I would have paid ten thousand dollars, cash, to have us both animal naked, with no cloth blocking our bodies at their most essential points.

I rubbed my cheek down his, tucked my face into his neck and bit at him there, running my tongue down to where it met his shoulder. I whispered words into his skin. "Let's go to your place."

The second after I spoke, I knew I shouldn't have. I should have let it happen, fast and sweet, right here. We should have crashed around the room, knocking down the flimsy cubicles. We should have had each other in the wreckage.

As it was, I felt him forcefully relax his grip.

"Just like old times," he said. He took a shuddering breath and set me on the desk. He pulled back, and I let him go. His eyes were open again, and almost angry. When he spoke again, it came out flat, not mad at all. Almost matter-of-fact. "We won't work out, Paula. If we start, we'll hit the same wall we hit last time, and you'll break my fuckin' heart again."

It was like being punctured. All the sex ran out of me. Now I saw the grime streaking the carpet, the peeling paint. I smelled burnt cumin. It was that last word, *again,* that got to me.

I hadn't known he'd been in love with me. Was that what he meant, when he said we'd hit a wall? That he had loved me? When he quit me, citing lack of communication, I'd assumed I'd done something to piss him off. When he stopped taking my calls, I'd assumed I'd pissed him off a lot. My focus after that was fixing our working relationship. I didn't give my personal relationships with men a lot of brain space. I specifically looked for relationships with men that didn't require any.

"Birdwine," I said. "I didn't know I broke your heart."

The very words tasted strange. They weren't the kind of words I said, but we were friends now, and I had started this. I'd reached for him first, and I had kicked the door shut. He deserved acknowledgment.

I should have answered my phone when Remi called me back last night, should have had him over for some auld lang syne. Instead, I'd called the ghost of an old love into this filthy room. I'd killed it a year ago, before I knew it existed. I found I didn't like it any better dead. This was not my kind of haunting.

I stood up, and I was instantly horrified at the crunchy feel of the carpet on my bare feet. I hurried to slide back in my shoes. While my back was to Birdwine, I straightened my clothes, smoothing down my skirt and then my hair. When I was more or less put back together, I turned to face him. He was standing quiet and calm by the desk. One big hand was rubbing at his temple, never a good sign. His hair was crazy rumpled, and I had a flash of what it had felt like fisted in my hands as I yanked on it, desperate to get him closer.

I dropped my gaze. We were supposed to be finding my dead mother. We'd agreed to try a friendship—a thing I deeply needed at this juncture. What the hell had I been thinking?

Truth be told, I hadn't thought at all. I had wanted; I had acted.

Finally I said, "I don't screw my friends, Birdwine. Not literally, not metaphorically. So that was an asshole move. I'm sorry."

I'd hurled my truly superior handbag onto the foul carpet in my eagerness. I picked it up now. I almost felt I owed the bag an apology, too.

"*De nada*," he said, though I wouldn't have blamed him if he'd walked off to find a MARTA stop and blocked me on his phone. By the time I straightened up, slinging the bag over my shoulder, he'd stopped his hand from worrying at his forehead.

"I'm not going to break your anything," I told him. I couldn't parrot that word back to him again. *Heart.* I didn't want to keep putting it out there. I didn't want to re-invoke it. "Can we pretend this didn't happen? Or chalk it up to the asbestos in this building? I got poisoned by asbestos."

That made him laugh. Just a little. "Yeah. Asbestos is a well-known aphrodisiac." When he spoke again, he was businesslike, but not cold. "Give me the keys. I'll drive so you can go through Worth's file. We can pick up looking for Kai right where he left off."

Now I did have a soft place. I felt my own heartbeat, pulsing in my throat. "Thanks."

I had to stay on the righteous side of any line he drew. Right now, that meant tossing the keys to him. He plucked them out of the air, and we left the filthy office and backtracked down the stairs, single file, to my car. It hadn't been stolen, and it still had all its hubcaps, so I decided to call that another win. I added it to cutting Worth off at the knees, and for the day, I was still ahead on points. Maybe I'd stepped too close to the edge of this new friendship with Birdwine, but winning was my dear and oldest friend. I could get back in bed with winning full-time, no complications.

We got in the car, the air between us still a little charged. I ignored the awkwardness. We'd had too good a morning to end on something sour or shameful. I pulled Worth's file out of my bag and held it up in Birdwine's peripheral vision, and he smiled. He liked winning plenty, too.

"Tell us, Vanna, what's in the prize pack?" he said.

"Stop by that Kinkos near your place. I want to scan the whole thing. You can have the hard copy," I said. While we were there, I could scan my mother's poem, too.

I flipped the file open on my lap to find the photo I'd already seen. I turned it like a page and found a full-body shot of Kai in the same top, same river in the background. Her back was to the camera, and she was watching a little girl throw bread to the ducks. Her brocade shirt was long-sleeved, paired with old jeans. She looked good from the back, but this was not the right thing to point out: *Hey, Birdwine, peep my genes. My ass could look this fine for another fifteen years.*

"Kai always said ducks were mean sonsabitches," I said. "Yet here she is, hanging with a bunch of 'em."

Birdwine shot me a look, like, *Really? We're making observations about ducks now?*

"They do bite," I went on doggedly. I didn't want it quiet in the car.

Though he'd not said it explicitly, I had no way to un-know this fact: a year ago, Birdwine had been in love with me. What had he been thinking? If a fella was looking for love, I was the wrong road to go down. I was the road, in fact, that was crawling with barbed wire and bears and dynamite, marked with huge signs that said THERE IS NOTHING FOR YOU HERE.

I sneaked a sideways look at him and found him pressing his fingers to his forehead again. Oh, right. Birdwine was an alcoholic; he had a known predilection for chasing after things that were bad for him. Things much worse than me. He kept on going back to something that would kill him.

As if he'd read my mind, or at least my line of sight, he stopped his fingers pressing his temple. He placed his hand deliberately back on the wheel; he knew his tells.

He said, "Yeah. I got my eight-month chip last weekend."

"Congrats," I said, although he'd said it as a warning, not a brag. He rarely made it past six months, and to my knowledge he had never gone a year. He was deep into a dangerous time.

"Is it all pictures?" he asked, changing the subject.

I flipped through more shots of Kai watching fat ducks getting fatter on the riverside.

"No, there's printer paper in the back. Notes, or—" My voice cut out abruptly as I flipped to the next picture. Kai now had her arm around the duck-feeding girl. I looked closer. My breath caught.

"What?" Birdwine said.

"Oh, shit," I said. "Are you kidding me?"

She was a pudgy little white girl, though her skin tone and her mass of dark hair said she might owe some genes to Mexico. I flipped again. The next shot was a close-up. She was snuggled under my mother's arm, and her eyes were spring-green Kai-shaped crescents that curved into narrow moon shapes as she smiled. I hadn't needed the close-up or the eyes to know. I'd already

162 • JOSHILYN JACKSON

recognized the very shape of her, those long storky legs, that squashy middle. It had been my shape at her age.

"Fatty-Fatty Ass-Fat," I said to Birdwine. I sounded like I might be strangling. The shots were eight months old. In another year or two, her body would begin to change, that soft belly slowly shifting up and down into its proper places. Damn, but my mother had some mighty genes.

"I'm pulling over," he said, and turned hard right into a gas station parking lot.

Birdwine shut the car off, and I shoved the picture into his hands. His face changed from curious to curiously blank. I couldn't get a read on him at all.

"Paula?" he said. "Who is this kid?"

"I don't know," I said, but I knew one thing about her. "She's Kai's, though. Look at her. Apparently my mother drops a fucking baby every time I turn my back." I scrabbled through the folder, scattering pictures and papers over the floor, searching for a name. Worth sat on this, too. "I'm going to sue that guy. No, I'm going to kill him. Take me back, I need to kill him, now."

"Who is that little girl?" Birdwine said, and his voice had an odd urgency.

"She's—Hana," I said. I'd expected something like Lakshmi, or maybe Dharma. "Hana May." And when I said the whole thing out loud, I got the reference. It was a feminization of Hanuman. The monkey god, impetuous but so intensely loyal, had always been a favorite of Kai's. I kept reading.

Age nine, so she might be ten by now. Father unknown, although I saw Kai had a boyfriend. Big shocker there.

I'd found all this on a fact sheet Worth had made. This was all the info the asshole had been able to cobble together in a day, nutshelled, stuck in a file, and handed out in tiny bites to keep the money flowing.

"Where is she? Where is she?" Birdwine muttered to himself, scanning the paper over my shoulder. He looked sick. Sick as me, even. Sick down to the root of him. He jabbed his finger at the middle of the page. "There. An address."

A real street address, not Kai's PO box: 1813 Bellman Avenue in Austin. Unit B, so it was some kind of apartment. There was a number listed, too. I went for my phone, but Birdwine got his out first and started punching it in.

I needed to read Kai's note again. I scrabbled in my bag, hunting for the envelope, and why did I have so many lipsticks? It had settled in the very bottom.

No, thank you. I have enough money to last me the rest of my life.

That was a joke. The cancer got everywhere before I noticed, so "the rest" will be quite short.

My hands shook. These pictures had been taken in November, and Kai looked good. A little older than she was, a little on the skinny side, but good. I'd gotten the note in February, and she'd written that she had *Weeks, if I am lucky.*

How lucky could one woman be? More than twenty weeks had passed, bleeding into months. So she had to be dead. Didn't she? Surely she had made arrangements for her youngest child, knowing how short her time was.

Kai had moved fourteen times in the last decade—I had the list of PO box addresses to prove it. Worth hadn't found so much as the father's name, and he hadn't written down Hana May's last name. Was it Vauss? I saw on his sheet that my mother had lived in Austin under the name Kira Redmond. Had Hana been a Redmond, too? What was she now?

"It's out of service," Birdwine said, disconnecting. "No new number listed."

I looked back at my mother's note. *I am going on a journey, Kali. I am going back to my beginning . . .*

The beginning. That could mean she was taking Hana to her parents. But I did not believe it. They were deep into their seventies, if they were even living, and

PS, they were racist assholes. She'd given Julian away to keep him from them; she would not inflict those people on her third child. So what was the beginning? Damn Kai and her love affair with mystic, cryptic bullshit. Sometimes poetry was not the answer. I'd go so far as to say it never was.

"*Death is not the end. You will be the end,*" Birdwine read over my shoulder. "Did she mean to bring the kid to you?"

"If so, she botched it," I said, so fraught I sounded furious. "I tend to notice orphans landing in my lap. Exhibit: Julian."

"But she says she's going to see you?" Birdwine said, pointing.

We will meet again, and there will be new stories.

"That doesn't mean in this life," I said, and read the final line out loud. "*You know how Karma works.* Kai believed in reincarnation."

"She knew she was dying, though," Birdwine said. "She must have had a plan for the kid."

"I hope so, but . . ." I said. "This is one crazy note. They'd lived in Austin a few months when Kai was diagnosed. Can you find someone you'd trust so much, that fast? Someone to raise your child? What if—"

There was no good way to finish that question. *What if* had so many awful answers. I knew what happened to young girls when they were unmoored and left to the mercy of the world. The lucky ones grew tough in foster care. Others landed on their knees inside thickets of azaleas. Either way, their little-girlhood got used up. And those were the ones who lived. Others disappeared right over the edge of the planet, falling past the world turtle into an endless darkness. "Bird-wine—"

"Don't," he said, three fingers pressing so hard into his temple that the skin went pale around them. "No need."

He said it like he knew I was about to beg him. And I was. I was about to beg, and tell him that he couldn't drop me off and put finding Kai's corpse in his to-do stack. He couldn't send me emails titled "Here is the information." He couldn't dive into the nearest bottle, either. It wasn't about me now, or whatever misguided love he'd thrown at me once, or my questionable ability to keep my pants on. That was all crap. Hana made it crap.

A wild tide of feeling had risen in me, both new and horribly familiar. My family wasn't only me. I hadn't felt this way for almost twenty-five years, not since I sent Kai to prison. I hadn't even felt this with Julian, a grown-ass man who'd had a second family all his own. It was a sudden doubling of myself that echoed in the very air around me. I knew what it was to be a child, and lost. I was from that tribe.

I had to make sure that my little sister didn't permanently join it.

"This is something I *can* fix," Birdwine said with odd intensity. I thought he was talking about us, saying even though our onetime love affair was wreckage, he'd help me make sure my sister was safe. But when I looked at him, I saw his gaze was set into the middle distance, and whatever he couldn't fix—it didn't seem to have much to do with me at all.

"What do you mean?" I asked.

He blinked and then refocused on the close-up picture of Hana.

"I mean, I'll find her." Those were to me the three sweetest words in all the English language. He looked at me and gave them to me again. "I'll find her."

Chapter 6

Kai's *Ramayana* comes in a large orange envelope with a brad at the end. It's only a few pages long, so she could have stuffed it in a business envelope if she didn't mind bending the pages. She's illustrated the margins, though, drawing an endless blooming vine of curls and spirals. This kind of envelope comes from the prison commissary, and it costs extra stamps to mail. Either she traded for it, or it's courtesy of Rhonda.

Joya and I sit side by side on my narrow bed to read the *Ramayana*, backs to the wall. Joya's small-boned and big-eyed, and with her hair in little braids she looks younger and sweeter than she is. She looks younger and sweeter than me, for sure, though she's a grade ahead. We sit close, so we can read at the same time. It starts like this:

Just as the serpent's wife is torn, from hearth and
*   home and all true love,*
And by the eagle's claw is borne, away to places
*   still unproved,*
So Sita was torn from Rama. Her heart was low,
But the chains around her could not break her will.
She denied the demon that had found her, and was
*   faithful still—*
And though this happened long ago, it's happening
*   now.*

Joya makes a fart noise with her mouth. "Why are moms so fulla goo?"

"Dunno, but damn," I agree.

We like to say things to each other about how mothers are, because we each still have one. This is what sets us apart and makes the other girls in our cabin hate us, except Candace, who is too weird and broken to get that she's supposed to. Joya and I are a tribe. We even have a name; Candace calls us Gotmamas.

"Why?" I asked her, hearing it as one word.

"Because you two both got mamas, duh," she said, then flinched, like saying *duh* might earn her a slap. It probably did, back where she used to live. But I smile at her. I like it. It names all the places I belong: with Kai, and in this tribe of two with Joya.

The rest of the poem is the same, overblown and rhyme-y, with Sita as a thinly disguised Kai. Dwayne is her unlikely, redneck Rama. Sita-Kai is a veritable cup of love, so full she has a love meniscus. She is steadfast and faithful; Rhonda does not appear in any guise.

The last page after the poem is a colored pencil sketch.

"Oh, hey, now. This is good," Joya says.

It is, actually. Much better than the poem.

"Kai draws for a job, sometimes," I tell Joya. "She sets up an easel in a city park or near some tourist trap, anyplace with good foot traffic. She draws people thinner than they are, or with a smaller nose, and she dresses them like princesses or astronauts. She gets twenty bucks a pop."

In the picture, Sita kneels in the top right of the page, smiling and serene. Her lap is full of lotus blossoms, cradled sweetly to her belly. Kai is good at faces in particular, and in case the poem wasn't clear enough, she's given her own face to Sita. Rama has the sky-blue skin that shows his divine nature, but his features match Dwayne's. Kai has even given this god-prince of ancient India a mop of Dwayne-ish, honey-colored curls.

"Can I come back in yet?" Candace pleads, from the other side of the door.

Joya kicked her out when the mail came, and she skulked off to bathe. Technically this room is half hers, but less technically, she's scared of Joya. Candace is currently the only white girl in our cabin, and she is very, very white. She comes from way out in the methlands of west Georgia, and her skin is milky and her hair is butter-colored, as flossy as cotton candy. Where she's from, black and white don't mix, so it's weird that she's glued herself to me. Inside me, black and white have mixed all the way, with a big scoop of Asian and who the hell knows what all else thrown in.

"Fuck off, Candace," Joya hollers back, and at the same time I say, "Get away from the door."

The demon Ravana is drawn crosswise, with a low worm's body that blocks Sita in the corner. Each of his ten heads is perched on a long neck that stretches straight down to his body, forming bars. In this production, the part of the demon Ravana is being played by the Georgia prison system.

Rama has most of the page. He is moving purposefully toward Ravana, scimitar drawn, ready to attack the demon. Here the margin vines are covered mostly in blooms, but I am looking closely. I see a clot of pointy leaves hidden near Rama in all the flowers, and I am Kai's child; I recognize the shape.

"Pot leaves," I say to Joya, pointing.

I think it's funny, but her eyes narrow. She takes the poem and starts flipping back through it.

"Do you think she's sending him a message? About the drug charges, or . . ."

"Naw. It's just a joke."

Joya says, "I hope so, because if she's telling him to mess with the drug people, they will kill him. They will kill his whole ass, all the way."

I shake my head at her. Dwayne's friends sell mustard sandwiches and acid in the parking lots of concert halls. They shoplift and rob empty houses, sure—they're assholes with peace sign tattoos. But they would kill people only by accident, driving drunk or stoned.

"Crack people aren't the same as pot people," I tell her. Joya's mom was on the pipe before she went to rehab.

Joya snorts. "No such thing as Drug-Lord Lite."

"There's no secret message about drugs," I say, reading back through the lines. I don't want to send the poem, but not because I'm scared of hippies. It's all the goo—was Kai really this big into Dwayne? He was nice and all, but the truth was, we were camping in a bus. She'd fallen for him at least partway because the nights were getting long and colder.

Joya mistakes my silence for waffling. "You still can't mail this. If they catch Kai using you to get to

Dwayne? Shit, they won't blame you. It'll all be on your mom. She'll get TPR'ed."

This is shorthand for termination of parental rights. Joya's voice trembles just saying the letters.

"Now can I come in?" Candace calls through the door, louder and more plaintive.

"Yeah, ho, if you wanna get beat down," Joya says. "Git your ass back in the toilet."

She says it really black, poking at me with her elbow. I have to smother a laugh. She talks like this with some of the other black kids, but sometimes she likes to turn it on for Candace; it makes Candace just about wet her pants.

There is silence from the other side of the door.

"She won't move away," I whisper. I mime Candace, making my lips into a thin line, pressing my ear to an invisible door.

"You want me to move her? I'll pop her head right off her body like a shrimp head," Joya says.

It's not an idle threat. The other two girls in our cabin tried to bully Joya when she first arrived. Shar and Karice came at Joya in the common room, smiling mean, ready to teach her the pecking order. They expected her to shrink and cry and take a quiet slap or two. She was outnumbered, and she's so small and cute. Mistake. Joya leaped right at Shar and grabbed her hoops. She jerked them through her ears, tearing the lobes clean through. When Shar fell down screaming, Joya hurled her tiny body on Karice and bit her on the face, then punched the bite until Karice went fetal. Joya stood up, not a scratch on her, just as Mrs. Mack came running in. Joya told Mrs. Mack that Shar and Karice had been fighting with each other, all the while staring down the bleeding girls, daring them to contradict her. No one did.

"Candace isn't worth getting in trouble over," I tell her, then call, "Just a minute."

I get up and pull my footlocker out from the under the bed. It's the only thing I own that locks—not that the lock keeps Candace out. I open it and start unpacking pictures, my peacock feather earrings, a braided piece of mane I clipped from Hervé's big bay gelding. I want the *Ramayana* lying flat on the bottom, so it won't get wrinkled.

"Y'all! I'm standing out here in a towel!" Candace whines.

I pack everything back carefully, and then I let her in. For the next few nights, I feel that poem's presence every time I try to sleep. It's like I've let something alive and dangerous move in under my bed. I toss and dream. My food tastes flat and all the textures are slightly off. I should burn it, but I don't. Kai asked me to mail it, but I don't do that, either. The tremble in badass Joya's voice when she said *TPR'ed* stops me.

The day before my next court-appointed phone time with my mother, I can't sleep at all. There's a street-light right outside the window, and its brightness feels like a searchlight. I could tell Kai that her poem never came. I could tell her a dog got it. I could somehow blame Candace. On the phone, I could sell it, but what happens when she comes to get me? Like most excellent liars, Kai has a nose for truth. Lying to her face is the hardest kind of lying.

I hear Candace's bed creak, as if thinking her name was enough to summon her. My bed is too full of churning worry to have room for Candace. I scootch to the edge, making my body into a wall against her as she creeps silently across.

Lying won't actually fix the problem. If I tell Kai it's lost or ruined, she can rewrite it and resend it.

Candace hovers, and I pull my blanket up over my head.

"Can I get in?" Candace whispers, as if my blanket isn't answer enough.

"Go die, Candace," I say, mean as I can, but she's impervious. Her spongy body can absorb superhuman amounts of mean.

"I have lickem sticks," she wheedles.

Lickem sticks is Redneck for Fun Dip, my favorite candy. I unturtle from my blanket to see if she really has some. She holds up the little packets. Lime is missing, but she has cherry and grape.

"Where did you get that?"

"Jeremy." Jeremy is a pimply high schooler who lives in one of the boy cabins. He has a constant pants tent and dead eyes.

"Ugh, it probably has perv juice on it," I say. He'd never give her candy, not unless she did something for him. Or to him. That makes me want to pinch Candace as hard as I can, but I settle for telling her, "You're so gross."

Candace shoves her flossy hair behind her ears, truculent, and changes the subject. "I think your mom's poem is real good. It's real romantic."

That has me sitting up, fast, and I do pinch her. "Stay out of my stuff!" She takes the pinch and waits for the next one. She'll take that one, too, and keep on waiting, resigned to it before it even happens. "How'd you get my combination?"

She ignores the question. "I know how you can send that poem to Dwayne and not get your mom in trouble."

"And stop eavesdropping," I say. I blow air out my nose, mad. There are no bounds to Candace's wormy snooping. But now she has two things I want. I sit up and scoot over to make room for her. "Gimme cherry."

We prop up on our thin pillows, licking the bland white paddles and dipping them into the packets of colored sugar. I try to keep an inch between us. Candace isn't loyal. She talks shit about me with the white girls from the high school cabins. But at night, she's like the love vine in Kai's margins. She twines and weaves and clings until I'm flat strangled. I have to keep peeling her off, or she'll grow right up my nose.

She regards me over her candy paddle, her mouth corners turned up to a sly and waiting angle. Her mouth is full of sugar and ideas.

"How?" I say at last.

"I'll whisper it," Candace says. She knows how to milk a quid pro quo.

My mouth sets, but I hold myself still as she closes that last inch between us, pressing in close. I can smell faux grape on her breath.

"Write him a long, long boring letter, like about what you saw on TV, and talk on a lot about how you're working on a poem for a school project. Then you put the poem in, but you recopy it."

"Mmm," I say, noncommittal, leaning away.

She leans with me, propping her head on my shoulder so that her pointy chin digs at me. "If it's in your writing, and if you burn up the original, they can't trace it to your mom at all."

Dammit, it's a good idea. Candace is such a mouth breather, I forget how crafty she can be. I owe her now, so I don't kick her back to her bed when the candy is gone. I turn my back and she presses herself against it. She is out cold in two minutes, limp and still as a corpse.

She never sleeps like this in her bed. She cries and kicks her feet, saying, *No no no,* and *I don't like it.* Listening to her moan and beg makes me feel queasy in my stomach. I wonder if I cry out in my sleep, as pitiful as Candace. I have my own bad nights, when I dream that 911 call.

What is your emergency, the dream-operator asks, and I see cop cars already zooming past the Dandy Mart, hundreds of them, zigging fast like a long line of black roaches. *I don't have one! I don't have one!* I yell, already too late. I see red light, like firelight, rising from behind the kudzu. I hear my mother screaming, and that always wakes me up. I could never, even in my dreams, un-tell the story that I told that operator.

Now Candace is so hard asleep that her head is sweating like a baby's. I can feel it dampening my T-shirt. I stay awake much longer, crammed against the wall in a bed that is gritty with spilled sugar.

By morning, I have decided. I go to Mrs. Mack, and I squeeze out some tears. I am Kai's child, and I know to start with true parts: "He always called me Bossy Pony, and he helped me with my math." The true parts are a foundation that let the lie stand tall and strong: "I know he's not really my dad, but he's the only daddy I've ever known." And then on top of this structure, I set the thing I'm angling for: "If only I could write him. I want to know that he's okay."

Mrs. Mack gets his address for me, even gives me stamps. It's easy.

I follow Candace's plan exactly, mailing Dwayne a long, dull letter that includes the poem, masquerading as a school project. I can't send the drawing. I lack the talent to reproduce it, and the original is way too traceable to Kai. I won't risk a TPR. Dwayne will know the poem is from her, anyway. She tells stories from the *Ramayana* all the time, and the poem reads like hers.

Destroying both the originals would be safest, but my mother wrote the poem, and she drew her own familiar, absent face on Sita. I hide them in the very bottom of my footlocker and change the combination on the lock. Again. Not that it keeps Candace out. It's a mystery, how she keeps breaking in.

I solved it two decades later, when I got out Kai's *Ramayana* for Julian. I'd pulled the footlocker down from the top shelf of my closet, then realized I couldn't remember the combination. Hell, I couldn't remember the last time I'd opened it. I tried my birthday, the day that Jimi Hendrix died, and a host of my old zip codes. I got so frustrated that I rattled the lock, then let it go with a spiteful, sideways jerk.

The cheap thing popped right open in my hands. I stared at it stupidly for a second, and then I started laughing. I closed the lock again, then I pulled and jerked at it, trying to re-create the angle of that sideways tug. It took me less than a minute. Damn that Candace. Joya and I had wondered if her giant bat ears let her hear the tumblers or if she'd been an international jewel thief in another life. I could have changed the combo to the infinite solution for pi and Candace still would have rummaged as she pleased.

Now Kai's illustrated *Ramayana* sat on my breakfast bar with my other childhood souvenirs, and Julian was on his way. The braided bit of horse's mane was gone, likely unraveled long ago, but everything else was laid out like a mini-museum of mother relics. The exhibits were pitifully few, but that hadn't stopped me from straightening and reordering them nine times. He was a solid twenty minutes late.

If he showed, this would be our first face time since our disastrous introduction in my office, when I'd freaked out and Birdwine had threatened him. We'd messaged back and forth a little more on Facebook. I'd told him about getting his file from Worth, the expurgated version. So expurgated it was like a novel boiled down to haiku, but I'd attached the scanned-in pictures of Hana with our mother at the duck pond. He'd responded, *Wow.* Then an hour later, *That's a lot to process.*

No shit.

These interactions gave me no real sense of the kid.

This morning, his message read: *I keep looking at the pics of Hana. What should we do?*

I messaged back, *I gave Birdwine a plane ticket to Austin, my AmEx card, and carte blanche. He'll find her.*

Is he in Austin now? What can I do to help? Julian pressed, so I told him everything I knew. It wasn't much.

Birdwine had checked in with me yesterday, after he visited Kai's tiny apartment on Bellman Avenue. Her boyfriend, Dave Tolliver, still lived there. He thought her last name was Redmond, and that the kid was named Hannah Redmond. On February nineteenth, Kai and Hana had packed most of what they owned into his old station wagon and disappeared while he was at work.

This was a classic Kai breakup move. She'd abandoned everything that didn't fit in the back of the wagon. I had Birdwine pay Tolliver for the car—it was only worth about twelve hundred dollars. In return, Tolliver gave Birdwine everything she'd left behind. He had four big boxes in his storage locker in the basement, mostly books and mail and photos, held hostage in case Kai resurfaced. Birdwine had sorted through it all piece by piece, reading the story in the lines between notes from her doctor, empty prescription bottles, scribbled phone messages, photographs, unpaid bills, and, of all damn things, a pamphlet about cancer. I tried not to imagine some chilly, white-jacketed stranger handing Kai a tri-fold glossy about the thing inside her that was killing her.

Instead, I told Birdwine, "When we moved like that, sometimes there was another man."

"Maybe not this time," Birdwine said. "It's bad. How much detail do you want?"

"Keep it dry, like it's any other case," I said. The mere idea of the pamphlet—that such a thing existed—had almost undone me.

There was a silent moment on the phone, then Birdwine said, "But it's not any oth—"

"Please," I said. The single syllable came out sharp, staccato as a gunshot. "Bare bones on this, Birdwine, from here on out."

"Okay. So. The cancer started in her lungs. She's had emphysema for years, and by the time she figures it's more than that, it's everywhere." Birdwine fell right into his regular rhythm. I knew his hands would be rolling in that way he had when he laid out a hypothetical. His voice was brisk, almost clinical, like I wanted. "Liver, bones, brain. She's starting to have delirium, delusions. Her decision making is impaired. She's on some heavy-duty medication, acting weird, and someone calls DFPS. That's Texas-speak for child protective services. Dave says it wasn't him, and I believe him. He had it pretty bad for Kai—he didn't even call the cops about his car. Could have been someone from a homeschool playgroup Hana went to. I don't think there was another man. They bolted because DFPS spooked her."

The longer he talked, the more my heart raced, and my lungs had started to feel sticky. His story changed the odd parenthetical sentence written up the side of my check. (Obviously I don't want you to come here). I'd thought it meant she didn't want to see me, but the journey she mentioned in the first half of the note was literal. Perhaps she'd only told me not to come because she wouldn't be there.

I said, "But Kai knew she was dying. It's not like she'd take off on a pilgrimage to see the largest ball of twine. She must have had a plan for Hana."

"Yeah, but what? Not one DFPS would approve of, or why go?" Birdwine asked.

I had no idea. Read in the light of dementia and heavy medication, Kai's note read less like hippie-dippy mysticism, more like a dangerous combination of terrified and crazy.

"So what's next?" I said.

"I can follow up with the mothers from the play-group and DFPS, and I got a few known associates from Dave. I have your list of PO box addresses, so I know where she lived before. Dave gave me the tag number, and I can trace her that way, maybe. Anything you can think of that would put me in a direction?"

But there wasn't. Not after fifteen-plus years of sec-ondhand stories and silence.

"Birdwine," I said, and stopped. I had two words stuck in my throat, pounding with the rhythm of my heart: *find her, find her, find her.*

"I got this," he said, soft, calm, deadly serious.

It was as if he could feel my heart's urgent drumbeat through the wires, as if it were driving him as hard as it drove me. He was all in on this search, as invested as if it were personal. Perhaps he had some motivation of his own, but I was too abjectly grateful to question it. I simply took it, and then braced my body for the bad part that came next: the wait.

I sucked at waiting, but I had no other options. Hana had disappeared deep into Kai's world. I'd grown up there. Names, relationships, and identities were fluid. Adherence to the law was optional. There were no safety nets. There had been nothing to catch me when Kai went to prison. She had vanished, ill and drugged, and Hana could have landed anywhere in the whole country. Kai was almost definitely dead by now. Anyone, anything might have Hana.

The buzzer sounded, and the sound almost shuddered me right out of my skin. Julian was half an hour late. I punched the code to let him into the building, then started pacing back and forth, kitchen to front door and back. My heels banged the floor in a nervous tempo that had Henry sticking a disgruntled face over the sofa, wondering why I was vibrating the floors. The angle of his ears changed to alarmed as I stomped past again, and he ghosted back to the laundry room. He had a hiding spot behind the dryer.

Julian was taking so long to reach my floor, I wondered if he was using the stairs. I paced another circuit. Maybe he'd died on the journey through the stairwell, and I'd never see him again. That was the current theme in our shared gene pool. I walked to the front door and jerked it open.

There he stood. He was taller than me, but my heels were high enough to put us even. His eyes widened, and he startled like a deer. His hands flew up. If he'd been psyching himself up to knock, he hadn't made it quite yet.

"Hi," he said.

"Hi," I said back. "Did you want to come in? Or knock? Or . . . ?" I meant it to be funny, but nervous on me often read belligerent.

"Yeah," he said, but he made no move to step across my threshold. He swallowed audibly and scrubbed at the side of his face with one hand, like Birdwine fighting off a binge. "I need to say something first. I've been standing on your mat trying to decide how to apologize for the way things went when we first met. I should have realized you were my sister earlier." The words kept coming in a tumble, as if he were a year-one kid in law school, botching his first overpracticed opening argument in front of a mock jury. "But I thought—I mean, I assumed—but not because I'm—"

"I have no idea what you're saying."

"All the way here I practiced, and then I sat down in my car, sweating and practicing, but I'm blowing it, huh?" He took a second, gathering himself, and then he looked me in the eye. "I'm trying to tell you, straight up, I'm not a racist."

It caught me off guard. I'd forgotten that awkward moment; he'd assumed his sister would be white because he was. He'd apparently been dwelling on it, building it up in his head, and now he was being so relentlessly earnest it was both sweet and unsettling.

I said, "Glad to hear it," to close the topic.

He must have taken it as sarcasm, though, because his skin washed pink.

"No, but I'm *really* not. It doesn't matter to me that you're—" He didn't know quite what I was, and he floundered. To be fair, no one ever did. He finally ended with "—whatever you are." I felt some hugely inappropriate laughter bubbling up and squelched it. I wasn't sure what my face was doing, but it couldn't have been good, because he babbled on. "I didn't have that kind of mom and dad. Not at all." His voice rose in pitch and volume as the words rushed unstoppably out. "I can see why you'd think that, because I went to Berry College, which is WASPy, I know, but my girlfriend there was black, and it wasn't—"

"My last girlfriend was black, too," I put in, to stop him talking. It worked. He froze.

"Oh, I'm sorry. I thought . . ." He trailed off and gulped and said, "I didn't realize you were gay."

"I'm not," I said, and then I *was* laughing. I couldn't help it. "I'm screwing with you."

His eyes got even wider, and he sputtered, "Well, I'm not homophobic!" He looked ready to burst into tears on my welcome mat, and what was wrong with me?

"I'm sorry, it's not funny," I said, though I was still grinning. "It's just—look at my suit."

His gaze dropped to my jacket for a second, and then he looked back to me, confused. "It's, um—it's a really nice suit?"

"I know, right?" I said. I'd dressed like I was heading into a particularly bloody deposition. I'd blown my hair out and put on matte red lipstick. "I've gone Full-Dress Bitch on you. Look at these shoes. The only word for heels this high is vicious. And you're a wreck, and none of this is helping." I turned to the side and kicked the shoes off, and stepped down, barefoot.

I hadn't been nervous, I realized. This kid carried the weight of my life's largest unpaid debt, and I was terrified of him. I hadn't recognized it, because terror wasn't one of my usual modes of operation. But I'd dressed to battle monsters. I'd even laid the relics of our shared heritage out in regimented rows, the way a prosecutor lays out evidence. Now, as he trembled in the hall, I was a little calmer, like a lady who realizes the little garden snake might be more afraid of her than she is of him. Maybe.

I said, "Let's restart, okay?" I took my jacket off and draped it over the table by the door. Garden snakes could be charming little animals, given half a minute and some hospitality. This was a simple meet. All I had to do was figure out what he wanted, and then give it to him. It wasn't that different from my day job, and—the last six months aside—I was very good at that. "First, I don't think you're racist or homophobic or any other -ist or -ic. I don't have a sense of you at all. So come in, and let's change that." I stepped back to let him enter.

"Thanks," he said. He still had worried eyebrows, but he no longer looked like he might vomit. He stepped awkwardly in and paused, his breath catching as he saw my wall of windows. "Wow. That is a view!" He looked around, taking in the way the high ceilings, the stark white walls, and the clean lines of my furniture acted as a backdrop for the boldly colored abstract art I favored. "Your place is really, really nice."

Meanwhile, I was studying him. He had enough familiar features to give me déjà vu: my mother's eyes, wide brow, and length of bone. He even had paler, hairier versions of my long-fingered hands. It was disconcerting.

I looked back up to his face and found he was now examining me just as intently. He blushed and shook his head. "Oh, sorry. This is weird. We have almost the same nose."

He was right, though I hadn't seen it until he said so.

"Weird as hell," I agreed, because it felt that way, even though it was actually exactly how biology worked.

Another awkward pause, and he said, "Any more news from—I forget his name. The spooky guy you sent to Texas?"

"Birdwine. Not yet. But he will find her," I said, very brisk, and changed the subject. "Speaking of PIs, when we went to see the one you hired, I asked him to rethink his life choices. He issued you a refund."

I had Worth's check tucked in my skirt pocket, and I pulled it out and passed it to him.

His eyes widened as he clocked the amount.

"This is more than I—"

I was already waving that away. "Call it damages. I would have taken his ass to court and made him pay more, if I thought he had it."

He stared at the check, his lips pressed tight together with some feeling or another. He finally said, "I can't tell you what this means. Really. When Mom got sick—" He stopped and shook his head.

"Forget it," I said. Birdwine had been right about the kid's fiscal hole; this meet that had me so on edge might have a very simple ending.

He started to put the check in his wallet, but then paused in the middle of tucking it away. "Oh, sorry, but the check is to me—do I need to pay you some? I mean, you went and lawyered at him."

So much for simple. He needed every dollar there and more, especially if he wanted to go finish up at Berry. Yet here he stood in my half-million-dollar loft, staring at a white sofa that had cost more than the amount on Worth's check—a sofa that I'd bought to match my cat—offering me a percentage. If the kid was playing me, he was a virtuoso.

"You got the friends and family rate," I said. His smile sparked at the word *family*, and dammit, it was possible I liked him. It felt uncomfortable and way too personal to like this kid I owed, this kid wearing manly versions of my nose and my hands. "Can I get you some coffee? Or a Coke or something? Or it's after noon, you want a beer?" I could have used a beer myself, because it was now clear that whatever we ended up being to each other, he wasn't a problem that could be solved whole, today.

"I'd love a Coke," he said.

He followed me left toward the kitchen, but paused when he saw all the things I'd spread out on the breakfast bar. "Oh, wow." He went right to Kai's *Ramayana* and picked up the drawing, peering down at Sita. "Did she draw this?"

"Yeah. It's a self-portrait," I said, going to the fridge. "The blue guy with the scimitar is one of her old boyfriends. Math says he might have been your dad."

Julian leaned in close. "Well, if he was, I didn't get his coloring."

I popped the cap off two Cokes and came around to sit beside him, saying, "He went to prison on a drug bust. Kai had me send him a copy of this poem, and if you look, here, and here—" I flipped through the pages, pointed to a line that read, *Sita's belly, full like the moon with love* and another that read, *Sita waxed, love growing with each passing moon.* "Plus, in the drawing, Kai has her whole lap full of lotus blossoms. See how she's cradling them? Her hands, the way the thumbs and fingers touch? It's a symbol of fertility. She was letting Dwayne know that she was pregnant."

Joya had suspected that the poem was a code. Of course it was; Kai wouldn't have risked TPR to send a mash note to a boyfriend.

"Holy crap," Julian muttered. "Why would she do that?"

"I don't know," I said. "Adoption laws in Georgia are tricky, and when she sent the poem, Dwayne was not established as your legal father. I think—best guess here—she didn't want to name him as the father and give him paternal rights. Not unless he came up with some great plan. She was almost halfway through the pregnancy when she had me send this. Best as I can tell from memory and the dates on your adoption records, she was only a few weeks away from choosing the Bouchards and going forward with the adoption. Maybe she hoped he'd work some kind of miracle? In the poem, Rama saves Sita—he comes in with an army and another god, Hanuman, and he sets her free. I think, bottom line, she didn't want to give you up."

Julian digested that, then said, "You really think that this guy was my bio dad?"

I shrugged. "I don't know. I think it served Kai's interests to tell him he was, in case he could help her. You can explore that, if you like. Just pick a better PI than Worth. All I can tell you is, I mailed Kai's poem, and I never heard back from him."

We sat in a silence that was oddly wistful on his side, uncomfortable on mine. Kai had entered prison as full of luck and fortune as she'd ever been, but she came home empty. Under the ashes and the soured red wine, she'd smelled like loss. Her gaze was blank and distant. I'd gotten wild with boys and beer and petty crime, acting out, trying to recapture her attention. Anything to wake her up, make her eyes focus on me again.

I never knew what I had really cost her until this boy-child named after Ganesha showed up at my office.

Julian set the drawing to the side and reached for the stack of early photos. I watched over his shoulder, narrating as he flipped through. I pointed out teenage Kai posing with some other hippie wannabes, showed him the ranch home outside Dothan where she grew up with our shared, sour grandparents. Then I walked him through a string of photos of our gypsy life after we left Alabama.

"Do you have any of the guy, the one she sent the poem to?" he asked.

I didn't. I had no pictures of any of Kai's boyfriends, I realized. Not directly. In the pictures I'd chosen to keep, the boyfriends were present only as objects in the background, setting tone. Here was Kai folding into a pretzel on Eddie's purple yoga mat. Kai drinking chicory coffee at the café under Anthony's apartment. Four different pictures of Kai and me on Hervé's horses.

"Sorry," I said. "I don't think I do."

Julian's head cocked to the side, and he looked so wistful. "It's okay. Maybe it's better. I've already lost three parents this year. That's weird, huh? Even if I hadn't been adopted, I still would have ended up an orphan."

But not an only child, I thought.

If I had never dialed 911, we would have grown up together. I tried to imagine it—a world where Kai never went to prison, and I didn't land in foster care. Where I never learned to hit hard before I could get hit, and where I had a baby brother. I would have fed him, rocked him, read to him—all the things much older sisters do. People come to love the thing they serve, and so I would have loved him. Who would I be, if I were sitting by Ganesh instead of Julian?

It didn't matter. That was a world that never happened, and now here I was with this sad boy, each of us folded up alone inside our separate histories and sorrows. I felt I should do something. Hug him? Pat his shoulder? But I wasn't touchy-feely by nature, and he was grieving his adoptive parents more than the mother that we'd shared. To be fair, I was having a hard time learning how to grieve for her myself.

"It's weird to think that I was born in prison," Julian said. "I'm sure I'm not processing it right. Or at all. It feels distant. It's like hearing your great-great-grandfather was a bootlegger or a pirate. It's fascinating, but really fictional. I mean, I had my own mom and dad, you know?" He shook his head and half turned to me. His eyes had gone very red. "I do get that it's real life for you."

Then he did the thing I couldn't manage. The kid leaned in and hugged me. A real hug, committed. I stiffened up—I couldn't help it—but he was clearly a dog person, so I didn't pull away. It went on for several seconds, Julian patting at my back like he was burping me.

I stared over his shoulder at the collection of items from my footlocker. There wasn't much there. I tried to be still, feeling his heart beating inside him. Awkward as the contact felt, the kid was larger and more alive than my whole childhood. My childhood barely took up half the breakfast bar.

My cell phone started ringing on the charger in the kitchen, and I almost leaped backward, relieved. Julian ducked his head, embarrassed.

"Oh, sorry, I—"

"No, no, it's fine. But I should get that. It could be Birdwine."

He sat up straight, nodding, and I went around the bar to answer it, still feeling faintly surprised at the sound. Half a year ago, that jangling ringtone had been a near constant noise, announcing calls from partners, friends, employees, opposing counsel, clients. Not long ago, I was so used to the feel of a Bluetooth in my ear that I sometimes fell asleep in it.

I picked up the phone and looked at the screen. It wasn't Birdwine. The screen said OAKLEIGH WINKLEY.

How unexpected. I'd programmed her info in back when Nick first signed her, thinking I'd be sitting in on most of her proceedings. Instead, I'd botched it and lost her. Now, not even a week later, she was calling me.

I held my finger up to Julian and said, "I have to take this. It's a client." I'd said those words a thousand times, but it had been a while. They felt good and familiar in my mouth. I slid the green bar sideways and said, "Paula Vauss."

"Oh, good, you're there," Oakleigh said. Her kittenish lilt had quite an edge to it today. "It rang five times at least. I was so sure I was going to voicemail."

"Hello, Oakleigh, what can I do for you?" I said.

"I might be in some trouble? The police want to talk to me. A man just called me, a policeman," Oakleigh told me, and I recognized the edge then. It wasn't bitch. Oakleigh was experiencing fear, and she wasn't used to it. I'd welcome her to the club, except I didn't want to be in one with Oakleigh. "I could call that other lawyer, my new divorce one, but I don't think he does things with police. Then I remembered Nick saying you did, like, crime things, like, for charity?" I almost smiled, because that was so like my partner. He'd been impatient and then angry about my string of destitute criminal clients, but not so angry that he wouldn't spin it to make us look good: *Paula's pro bono exemplifies our firm's commitment to giving back.* Oakleigh was still talking. "He said that's why you missed my deposition, so I dug your card out of my purse—"

"Why do the police want to talk to you, Oakleigh?" I asked.

"My ex—my almost ex. I mean, my husband. He's in the hospital, or he was earlier this morning. He thinks I tried to kill him. He told the police I did, anyway."

I blinked, nonplussed. Julian had perked up at the word *police* and was looking at me with his eyebrows up and questioning. I took a beat to formulate a careful question.

"Why would your husband think that?" I got the tone right. Calm and nonjudgmental.

Oakleigh made an angry huffing noise and said, "Oh, it's his own damn fault. He's been sneaking back into the house and doing things. Doing awful things, and now I'm missing spin class! But most of his clothes were still here, so—look, it's really kind of compli- cated. And I don't know when the police will get here. Can you please come over?"

"The police want to talk to you at home?" I asked.

Julian stood up, eyes very wide now, watching me like I was a movie with a twist. It was cute, so I shook my head at him, wry and wise, like this kind of thing was happening to me every other minute.

"Yes, I told you. They said they'd be by this afternoon, which in retrospect is super unspecific," Oakleigh said.

I wasn't alarmed. If Oakleigh had taken a shot at Clark or put bleach in his margarita, the police would not call and set up a polite appointment. They'd show with no warning, to see her fresh reactions. They would haul her ass in and ask stern questions in a box. This sounded to me like a dumb-ass domestic squabble—something any good divorce attorney could handle. On the other hand, getting Oakleigh Winkley back in our firm's fold would be a coup. It would go a long way toward making things right with my partners, and I wanted that.

"Can you hold? I need to see if I can move my two o'clock," I told Oakleigh. I hit the phone's mute button without waiting for an answer.

"You have to go?" Julian said.

"I do," I said, with genuine regret. I'd gone stiff when he hugged me, then bounded backward and away at the first opportunity. I didn't want our time to end on that note.

"Oh, no! But we didn't even get to Hana yet." He kept bringing up Hana, but there was nothing to discuss. Birdwine would find her for me. He had to, and that was all. "I don't have a shift at work until tomorrow. Can't I wait here until you're done?"

I felt an immediate internal balk. I couldn't give this kid free run of my loft. It seemed more intimate and invasive than the patting. He would make nice with my cat and go through all my closets. Not that I would blame him. If he left me alone at his place, I would surely rifle through his drawers. We were curious about each other.

If he were five years younger, I'd give him forty dollars and drop him off at the mall or the movies until I was done with grown-up business. I wasn't sure that would fly with someone in his early twenties.

I said, "You could come with me."

"Really? To a police interview?" he said, his voice rising with excitement.

"Why not?" I said. Now he was practically bouncing on the stool, and what the hell. I hadn't checked the calendar. It might well be Bring Your Puppy to Work Day. "You'd need to keep your mouth shut, but it won't take long, and I could take you out to dinner, after."

"Yeah. Cool," he said.

I found myself smiling, and I realized I actually wanted him to come. Part of it was injured pride. When we first met, I'd been shaking in the center of a full-blown panic attack. Today I'd started out scared into pure bitchdom, then ended stiff and almost weepy. I wanted him to see me more myself. I took the phone off mute.

"I can clear my afternoon," I told Oakleigh, walking over to my office area. "But understand me: If I take this on, then I'm your lawyer, period. You ditch the new guy, and my firm handles your divorce."

"Fine," she said, so relieved she sounded downright eager.

"I'll bring a contract over. You need to sign before you tell me any more about what you did or didn't do." I swirled the mouse to wake up my computer.

"Okay, wonderful. Hurry, please. The policeman said—"

I overrode her. "And I'll need a retainer." I started our standard client contract printing.

There was an awkward pause. "Well, but, my funds are limited. Clark's being so unreasonable." I let my own bored silence speak for me; this point wasn't negotiable. "I could swing maybe twenty-five thousand? Is that enough? Just to start?"

"Fine," I said, like I was doing her a favor. Money was so relative. In Oakleigh's mind, a mere twenty-five thousand lying around spare was tantamount to being broke. I wondered what Julian would make of that. I started an intern form printing, too, while I had my work files open. I'd need to hire Julian for today if he was going to sit in on a client meeting. "I'm on my way. And Oakleigh, if they beat me there? Be sweet, offer coffee or tea, but stall the interview. Tell them I'm coming." If anyone could turn a simple domestic into something serious, it was Oakleigh Winkley, swanning about all privileged and unsupervised with cops.

"Just hurry," she said, and we hung up.

I got the forms and went to the door, where my jacket and shoes were waiting, glad that I'd gone full-court bitch this morning, after all. I could be ready to walk in three minutes. Julian followed me.

"It should be interesting," I told him as I got back into uniform. "At the very least, we'll learn the proper shade of nail polish for a police interview."

He smiled, a little bit uncertain. Well, he hadn't spent quality time with Oakleigh Winkley. An hour with her, and he would get the joke.

"I'm glad. I was so interested in the pictures, you know, I got distracted," he said.

"From?" I said, smoothing down my skirt.

"Hana," Julian said, like it was obvious.

I shot him an irked look. "I told you. Birdwine—"

"Is finding her, I know," Julian said. "That's great, but then, what happens after that?"

I was grabbing my bag, turning toward the door, but his question froze me in my tracks. Everything after *find her* was a blank, and her present was distorted by the lens of my own past. Thoughts of Hana sent me back in time, back to when I'd been the lost girl.

I found that I could not imagine an after. How could I? Hana was suspended in the now, like Schrödinger's cat. She was both alive and dead, safe and scared, hungry and well fed, sleeping easy and crying in the dark. I'd been blind to even the idea of Hana's future. I'd only seen her teetering in an uncertain present.

Julian's simple question set me reeling, and I understood that Hana and I, we were not the same. I'd been a Gotmama, a loved girl with a lifeline. When my mother was taken, it was only off to jail. I'd had total faith that Kai would come for me. What faith could Hana have, once Kai was dead and gone? Hana was stuck wherever Kai had left her, with whatever brain-addled arrangement Kai had made—or failed to make.

Hana didn't know that I existed, much less that I was looking for her. She didn't know that anyone was looking. Hana wasn't like me. She was like Candace, Shar, Karice—every lost girl in the world who felt herself unvalued and unsought. She had no way to know that somewhere in the world, right now, her name was being called.

Chapter 7

A long time ago, this happened, and it's happening now. Raktabija, the Red Seed Demon, arose against the Earth. He came to burn it and warm his great red feet among the cinders.

The armies of the Earth rose up, swords lifted to protect their mother. They ran at him, and they cut him in a thousand places, all at once. The Red Seed fell, and the army cheered.

But even as the armies celebrated, the Red Seed's blood was soaking into the earth, and the earth is such a fertile mother. From every place even a drop had touched down, another Raktabija sprang up, full grown, swords drawn, so that the thousand cuts became a thousand demons. The armies of the Earth fell back, with a host of Red Seeds now assailing them.

They fought so bravely, all Earth's sons, but it did no good. Each time they cut a demon down, the blood would spatter. Each drop would spawn another from the soil, and another, and another, until the armies of the Earth were outnumbered. Their bodies lay in heaps upon the ground, and soon they would all be destroyed.

It was then that Kali came. She came not because she had been called by men; all human beings call out to their gods, and very few get answers. Kali came because the heart of Earth herself was groaning.

The demons were afraid when they saw Kali, until they realized she had no swords. Only bells. How they laughed and pointed, to see a champion so armed. She had tiny bells tinging on her fingers, larger ones chiming on her wrists and ankles, and great, deep bells roaring as they hung in a cinch around her waist.

They laughed, but they did not laugh long. Kali began dancing to the music of her bells, and as she danced, she let her long tongue unfurl from her mouth. It snapped like a whip, keeping time. It whirled like a dervish. Her tongue did its own dance to the tintinnabulation of the bells, and it was redder and faster than all the legion of the Great Red Seed.

The armies of the Earth rallied, and began to cut the demons down. Kali danced among them, whipping and whirling her red tongue, lapping blood from the air before it could fall. She licked up every drop, so by the time each demon died, he was a husk, as empty and transparent as a plastic bag. The drained bodies of the Red Seed were so light, so empty, that they flurried in the air as Kali's feet danced through them. Earth's armies reaped and mowed, and Kali drank and drank, until all the Great Red Seed was only dandelion fluff, riding the winds in swirls and eddies.

"Bitch, get off the phone," a female voice says on the other end of the line, so loud it crackles.

Joya and I startle at the interruption. We are huddled side by side on the floor of the pantry with the old phone set to speaker, our heads cocked to listen to my mother's story.

We look at each other wide-eyed, and then Kai is back.

"It's okay. Rhonda's talking to that rude woman about manners. Oh, wait—one more second."

We hear muffled, angry conversation through the speaker.

Joya hugs herself and whispers, "Shit, your mama can tell a good story."

"Yeah," I agree.

My mother's stories do not have a Disney version; if they're spooky, then she tells them deep-down spooky. Maybe too spooky if she is going to be this far away, fighting about phone time with a mean-voiced lady who might be dangerous.

"I'm back. We have a few more minutes," Kai says.

Joya asks Kai, "Is that the end of the story?"

"No," Kai says, at the same time I say, "Yes."

I don't want my mother to gain a mortal enemy because I kept her talking. I want her safe. Also, I like it when the Red Seed tale ends here. If it were night-time, and Kai were tucking me in bed, she would now say, *Each of those demon-dandelion tufts is a wish for you. Close your eyes and make them.* I'd be fast asleep before I ever finished wishing.

I don't like Kai's favorite end, where Kali, drunk on demon blood, cannot stop dancing. She's so wild and mighty she begins to crack the earth itself. She cannot be stopped. The armies quail, and all seems lost, until her lover comes. He lies down directly in her path, and when her bare foot touches his chest, she stops at once. *Lest she crush his precious heart,* Kai says in that version, and that's my cue to make a puking noise.

"Do you have time to finish?" Joya asks, ignoring me.

I shoot Joya an irked look. She's supposed to be sitting outside, guarding against Candace's big ears. But then Kai started to tell "The Red Seed," and I invited her in. I thought Joya should hear it, especially since a new kid has moved into our cabin. Kim is a hulking girl with heavy, scowly eyebrows, and she's posse'd up with Shar and Karice. The odds have shifted against the Gotmamas. Shar is giving Joya stink eye every time their paths cross. Shar still owes Joya plenty for her earlobes, and Joya's mama has completed rehab and moved into a halfway house. Shar is running out of time to pay her back.

There is power in my mother's tales, and this story is a mighty call to rally; I wanted Joya to have a share. "The Red Seed" is the story I hoped for the day those Paulding County white girls named me Fatty-Fatty Ass-Fat. If Kai had told it that day, I might have gone back to school with bells on my wrists, ready to take on the world. Instead, Kai told "Ganesha's Mouse," and I called 911.

"She needs to get off the phone, before she gets in trouble," I tell Joya, loud enough for Kai to hear me plain.

"But I want to hear the end," Joya says.

"Every story has a thousand ends," Kai says. She sounds calm, or maybe she's just tired. "I could tell you an end that even Paula doesn't know."

"Oh, please?" says Joya, and now my interest is piqued. I like to stop when Kali wins the battle, but Kai likes romance. There is no third ending that I know.

"Long ago, right now," Kai begins, "Kali has a new-born boy—"

"Wait, she what?" I say.

I've never heard a tale where Kali is a mother. She's The Mother, sure, the one who burns the ancient forests down. After, from the charred ground, the new grass grows in sweeter and greener than ever before. But I can't imagine Kali as some mommy, using two of her many hands to change a diaper while the human bones tied to her wrists rustle and scrape.

"She said Kali had a baby. Shut it," Joya says, and Kai begins again.

Long ago, right now, Kali has a newborn boy. But Kali is drunk on the Red Seed's blood. She dances her victory so violently against the earth that the big bells at her waist sound like artillery. Her finger bells ting so high they hurt the ears, and the bells on her wrists bark and clang. She dances so hard, the world begins to crack at its foundation. The cities shake. The oceans churn and foam.

The bravest soldier snatches up her tiny son and brings him to the battlefield. He creeps as close to

Kali as he dares and sets the baby gently on a pile of Earth's fallen soldiers. Then he runs. The bodies are cold, and the baby is naked. He is unhappy to find himself alone and so chilled. He opens up his tiny mouth and wails, a bare scrap of sound.

But Kali hears. She stops dancing, and her bells fall still. In the silence, everyone can hear the baby cry. She goes to him, running quick and light. The oceans calm, and the Earth shivers back together, knitting at the seams. She lifts the baby up and sits down on the heap of corpses. She begins to nurse him, rocking and singing. The bells chime sweet and quiet with her gentle movements. All around her, the white chaff of the demons begins to settle, landing in drifts like new snow. It blankets the carnage until all the world is covered, remade fresh and faultless. The only colors come from Kali and her son, nestled together on a white hilltop.

Kai stops speaking, and it is very quiet. This is the right way to end the story for the Gotmamas. This is the end where you are cold and all alone, and your mother comes and gathers you up. Even Joya's eyes have pinked. She breathes out a sigh, and then, outside the pantry, we hear a muffled sniffle.

I recognize the sound; it's that damn Candace, come to steal more of my conversations. Her allergies have betrayed her. Either that, or she's feeling some emotion that she has no right to feel. Joya is up in a flash, leaping out of the pantry with murder writ large on her face. I hear Candace retreating at full gallop, hollering, "Wait, wait, wait, wait, no, no, no!" and the pounding of their feet as they race across the rec room.

I take the phone off speaker, and in the quiet, I can hear Kai's breathing has constricted.

"Mama?" I say. I rarely call her Mama anymore. Not since she was with Hervé, and I got used to saying Kai. I wouldn't have called her by that name if there was a chance in hell that Candace was nearby to hear. It is a sacred word to me and Joya. "Mama, are you crying?"

"No, baby," my mother lies. She's good at it, but no one's that good. There is a pause, and I clutch the phone hard, leaning into it. I am so attuned to her breathing, to the quality of her silence, that I can sense her bringing herself in hand. Miles apart, I feel my mother's spine straightening, and it straightens my own. I feel her sad mouth willfully re-form into a smile. When she speaks again, her voice is brisk and cheery. "Baby-mine, my phone time's more than up. I love you. Take care of yourself, and I will see you soon. So soon. These last few months will go by in a blink." A lie, but such a good one. In that moment, she makes herself sound so sure, we both believe it.

I hadn't seen my mother for a year and a half. I'd had a birthday, grown three inches, and started my period. She had shrunk, emptied of my brother. Ganesh was truly gone by this time, already remade into a Julian.

Had she seen the baby? Held him? Nursed him? When they took him from her body, did they have to say he was a boy, or had she already known it, the way she knew I was a girl?

You had such a female energy, she always said.

Odd to think of myself that way, small and blind and tethered to her. In that time before memory, everything I touched was hers. I heard her voice from the inside, with no idea that she was a separate person. Back then, she had simply been the world.

This boy sitting in my passenger seat began his life there, too, in my abandoned room. When Kai told the new ending to "The Red Seed," had he been the baby she imagined? I didn't think so. By the time she told that story, she'd already sent him to the parents she had chosen, carefully, using Kai-centric criteria.

The Bouchards had been solidly middle class—a kindergarten teacher and an insurance agent—because Kai didn't trust the rich. In love, because Kai was big on love. A mother with a medical condition that pre-cluded bio kids and pushed their name down on adop-tion waiting lists, so Kai's boy would likely be their only, the single son that they revolved around. I glanced over at him, earnestly reading in the passenger seat. I took in his smooth pink cheeks and his curls. His eyes were wide and bright. He looked like the poster boy you'd pick to represent whole milk, or organic peaches. No baby had ever been set down in a place less like a battlefield.

We came abreast of a southern-style colonial Mc-Mansion, and my GPS announced we were at Oak-leigh's. I pulled in, glad to see my car was the only one in the long drive. The cops weren't here yet, and it was a good thing, too. I needed to get my game face on. All the way to Oakleigh's, watching my half brother trying to decipher the mud-thick legalese of the intern-ship agreement, I'd been thinking of Hana and of Kai's story of the Red Seed.

That baby on Kai's battlefield was me. In reality, I'd been all gangly limbs and bitchiness, with a rash of pimples on my forehead and my hip near permanently cocked at an insolent angle. But to Kai, I had been the beloved thing heard crying on a heap of corpses, tiny and cold. She had signed away the baby in her belly; I was all the baby she had left. She wanted to come for me and save me. I would fill her empty mother's arms, saving her right back.

I'd never understood that story fully, not until the boy she lost asked me what I'd do with Hana when I found her. Julian, wise in the ways of the nuclear family, had seen the situation from angles that did not exist for me. What the hell *would* I do?

My half brother stole a nervous peek at me as he flipped to the last page. I didn't have his frame of reference, especially for the word *family*. When I was a kid, family meant me and Kai, freewheeling through a revolving cast of lovers and friends who ultimately did not matter. I hadn't owned baby dolls or Barbies, but sometimes, when I was small, I had played house with Kai. I would be the mommy and feed her with my spoon. I must have thought that one day I would be a mother. Then I made the 911 call that put a crack in us. The crack spread and widened until my family fell into two parts, me alone, and her. I'd never tried to make another.

I was halfway through my thirties, and biology had yet to trouble me with even a mild urge to reproduce. I couldn't imagine that it would. I'd always joked that if my biological clock went off, I'd skip the snooze button and yank my whole alarm system out by the roots.

But the need to find Hana had hit me like biology. It was that basic, and that unreasonable. I wanted to find her in the same way that a starving person wants a sandwich, or a person underwater swims straight upward toward the air. All I had to do was think her name, and the world reversed. I'd know what it meant to be the lost girl, swamped in a wash of feeling much too strong to be mere memory. My heart would race, beating out the call to *find her, find her, find her.*

It was hard to see past it, because urges to breathe or eat or nurse the crying baby yell too loud for logic. They come from deep down in the most primitive portions of the brain. Julian had jerked me right into reality simply by asking the question. When Hana was found, what the hell was I going to do with her?

Raising kids was not remotely in my wheelhouse. Hell, I didn't even have a place to put her; I lived in a radically open space specifically designed for single residents. The lack of walls declared I was a loner louder than a thousand closed doors could. I had no room in my life, literally, no den or extra bedroom, that would allow for any kind of family.

Julian was still reading, drinking in every word. This was the same kid who had wandered the city with all his most important papers stuffed in a file. He had thrown them on my floor and then galloped off in a panic. Well, he was impetuous and emotional, but he'd been Raised Right, in the southern sense. He knew to put his napkin in his lap, to open doors for little old ladies, and to read contracts before he signed.

"It's an intern form," I said. "I need you to sign it mostly so privilege applies here."

"Yeah. And this is a really good idea," Julian said without looking up. "Today feels like good practice."

"Practice? For what?"

"Like, so we can learn to work together," Julian said. I opened my mouth to tell him this was only for today, but he was still talking. "We'll have to, when we find Hana."

I tried to make a noncommittal noise, but it came out like a hum in the midst of being strangled. He'd reset the angles, again.

He'd said *we*, as if he already had a place inside my nonexistent plans. As if he had the right to shape them. But he wasn't in my tribe, much less in Hana's.

This kid had grown up in suburbia, with a mommy and a daddy and a bike and probably a dog named Duke or Fido. He had three-quarters of a Berry College education and no frame of reference to imagine the world that Hana and I came from. He'd never set a toe into the places Birdwine would be looking for her. All we had in common were my mother's genes, diffused by different men and scattered into each of us. He was demanding a piece of a kind of pie he'd never smelled or tasted.

He handed me the signed form. "Ready," he said. He sounded downright perky.

I couldn't think about this now. He was right. I had a job to do that was the very opposite of the lunacy he was proposing. I vivisected families; this orphan was asking how *we* could create the very thing that my life's work was deconstructing. I shook my head at him and got out of the car, walking toward the job I understood.

He got out, too, following me to the wraparound porch. I forced myself to put aside his assumptions and focus. I rang the bell, smiling for the camera. I didn't spot its small glass eye gleaming at me, but security cameras were what rich people had in lieu of peepholes. I could feel it, that faint electric charge that crept across my skin when I was being watched.

Oakleigh jerked open the door almost immediately, scowling. Her glance took in Julian, his legal pad and pen held at the ready, and dismissed him as something secretarial. She skipped hellos and introductions and went straight to bitching, even as the door swung wide.

"I don't see why I have to talk to the cops. Clark's the one who broke in here and started this. Can we make a counter-thingy, and get *him* arrested? He's trespassing, moving and ruining my things—every day." The lather of fear I'd heard in her voice on the phone was gone, transmuted into anger. Julian leaned back from the blast, eyes wide. She turned and stomped away, and we followed her into the vaulted foyer. "I changed the security code. Twice. What am I supposed to do now?"

"Change clothes," I suggested. Her dress was red, and tight, and very short, worn with black boots that came up past her knees. There was a lot of slim, tan thigh showing between her hem and the boot tops, and as we followed her in, I caught Julian looking. He blushed bright pink and looked deliberately away. To be fair, I didn't know many straight men who could have kept their eyes trained purely up toward heaven.

"I already changed. When I called you, I was in yoga pants," she said, waving us forward. There was a sweeping staircase, and beyond that, a wide arch opened up into a great room. She angled to the stairs, climbed three steps, then paused and turned toward us. Almost posing. "Cops love this dress. Last month, it got me out of a ticket."

"Mm-hm," I said, hoping to all the gods we wouldn't get a female cop.

Then she turned to the wall and jabbed her finger at a patch of nothing. "Look at this!"

"I see white paint," I said. "This is Juli—"

"White?" Oakleigh interrupted, and now 10 percent of her rage was aimed at me. "It's Polar Vanilla, which is a very warm cream. But can't you see the square?"

She jabbed at the wall again. Julian and I leaned in like a pair of paint-shade critics, and then I saw the faint shift in the color. A small rectangular patch shone a little brighter than the rest, and there was a tiny nail hole at the top. "What you don't see is my Picasso sketch. And you don't see it because Clark took it down and stuffed it in the liquor cabinet to make me think that it had been stolen. What are you going to do about it?"

Oakleigh was treating me like the help and Julian like furniture. Time to get my girl in hand. I made my face look blank and bored and held out my contract in two fingers. "Nothing, until you sign this. And I need that check."

She rolled her eyes, but she came down and snatched the papers, then held out a peremptory hand toward Julian. He passed her his pen. She turned on her heel and stomped through the archway, leading us into the great room.

There a huge sectional sofa, ash colored and covered with an excessive number of black and white throw pillows, faced a fireplace big enough to roast whole pigs. Oakleigh walked around it to a Cheveret desk. She opened the drawer and pulled out a checkbook.

Julian was looking around the room with his arms tucked close to his sides.

"Relax," I told him, sotto voce.

He shook his head and whispered, "If I break a vase, I'll have to sell my car to replace it."

Funny to see him so intimidated by this show of money. He'd been this way to a lesser extent at my office and my loft, but when I was growing up, the Bouchards' suburban house would have looked down-right ritzy to me.

"Oakleigh doesn't seem to mind ruined things," I said quietly, pointing to the picture hung above the fireplace. It was Clark and Oakleigh's wedding portrait.

They stood together on a sweeping antebellum stair-case, Oakleigh in a huge dress that made her look like a poufy haute couture meringue and Clark in a bespoke tuxedo. It was my first look at Oakleigh's husband. Or bits of him, anyway. He was elegant and slim, with art-fully tousled blond hair and a chiseled jawline—pretty much what I'd expected. What surprised me were his devil horns, his Hitler mustache, and the blood-red slanting demon eyes with slashed black pupils that ob-scured the top half of his face. Oakleigh herself had no face at all, just a jagged black scribble of ballpoint-pen ink. Her whole head had been annihilated with such pressure that the canvas had rips and scours.

"There," Oakleigh said, tearing a check out of the book. She came across the room to join us, looking at the portrait. "Yes, you see? I shouldn't have drawn on him like that, but at least I'd pulled it down and stuffed it in the closet. He wrecked my face and hung it right back up. I left it to show the cops."

She handed me the check and the contract, both signed. The O in Oakleigh was huge, and the rest of the letters were as curly and fat as anime bunnies.

"Don't sign things you haven't read," I told her, putting them inside my bag.

She flirted up a dismissive shoulder and said, "I thought reading my contracts was your job."

"Fine. Next time I'll put in a clause that gives me your immortal soul," I said, and finally got a small smile out of her. I was giving her the benefit of the doubt by assuming that she had one.

Julian's gaze caught on the sofa and his face lit up.

"Kittens!" he said, and went right to them. There were two, one black, one white, nestled up asleep in a fuzzy yin-yang that I'd taken for yet another throw pillow.

It wasn't at all professional, and Oakleigh's eyebrows shot to dizzying heights as Julian plopped onto her sofa and pulled them both into his lap. He looked up at me, grinning and oblivious, scratching at the black one's ears. It burst into enthusiastic purring, and the white one yawned. Its eyes were bright blue. If Julian were my real intern or assistant, I'd be excusing us both and taking him outside to fire him right quick. But the sight of Julian snuggling fluffy baby things pulled me off my game. My heart rate jacked into that pulsing urge: *Find her.*

I heard myself saying, "I would have thought you were a dog person," and Oakleigh's disbelieving gaze widened to include me.

"Oh, yeah, for sure," he said. "But who doesn't like kittens?" He turned to Oakleigh. "What are their names?"

She snorted. "I don't know. Blackie and Whitey? I got them yesterday, after Clark broke in yet again."

Julian ran his fingernail across his pants seam. The black one heard the noise and pounced. Whitey had to see Blackie jump before he noticed the wiggling finger. He was probably deaf, like Henry.

I didn't quite have myself in hand, and I couldn't see the connection between home invasions and getting kittens. "Wouldn't a Doberman be more to the point?"

"No, because Clark's allergic to cats," Oakleigh snapped.

She was still bristling because The Help was plonked on her sofa, playing with her baby animals. The odd part was that I bristled right back at her, even though she was a client, and Julian was out of line.

So this is what nepotism tastes like, I thought. I found I didn't mind the flavor.

"Oakleigh," I said, sharp enough to reclaim her attention. "How allergic? Touch-a-cat-and-die allergic? Or cat dander makes him sneezy?"

"How would I know? I never saw him go around cats. He was *allergic,*" Oakleigh said, as if she were speaking to someone who was very, very slow. "He didn't carry an EpiPen or anything. He did say being around cats made him miserable, so when he kept breaking in and ruining all my things, I got some."

"What's been ruined, other than the obvious?" I asked, glancing at the wedding portrait. I was skeptical that Clark had been in the house at all. I wouldn't put it past Oakleigh to ruin her own things, hoping to make Clark look bad.

Oakleigh flushed. "It's crazy. I got my hair cut, and when I came back, the Picasso sketch was missing. I thought maybe he'd done it before, when he emptied the safe, and I hadn't noticed. I changed the security code anyway, and I went out to dinner. When I got home, the alarm was still set, but half my shoes were in the bathtub. The shower was running. Nothing suede survived. That's when I found my sketch in the liquor cabinet. I changed the code again, and then yesterday, I went to pick up a ton of dry cleaning. I'd forgotten about it in all the chaos, and there was a pet shop next door. I went in and bought these kittens. While I was gone he—" She faltered, and her voice dropped to an outraged whisper. "I really, really think he peed into my makeup case. It's made me crazy, wondering what else he may have peed in. I keep throwing out food, and I'm carrying my toothbrush in my purse now. So this morning, I went to Pilates, and while I was gone, he came and scratched my face out and rehung our portrait, and I don't know what else yet. I'm scared to even look around. I'd left the dry cleaning draped over the banister. It was mostly his suits and his dress shirts. He must have grabbed it on the way out."

"He would have seen the kittens," I said, watching them tussling in Julian's lap. "Why would he take clothes?"

"Well, the clothes were all still sealed up in those plastic bags. They looked fresh cleaned," Oakleigh said. It was an interesting choice of words, to say they *looked* clean instead of simply saying that they were. She stared at the floor, and added, truculent. "Maybe he thought he'd better take them before they got all dandered up."

I quirked an eyebrow up. "You meant for him to take them."

"I didn't say that," Oakleigh said, now so disingenu-
ous she might as well be scrubbing a toe against the floor.

Julian shot me a puzzled look, but I was as adrift
as he was. I noticed his navy-blue pants were already
showing white cat hair. I kept Henry brushed because
so many of my clothes were black, and I still had to use
a tape roller every time I left the house. But Blackie's
fur didn't really show against the navy, I noticed, and
then I understood. Oakleigh had picked these charming dander factories for their colors.

"You ran the kittens through his clothes," I said,
surprised. Julian looked surprised, too. "You ran the
white kitten in and out the sleeves of his pale dress
shirts. And then the dark one, you ran him through the
suits. How many times?"

"Oh, I don't know. Kittens are silly," Oakleigh said.
"Can I help it if they like to play tunnels?"

"Holy crap," Julian said.

"And then you bagged the clothes back up and
hung them where he'd see them, and you trotted off to
Pilates."

"I didn't say that. But he shouldn't have been messing with my things." Her voice was prim and not without pride.

Now I believed that Clark was breaking in. People
in contentious divorces blame their spouses for rain

and hangnails and the chlamydia they know damn well they've gone and outsourced all on their own. But they don't lay elaborate kitten traps for the ex if they are the one doing the sabotage.

If only she'd rehired me after the first break-in! I'd have set up nanny cams and caught him peeing in her makeup. What a lever that would be in settlement negotiations. The kittens were a vicious return on his serve, more interested in hurting him than protecting her belongings. That put her a good six steps up the crazy stairs from standard divorce behavior. A BANK case was usually selfish people trying to keep the largest stack of goodies as they tore each other up. But she'd put Clark in the hospital. Had she known how much it would hurt him? Maybe. If so, it was crazy-smart. If he'd wheezed himself to death on a fine coat of kitten dander, well. I'd like to see the DA that could get around reasonable doubt on that one.

"Do you think I'm in trouble?" she asked, sulky and so twee it was almost baby talk.

I shook my head. "Oakleigh, if I let you get arrested for revenge-kittening, I will personally eat my law license and become a fry cook, okay? When the police come, look as demure as you can in that dress and let me do ninety percent of the talking."

"Is it legal to not mention that I let kittens play in his clothes?"

"We're not going to bring it up if they don't ask. And they won't ask that," I said, distracted.

So Clark wasn't robbing her. He was gaslighting, moving and ruining all her favorite things strictly to drive her nuts. I was now quite keen to meet this shoe-drowning, lipstick-defiling fellow and see what he looked like unembellished. The sheer, personal vitriol of his small-minded attacks put him at least as high up the crazy stairs as she was. Also, he had a secret way in and out of the house, and he knew down to the minute when she left home.

I said, "He's got eyes on you. You get that, yes? His break-ins happen fast, immediately after you leave."

"You think he's been watching me?" It honestly hadn't occurred to her. This supported my theory that she was only exceptionally bitchy rather than a criminal mastermind plotting the perfect murder via adorable baby animals. But it also resparked the ugly rage I'd seen earlier. "That bastard!"

"We'll report this to the cops, but I want to get my own PI in here to sweep your house for bugs."

"You think Clark's filming me?" Oakleigh shrieked, with such instant panic that it set me wondering who she was screwing. I'd need to prepare if there was a chance Clark had a sex tape to spring on us in mediation.

"I don't think so. Calm down. If he had video in here, he'd have seen what you did with the kittens."

She didn't calm at all, stalking back and forth in a lather. "So he has somebody following me?"

"Maybe," I said. He could well be watching her himself.

I needed Birdwine, but I wouldn't pull him off Hana's trail for Oakleigh Winkley. Not even if Oakleigh were on fire and he had the world's last extinguisher tucked in his front pocket. I wished instead that I had extra Birdwines, three or four, at least. Amazing to me that some people staggered through their lives with none. I would have to use Nick's guys to do a bug sweep and figure out how he was getting past her security system.

"How is he getting in?" Julian said. Bright boy, he had followed my same chain of thought.

"I don't know," I said. "But we'll find it. Then we can either close it down or put some cameras—"

"Screw that. Leave it open. Let him come. I am going to shoot him so much," Oakleigh interrupted, whirling to face us. "This is still America. I can shoot anyone who breaks in, right?"

Julian went very still, but I rolled my eyes.

"Please don't plot murders in front of me, Oakleigh. It will make it morally quite sticky if you do kill him and need me to defend you." I spoke in a bored tone that told Julian I wasn't taking her threat seriously. My firm passed the very ugliest of dissolutions to me, so death threats were de rigueur. I'd heard them by the hundreds, and I'd never had a client make good on one. Not yet, anyway.

"It's not funny," she said, very screechy. As she spoke, she was stomping across the room, heading for the entertainment center. "We have two guns, one in the bedroom and one down here." She jerked open a large drawer near the bottom and began pulling out old re-motes and rolls of cable, dumping them haphazardly on the floor. Then she grabbed a wooden box out of the back. "Clark got them for me, in case anyone broke in when he was traveling. Well, it would serve him right if—" Her voice cut out abruptly as she opened the gun box. It was empty. Her face went ashen and her eyes bulged like a pug dog's. Love betrayed was the ugliest thing alive, and as we watched, she devolved into its lowest common denominator. When she spoke again, her face twisted and froze in a rictus of loathing, genuinely deadly. "That bastard. That bastard. He stole my guns!"

We were now steps past regular, even for my cases. I rose and put propitiating hands out. "Okay, let's calm down. Close that up. Pack the things back in the drawer. The police will be along any—"

She wasn't listening. She was already running to the foyer. We heard her boot heels thundering up the stairs, no doubt going to check for the other gun. After another minute we heard her unleash a bloodcurdling string of curses, so it was missing, too.

"Holy crap!" Julian whispered. "Is she—"

I waved it away. "This is a bit much, with the kittens and the urine and the missing guns. But I've seen worse."

I wasn't sure I had, though, and I also wasn't sure I would have spoken in such a reassuring way to, say, Verona. But Julian looked so worried, and he wasn't truly an employee. He was something else.

"She said she'd shoot him," he said, still fretting.

We could hear Oakleigh stomping back and forth upstairs, doing what sounded like primal scream therapy while wrecking a dresser with a hand ax.

"I'm sure she would, if he were right in front of her this second, and she had that gun. They all mean it in the moment. But the moment passes, a thousand times out of a thousand and one."

"What about the thousand and first time?" he asked.

"You read about those cases in the paper."

"Should we—should you go up there?"

I shook my head and sat down by Julian to wait comfortably and billably on the sofa until Oakleigh wore out her fit upstairs. The cops did not concern me. I had yet to meet the Atlanta cop who'd spend more than five minutes on any assault charge where the weapon was a kitty cat. When they came, I'd file a report about the break-ins to have them on the record. Especially the guns. I didn't like the guns. I liked them even less in Clark Winkley's hands. A divorce this volatile, having either of them armed was a bad idea. There was always that thousand and first case. But at least the upstairs noises were abating.

"See? She's calming down."

"People don't act like this," he said.

"Sure they do," I told him, and was relieved that my protectiveness for the kid stretched only so far. I didn't want him genuinely frightened, but I also couldn't let his rosy worldview stand unchallenged. "All people have it in them. Don't ever get divorced, Julian."

He chuckled, a nervous noise, releasing tension. "I'm not even married."

"That's the only surefire way to avoid it," I said. And then, because he'd asked me the impossible—what *we* would do when Hana was found—I added, "Making a family is a dangerous business."

He looked up from the kittens at me, clear-eyed. "If you mean us, it's not the same thing as this. Not at all. We're looking for a little kid."

Damn, but the boy was direct. I considered him, poker-faced. Hana would be nothing like the blank slate of a baby, nor would she be a television ten-year-old. Real, live preteen girls were time-consuming, irksome, and difficult at best. I knew, because I'd been one. The specific one we sought had a complicated history. Did he think she would run and hurl herself into our arms, as delighted as a rescue dog? We weren't Kai. We weren't anything to Hana. I was invested because I saw myself, my own childhood, in her, but she wouldn't see herself in me. She wouldn't have a thing in common with sweet, sheltered Julian. I had a hard time imagining what his childhood would have looked like, and I was an adult.

"When you were growing up, did you have family dinner?" I asked him.

His eyebrows knit. "Well, we had dinner."

"At a table?" I said. "With all three of you there, and you talked about your day or your plans for tomorrow?"

"Yeah, but it's normal to have family dinner."

"Mm-hm. What did you do after?" I asked.

"After dinner? I don't know," he said. "We read or watched TV. Me and my mom liked board games. What? That's not weird."

"Do you think that's what we'll be like? You and me and Hana? Tuna casserole and Pictionary after?"

"No," he said, but then he added, "Not at first."

In those three words, I saw a whole imaginary future, cheery, tinged with pink, unfurling in his imagination. It bore no resemblance to what was forming in my mind: a lurching Frankenstein's family, cobbled from dead pieces. The kid hadn't seen a lot of ugly— his reactions to Oakleigh's fit proved that. He was not prepped for Hana, or for *After*, for a *We*. To be fair, I wasn't either, but at least I had a realistic grasp on *Now*.

"Julian, we might not find her at all. Even if we do, she's not going to be some Brady kid in pigtails. She—"

"I know," he interrupted, sparking to my tone. "I wasn't raised by Care Bears, Paula."

"Okay, okay," I said, light, trying to head off his temper. "But I'm guessing little birds show up to clean your dishes?"

"No, they don't," he said, even madder. "And my mom doesn't wear pearls to do the dusting, and"—he faltered, and his eyes got all glossy—"Didn't, I mean. She didn't wear pearls. We were just regular."

"I'm sorry," I said. It was a bad line of questioning for a kid who'd lost his mother so recently. Kai had chosen good parents—they might even have been great ones, if they hadn't gone and died on him. "I don't mean to upset you, but what you're calling *regular* is actually lovely and quite rare."

My words were meant to soothe him, but they had the opposite effect. A fat tear spilled down one cheek, and he set the kittens off his lap.

"You think I can't handle this? You think I'm too soft? Or too dumb? What?" His voice was thick and loud.

I had no idea how the conversation had gotten so out of my control, so fast.

"I think my client's right upstairs, and I shouldn't have opened the topic here," I said, firm.

He stood abruptly and walked past me to the mess Oakleigh had made. Blackie jumped off the sofa, following with Whitey in his wake. Julian knelt and began rerolling the cables with his back to me. I thought he was getting himself together, but then he turned to me and more tears were running down his face. His eyes looked so much older than the rest of him. He spoke again, low and quick, but with a great deal of intensity.

"I'm tougher than I look, you know. Maybe not a year ago. But now? After my dad was gone, there was only me. It was only me with my mother, those last weeks. It was . . ." He paused, the unspooled cable shaking in his trembling hands, seeking a word, but he couldn't find it. He changed directions, saying, "I changed her diaper. Near the end, in hospice. There was a male orderly that day. Always before, it was these three girl ones in rotation, and I stayed out of the way. But that day, the regular girl was sick or something, and this guy was working. He was an old guy, too, like, near her age."

As he spoke, his shaking hands kept winding up the cable. Blackie pounced at the moving end, cute and thoroughly unhelpful. I looked at him instead of at my brother's shaking hands as he talked on, unstoppable.

"I could smell it, you know? That she needed— I could smell it. I was going to get that orderly, and she started crying. Mostly she was out of it, but not that afternoon. She shook and made this awful clacking gulp noise, and I hated it, and I knew that she was crying, so I leaned over her and I said, 'What is it, Mama? What?' My mom and dad were high school sweethearts. No other man had ever seen her without clothes on, she said. She'd always gone to women doctors, even. She was so skinny then, like this little dried-up scrap of mother, and her skin was so loose on her it hung down in floppy creases."

Oakleigh was right upstairs, and now the kid was weeping openly. I was paralyzed in the face of all this naked loneliness and sorrow, and, worse, I couldn't help wondering—had Kai been so frail and helpless, at her end? Had anyone been with her? I didn't want to hear any more, but he kept on, relentless.

"She looked up at the ceiling, and she cried, and I talked about our old bird-watching log we used to keep when I was little, and I cleaned her up. I made myself not gag because I didn't want her to hear and feel bad. It was terrible, but I did it, because she was my mother. That's what a family is, Paula. That's what family does, except Hana doesn't have any.

"So that's what we have to be. I want us to make something good for her. We have to, and I don't know why you have to be so fucking scary. I'm trying to be friends with you, but every other minute I feel like you're laughing at me or that you hate me. You're what I got, though. And we're what Hana's got. We're the only things at all—"

His voice had risen at the end, but then it cracked and he dropped his head and wept his guts out. After six fraught seconds, he turned his back and began stuffing the remotes and the rerolled cable back into the drawer, pushing gently at the kittens. He was still weeping as they both tried to climb into the drawer in a fluffy bother. He got the drawer shut, then scrubbed at his face with his palms.

"I don't hate you," I said quietly. "For what it's worth, you're pretty fucking scary, too."

He only hunched his shoulders, snuffling and gulping. I had no idea what to do with a crying man-boy in the middle of my awful client's house, especially one who was telling me what a mother looked like when she was sick and slowly dying.

One thing was clear: Hana had hit him like biology, too. I'd miscalculated both his depths and his investment. I wondered if he heard it as a heartbeat: *find her, find her, find her.*

Meanwhile, upstairs, it had gone dangerously quiet. Oakleigh could come back at any second. I realized my discomfort was more on Julian's behalf. I didn't want Oakleigh's disdainful eyes to see my brother, tearstained and flayed open. I walked over and handed him my keys.

"I'm sorry," I told him in the gentlest voice I owned. "I'm very bad at this. Go wait in the car, okay? I'll finish here, fast as I can, and then we'll talk."

He took the keys without looking at me, and he made his own way out.

Damn, but I'd mishandled Julian, and misunderstood him, too, on several levels. I had to make a room for him, as well as Hana. Metaphorically, at least. But not right this second. I took a long, slow exhale and thanked the gods that I knew how to compartmentalize.

I called the offices of Clark's lawyer, Dean Macon, from my cell. I left a voicemail notifying him that I now represented Oakleigh. She came down when the cops rang the doorbell a few minutes later. The rest of the afternoon was simple, professionally speaking. Police interest in The Kittening was cursory, and we got our countercomplaints on the record. Afterward, Oakleigh swanned upstairs to take a bath, leaving me to call Nick's PI firm. I asked them to send a fellow over ASAP to bug sweep and find Clark's way in.

While I waited for the PI, I went out to the car. Julian was in the passenger seat, reading something on his phone. He peeped at me as I got in, embarrassed, though by now the tearstains had faded and his eyes were only a little swollen.

"I'm sorry I lost it," he said. "It's been a really stressful day."

I waved the apology away and said, with no preamble, "What if I hired you for the rest of the summer?"

He let out a startled bark of laughter. "Yeah, because today has gone so well."

"I'm serious," I said. "You could come in on your off days from the pizza place, once or twice a week. We could get to know each other a little more naturally, over time."

He looked uncertain. "I'm not sure I'd be good in a, you know, cutthroat kind of environment."

I realized I didn't even know what he'd been studying at Berry, and felt ashamed of how little I'd asked Julian about himself. Not at this morning's meeting, or even earlier, on Facebook. So I said, "What's your major?"

"Psychology. I want to be a therapist, eventually. I'm sure not cut out to be a lawyer."

"It's not always this high stress," I told him. "Take the internship. It's only until the end of summer. I can promise you some delightfully bland phone answering when Verona goes to lunch. There'll be quite a lot of very dull filing."

"Okay, now I'm sold," he said, but I had gotten a smile out of him.

"Did I mention it pays twenty bucks an hour?"

"Holy crap, I suddenly love filing!" He cut his eyes at the ugly colonial house. "For twenty an hour, I might even love Ms. Winkley."

Money was so relative. It was a fortune to him, but I could pay him out of my pocket, like Catherine did when she hired her oldest son for the summer, and never feel it. The job would let me funnel cash to him.

If the water got too cold, too deep, too full of sharks—hell, just too wet—he'd have the means to flee back to the sheltered world of Berry College.

I didn't think he would, though. The kid had metal in him, and he shared my driving urgency to find Hana. I had to respect that and find a way to merge our visions of the future.

"Deal?" I asked.

He nodded, and as we shook hands on it the guy from Nick's PI firm pulled into the drive behind us.

Turned out, Clark had removed an alarm contact from an upstairs bathroom window and reprogrammed the system not to register it. To reach the window, he had to sneak through a neighbor's backyard, climb a tree, and slither and roll across the back of the perilous, steep roof. The PI tested the route and found it possible, but dangerous as hell. Clark had to be both in good shape, physically, and in bad shape, mentally, to take it. He'd literally risked his life, more than once, to pee in Oakleigh's makeup case and spoil her shoes.

I had them plug the hole. As much as I'd love to install nanny cams, I didn't trust him not to creep in one night and strangle her. And that was assuming that she wouldn't get another gun and shoot him right on camera first.

The next morning, I took Oakleigh's check and contract to the office. I tossed them on Nick's desk, casual,
as if I were the Paula of yore, who delivered BANK
clients and retainers on the regular, and I was rewarded
with his familiar grin. In this brave new world where
finding Hana might have an after, I needed to mend
fences with my partners, stat. I'd need time off when
I had a sudden sister to resettle. I spent the next ten
days getting current on our every open file, reconnect-
ing with our client list, and billing monstrous strings
of hours. As I got my files in order, I had a disturbing thought: perhaps this was what nesting looked like,
when I did it.

I felt eyes on me all the time, though, that faint
electric skin-crawl that haunted the watched, as Nick
kept popping by to check things that did not need
checking. As the days rolled past with zero panic attacks, and I took on exactly zero pro bonos, both my
partners relaxed. The chilled air of our offices re-
warmed.

When I felt anxious, when my heartbeat sped up,
beating out the call to *find her, find her, find her,* I reminded myself that I was not alone in feeling it. Julian
was waiting, too, and Birdwine was on the job.

But when word finally came, it wasn't good. Birdwine sent an email, no title. Not even "Here is the

information," because there wasn't any. I could tell he was ashamed, because he didn't even sign it:

> *I traced their route through four states before I lost the trail. There's nothing. It's dead cold, Paula, and I can't do any more from here. I'm coming home.*

Chapter 8

Joya is sitting sideways on my bed. The rooms here are small, just enough space for two twin beds, a shared dresser, and a closet. There's a common room downstairs with desks for doing homework, an old navy-blue sofa and loveseat, and some big donated beanbag chairs, but Shar, Karice, and Kim have practically peed in a circle around that territory. Joya rooms with Kim, so we default to my room. We can kick Candace out and lean on the wall, shoulder to shoulder, feet hanging off into space. After a year and a half, my place on this bed is so established I can feel a faint, butt-shaped dent in the mattress where I fit.

I'm out of place today. I have moved up, much closer to the scratched headboard, and put some space between our shoulders. Joya either doesn't notice or doesn't care. She's so happy she's having a hard time sitting still. I look down at our bare feet, my two, then a space, and then her two. She has doll feet, very small with round toes. She flexes them, back and forth, like they are waving. Happy feet, waving good-bye.

"You're bouncing the whole bed," I say. My feet are bonier and longer and very, very still.

"Well, you're bitching up the whole room," Joya fires back, but she's smiling and I'm not.

Our voices sound so loud in all the quiet air. We are truly alone, with the whole cabin to ourselves. It's rare to be the only two people in a building here, but everyone else has gone to the dining hall in the center building. Mrs. Mack said she'd bring me a sandwich if I wanted to skip the meal and hang with Joya. Joya's going to a real restaurant with her mama. They will have a celebration meal of fried steak and mashed potatoes and pie, because Joya is not coming back. Everything she owns is packed up, sitting in two bags in our cabin's common room.

The longer we wait, the more bitter and darkhearted I become. It's like I am steeping in something awful. I should have given her a quick squeeze, said bye, and gone to dinner.

But that would have meant sitting alone in the dining hall. At meals, the black kids and the two white boys who talk and dress black have the tables near the windows. The white kids, including Candace, have the tables by the door. There are only four Hispanic kids. They keep to themselves, sitting on one end of the eight-top nearest the kitchen, talking Spanish. We Gotmamas own the other end of their table. We've been a tiny nation to ourselves for over a year, but the problem of being a Gotmama is now clear to me: Someone's mama is coming. It isn't mine.

Sitting alone in the dining hall, I would at least have hot garlic toast. Here, my guts twist, hungry in all kinds of ways, watching Joya get what I want most.

"I'm missing spaghetti night," I say, mean enough to spark her back.

"Can't you be happy for me?"

"I am," I say. I wish I were.

"The way they've worked my mama over, it could have been you leaving first just as easy."

"I know."

Her mom got out of rehab months ago, but they made her move into a halfway house. All Joya got was supervised visitation. Her mama had to get a job, keep it, pass her weekly pee tests, save a certain amount of money. Every time she hit a goal, it felt like they'd add on another. But now she has her own apartment down south of the city with a dedicated space for Joya. Last month she got Joya for an overnight, and then for two weekends. Now, tonight, she's finally taking Joya home for good.

"So stop being a piss," Joya says.

"I'm not," I say, pissy. Kai still has three months to serve, and who knows how long we'll get jerked around when she gets out. "Or if I am, maybe it's because you're leaving me with such a pile of shit."

"What does that mean?" Joya says. She's too deep-down happy to get snippy fast, but I keep pushing.

"I mean Shar and Karice. You're the one who beat them down, but Shar never got you back. When you go, they'll come at me."

She dismisses that with a wave of her small hand. "Bitch, please, like you can't take them?"

I could take the two of them, actually. I'm pretty sure. Joya did, and I'm taller and stronger and almost as mean. But they aren't two anymore. "They have Kim now, too."

"Kim's not so tough. Just take your earrings out. Don't wear even studs until you settle with them." She sits up and curls her legs under her, getting into it. Joya likes tactics. "You have to hit Shar first, right off, hard as you can. Go for the face, she likes being pretty. You get her down, the other two will scatter off like bugs."

"I can handle myself," I mutter.

"Yeah, you can," Joya says. She looks at me, sizing me up, and then nods. "You be all right." It isn't an assessment. It's a command.

"You be all right," I order her back, and it comes out only a little bit resentful.

Shar and Karice don't really matter. I've been in fights plenty. They aren't what's wringing out my guts. I want Kai. I want Kai to come for me so bad it feels like a hundred mean hands twisting every organ in my abdomen.

I don't want to talk to Joya anymore, at all. I should move back down to my habitual place, sit shoulder to shoulder with her like always. If I would do this simple thing, we could run out the minutes in silence. Joya's not one for tears and speeches.

I can't, though. I can't make myself sit close to her. She isn't Joya anymore. She's some girl who is leaving me, some girl who's getting everything I want.

Joya seems to think we're good, though. She's helped me plan a Shar defense, so we must be golden. She creeps a little closer. Her eyes are very dark brown, but they look black in the dim light.

"Paula? Imma call you, okay? We'll still see each other."

I twitch one shoulder, noncommittal. She's throwing me a crumb, but I've been moved around enough to know it isn't real. She might call once or twice. She might ask to visit. But her apartment is forty-five minutes away, in a different school zone, and her mama has a full-time job. Time is short and gas is pricey. The truth is, we are finished with each other. She wants to pretend different and have some kind of moment? Screw her.

"I mean it," she says, pressing.

"We'll see," I say, with some finality. I need her to shut up now.

"My mama's got a car. She'll drive me here to visit."

A lashing blackness rises in me as she says what her mama has; what her mama, who is coming for her now, will do.

"You won't come back here," I tell her. "I wouldn't, and you won't, either. Not unless your mama fails a pee test, and they drag you back."

Joya's eyes narrow. It's the thing we're both most afraid of, and I've named it. We never do that to each other, talk about how her mama could go back to the pipe, how mine might not get early release. These things could take our mothers from us, and we don't invoke them.

We talk about how mamas are, and what we'll do and say when ours come for us. I've heard a thousand times about this dinner Joya's going to eat tonight at

Demy's Blues-N-Burgers. I know Demy's has signed pictures of Hound Dog Taylor and Muddy Waters on the wall. She's described the potatoes mashed with Cheddar and chives so many times, it's almost like I ate them myself a long time ago. She knows when Kai comes, our first meal will be her famous pancakes with the orange zest in the batter. Kai always helps me paint my room, and we've endlessly debated the color I should choose. We plan our lives with mothers in great detail, as if their coming is dead certain. Nothing else is bearable. It is a silent pact that binds us, makes us into Gotmamas. I'm breaking our most secret and un-stated rule.

"She won't, though," Joya says, and it's more than a warning. It is a window, an offering. She's made a space for me to take it back.

"I hope not. But, damn." I shrug, all world-weary, like I regret her mama's chances are so slim.

Joya scrambles up onto her knees and rears as tall as she can go. It isn't very tall. "She won't though, and you know she won't. Say she won't."

I have a bitter flavor in my mouth, but it's rich, too, as savory and sharp as lemon butter. I rise to my knees as well, taller than her, and I tuck my hair behind my ears, so she can see I didn't need her stupid tactics. I already have my earrings out.

"I'm just being honest," I say. "It's dumb to have this big good-bye, when you'll be back in six weeks. If your mama even makes it that long."

She shakes her head. "I'm smoke, bitch. I am gone, and your sorry ass is stuck here." Her voice is loud and her black eyes shine, welling in her weakness. I've gotten to her, and I can't help how good it feels.

"For now, but you don't see me crying about it," I say, sneering. I say it like I'm tougher, though no one is. Not anyone I've ever met.

She leans in, closer. So close I feel her hot breath touch my face. "You will cry, though. Your lesbo mama likes that prison. She don't want to come for you. She'd rather stay dyked out in jail."

My lips peel back, inadvertent. She knows the thing with Rhonda hits me low. I don't want Kai to be so lonely that she needs a prison boyfriend, or worse, for her to trade her beauty and her sex for more phone time and outsize orange envelopes and stamps. That's why this fight is so very dangerous. We know all each other's soft places. I hit her back in one of hers.

"Well, your mama will go back whoring. They always do."

"Who always does," she says. It is a challenge, not a question. She is daring me to say it. There is the promise of pain in her voice, and I want it. I want her to come at me with tooth and claw. It would be better to feel this tearing outside, on my skin.

"Whores," I say. It's low and it feels good to be low. "Whores like your mama, the whore."

I am ready in my body for her to come at me. I want her to hit and hit me. I deserve it. I've said the lowest thing that can be said.

I can't imagine a force strong enough to keep her from launching, but she finds one. Her eyes gleam like chipped onyx. She tilts her head sideways and leans in, taking five long seconds, like she's coming in slo-mo for a kiss. She slips sideways though, putting her mouth near my ear.

"You take it back. You be so sweet and kiss my ass, because I know what you did. You snuck your mama's poem to her boyfriend." This is harder than fists, this hot whisper of breath brushing my ear. "I could tell. I could beat you down right now, take that footlocker. You kept that poem, and it's proof. Then she won't get early release. They'll keep her ass. You'll be here until you age out."

Everything in me goes dark. I don't breathe or speak. She could do it. I've pushed her too hard.

Her body stays close and feels coiled, ready now for me to make it physical. I am bigger, but she is so damn tough. If I lose, I have no doubt she'll do it. She'll take the footlocker, and she'll screw Kai to the wall.

I lean back, so she can see my eyes. I show no fear. I know Joya. Her instinct for finding soft spots is unerring. So I can't have any, and that's all. I stay cool, and shake my head, wry, like she's said something so weak it's funny. I make my mouth curl into a little smile.

"I don't care if my mama dies in there. I'm the one that put her into prison in the first place."

I say it soft, but even so, it comes out powerful. The truth always sounds so very, very true. She hears it, ringing clear and loud as bell song under my words. The truth at the center is the thing that sells the lie.

"What?" she says. She even blinks. I've shocked her out of the advantage.

"I called the cops, dumbass," I say. These are the words I've never said out loud. This is the biggest truth, the secret one, alive in the bitter depths of me. It feels so good to say it, to confess it to this girl who will not give me absolution. She will hate me for it. I've done a thing that she would never do. "I turned Kai in."

She rocks back all the way onto her heels, kneeling on the bed now. "Why?"

"Because she fucked with me," I say. I let that sit there. Joya already knows one secret that could ruin us; now I am handing her another, even worse. It is a risky strategy, and this is the part I have to sell to make her back down. I lean in close. Each word is barely more than breath. "I kept that poem to be *my* leverage. I'll show it to Kai's damn parole officer myself if she tests me." I pause. I want to be sure Joya understands this last part. This is the part that matters. "There's no limit to what I'll do to somebody who fucks with me. You understand? No limit. I sent my own mama to jail because she moved me out of Asheville, and I kept that poem so I can do it again. If you start with me—what do you think I'm going to do to you?"

She stares into my eyes, uncertain, teetering on the cusp of disbelief and violence. I don't blink. Not at all. I don't move or waver, and then her eyelids come down, shuttering closed.

"You a stone col' narco bitch," she says, her grammar and inflections gone into that way she talks with other black kids. It's the way she talks to Candace to scare her and to shut her out. She's never talked like this at me. She opens her eyes, and she is a stranger, waving a hand between us. "We done. I don't need your sorry ass for nuthin' anyhow, because I'm gon' go home."

I sink back, too, shrugging like it makes no nevermind, but there is truth inside her blow, weighting it. All Joya really has to do to win is leave me here, and we both know it. She jerks her chin down in a single nod, and we are done with each other. She gets up off my bed and goes downstairs to wait with her bags. I am Rome, burning behind her. She doesn't look back, and I don't cry. The Gotmamas are char and ash, so wrecked it's like we never were.

I never saw Joya again. I didn't talk about her, and I tried not to think her name. Not until I got all that good, free university therapy while I was in school. My Emory counselor was the one who said the way we ended things was not uncommon for kids like us. She said we'd lost enough in our short lives to want to cauterize our wounds before they happened. We burned our connection closed before we felt the holes.

Years ago, I had a client who reminded me of Joya. One of my earlier pro bono girls, a payback to karma on top of Kai's monthly checks. This one was barely eighteen, built small with milk-chocolate skin and eyes so dark brown they looked pure black from any distance. She'd been Stockholmed into calling her pimp her boyfriend, and she was about to eat a ten-year sentence, covering his ass.

By the time I was done, the pimp did his own time, while my client walked with court-mandated counseling and five years' probation. She hugged me when it was over, trembling, her body as delicate and small-boned as a sparrow's. That night, I drank a little too much bourbon, and I called Birdwine. I told him I had a job that billed to me, not the firm, which usually meant it was part of a pro bono case. I gave him Joya's name.

I should have known better. Hell, I knew the recidivism rates, knew how seldom stories like Joya's got a happy ending. Statistics said once her mama got back in her old environment, she would find old friends, slip back into old habits, and sink Joya with her. The daughters of crack addicts and prostitutes almost never find their way to dental hygienist school, much less Yale. But Joya was so tough. I hoped. Hoped stupidly and very hard. Hard enough to ask the question.

Birdwine found her fast because she had a sheet. Drugs and prostitution. She'd died in south Atlanta at nineteen, caught in gang crossfire.

He said, "I don't have a lot of details. A black working girl, it's not like the paper's going to spend the inches." His gruff, blunt voice was suspiciously gentle. "Want me to keep digging?"

There was the briefest silence on the line between us. On my side, it was filled with the most foolish longing; I wanted him to track down the waiter who had served Joya's celebration dinner at Demy's Blues-N-Burgers all those years ago. I wanted to know if she and her mama had a good time. I wanted proof that our breakup hadn't soured her pleasure in seeing her mama's car pull up or spoiled the taste of those cheese and chive potatoes.

But almost as fast as I could feel it, it was laid to rest. I knew better. I understood firsthand how much it took to mar the joy of someone—the best and dearest someone in the world—coming to get you, just as promised. Whatever happened later, that dinner would have been so good.

I said, "No. Send me a bill."

"This one's on me," he said, and then added, right before he hung up, "Sorry about your friend."

Either his investigation had been thorough enough to connect us, or he'd simply read me and decided it was personal. Either way, pretty savvy. That was when I decided he was worth working round his binges. I'd since used him for everything that mattered, and I'd never regretted it. Not until now. Not until he emailed me that he'd lost Hana. She was free-falling, lost in the same world that had eaten Joya. I wanted to interrogate Birdwine, dig through his file, see if anything would resonate. But Birdwine was unavailable.

I knew where he was. When Birdwine went missing, it was never a mystery. He always went to the same place: Drunk. Drunk wasn't on Google maps, and a trip to Drunk took as long as it took.

I was impatient, but not angry. Birdwine was what he was, and anger wouldn't change it or get me what I wanted any faster. As soon as he surfaced, I would jolly him along and get the information. If that failed, I'd peel it right out of his hide.

Three times a day, before work, at lunch, and after a working dinner at my desk, I went and sat at Birdwine's place. I didn't wait in my car, either. The first morning, I'd wormed through the dog door and gotten Birdwine's spare key out of his office desk. Looper would have eaten the face off any stranger who tried this move, but he was thrilled to see me, thrilled to nap beside me on the sofa, thrilled to breathe in and discover afresh that the world was full of air. Dogs were such easy marks.

The third day of my vigil coincided with one of Julian's days off from Mellow Mushroom. He appeared at noon for more "internship." I was slammed, and so I gave him to Verona. Around seven, I sent him to pick up Chinese so I could work through dinner, and I asked if he would stick around and go with me to Birdwine's.

I'd meant what I had promised in my car at Oakleigh's. On the days he came to work with me, I took him for meals, asked him questions, got used to his spastic tendency to dart at me and hug me every time we said hello or good-bye. I hugged him back now, trying to let him be my brother in a realer way than updating the *How do you know Julian* field on Facebook. But I also thought that it would do the kid some good to visit Birdwine's sketchy neighborhood.

The neighbors were a mix: black and white and brown, young and old, some squatting briefly on their way up, others scrabbling for a hold on their way down. Across the street from Birdwine's shabby craftsman, a taquería that smelled like horse meat and roach spray shared a building with a run-down barber shop. Two doors down, a thriving drug house did a busy trade. The whole street had an unstable danger vibe I knew well from most chapters of my childhood. Hana would know it, too.

As we turned onto Birdwine's block, I saw that the front door of his house was hanging open. Looper sat in the middle of the patchy front lawn, looking worried and long-suffering.

"Shit! He's home," I said, and pulled over to park. I hadn't expected to see him until tomorrow, at the earliest.

Julian had barely registered the ratty streets as we wound through them, but he sat up very straight when he realized we were stopping.

"This is where he lives?" Julian asked.

"Yep," I said.

As we got out of the car, I could hear a terrible crashing sound coming from inside. Looper ran to me and thrust his giant, square head into my hand. I patted him, and he immediately turned and ran a few steps toward the door, pausing to peer back, his eyebrows set to anxious.

"I know, buddy. Timmy's in the well," I told him.

Julian paused, half out of the car. "Is that—the big guy? In there?" He sounded nervous. I'd forgotten— the first time he met Birdwine was in my office. I'd had a panic attack and Birdwine had stepped to him, violence limned in the angles of his body.

"Yep." We heard a whomping crash from inside. Birdwine wasn't making a great second impression. "If a stranger was wrecking the house, Looper would be in there scrapping," I said. Looper's tail wagged when he heard his name, and he took another step toward the door, trying to get me to follow. I leaned against the car. "Not yet, buddy."

"How are you so calm?" Julian asked. He still had the passenger door open, and his head swiveled back and forth, peering up and down the street. I reminded myself that at dinner the other night, this kid had gotten in a lather because a Marietta neighbor let the dandelions take over his lawn. Baby steps.

"He's never killed anybody yet," I said. I'd seen Birdwine on the back end of his cycle before. I had no girlish notions, either fearful or romantic, about what was in the house. "It may not be pretty in there, but it isn't dangerous."

"I feel like we're being watched," Julian said, looking around uneasily, but he shut the door and came to stand beside me. "Do you feel that?"

"No," I said, but after he mentioned it, I realized that I did. I'd felt so watched at the office recently, I'd gotten used to the faint electric crawl across my skin. "It's probably the one-stop pill shop two doors down. The dealer keeps a close eye on the street." Not only for cops—sometimes ancient Mrs. Carpenter, who owned the house between them, went wandering down the sidewalk in her bra. Birdwine and the dealer both looked out for her.

My explanation did nothing to set Julian at ease, but at least it had gone quiet inside. I waited another minute, then decided to go in. I didn't want to give Birdwine time to pass out.

"You can wait here, if you like." I boosted off the car and held my car keys out. "I'll let you play the radio."

Julian paused and swallowed. The sun was almost down. "No. Let's go."

Inside, the living room looked like a bear had gone crashing through it. A wooden chair was reduced to kindling, and the coffee table was overturned and shoved half into the fireplace. There were gaping holes and shatter-spots in the drywall. It looked like the whole room had pissed him off, and he'd taught it better with a baseball bat. The bat itself was cracked and lying in the middle of the floor.

I could hear humming, loud and tuneless, coming from the kitchen. He seemed to be done breaking things, but he was still conscious. Good.

Looper jumped up on the wide plaid sofa and flopped down in a sprinkle of wall plaster, the flakes catching like snow in his dense fur. He put his shoe-box head on his paws and gazed back and forth from me to Julian and back again, eyebrows twitching. Whatever was happening at the back of the house was clearly a human problem. He would wait right here.

"Coward," I told him, and he thumped his tail. So be it.

As I walked back to the kitchen, Julian crowded up on my shoulder. He was nervous, but I got the sense he had my back. I'd underestimated him, again, thinking he'd chosen to come in with me because it was getting dark outside. The kid was a better dog than even Looper, loyal through and through.

We found Birdwine by his hideous avocado-colored stove. One of its electric eyes glowed deep orange, and a fry pan full of smashed eggs sat on the dead, gray burner next to it. Birdwine had his back to us, rattling the pan and humming, stirring eggs that weren't cooking at all. He peered owlishly over his shoulder as we came in. He was beat all to hell. His left eye was almost swollen shut, and blood had crusted at the corners of his lips.

"Mmm, Pau," he said, which I took to be a greeting. He was so drunk that turning his head set him swaying, like a man standing on a little boat at sea, riding the swells. "Ahmmakineg." *I'm making eggs.*

"I think you might be making deadly house fires," I told him.

He gave me a sloppy version of the big grin I'd always liked, the one that showed the gap in his front teeth. They were all still in his mouth, from this angle, anyway.

"God, I'm scared to see the other guy," Julian whispered, blinking rapidly.

"There is no other guy," I said.

Birdwine came back from binges with cracked ribs, loose teeth, and new, exciting angles in his long nose. I used to worry that he'd accidentally kill someone. He was so big, and he knew how to fight. But he never once had broken fingers or even bruises on his knuckles; he closed his sprees by pissing people off, and then taking the beating.

The kitchen was large, with room for a butcher block table and two chairs near the door. Birdwine's old laptop, a huge slow thing I called his Craptoposaurus, was sitting on it, open. I went over to it and checked the screen.

He was logged into Facebook, which was odd enough to make me do a double take. Not a social media guy, that Birdwine. Unless he had been trying to work, drunk, and this page was related to Hana? I wanted to slide into the closest chair and start digging, but Birdwine's sleeve was dragging dangerously near the lit burner. I left the browser open and went to get him.

"Julian, would you finish the eggs? You can make eggs, right?" I said, taking Birdwine by the shoulders, turning him away from the stove.

"Everyone can make eggs," Julian said, overly hearty.

I steered Birdwine across the kitchen. He was unwieldy and out of balance, but he shuffled in the direction that I pointed him.

"Look, Birdwine, it's Julian, remember him?" To Julian I said, "And get him some water."

I dumped Birdwine in one empty chair, then went back to the other myself, the one close to the computer. Facebook was open to the page of a woman named Stella Martin. Her feed was full of pictures from what looked like a family beach vacation. I didn't know any Martins, but the first name rang a faint bell.

"There's so much shell in here," Julian said. "I think it's all the shells."

I glanced at Birdwine, swaying in the chair.

"Forget it. Turn the stove off and bring the water," I told Julian, and then muttered to myself, "Stella, Stella, Stella. Who are you?"

"Stellaaaaa!" Birdwine bellowed, sudden and loud, in a drunken Marlon Brando. Julian jumped and dropped the egg pan into the sink with a clatter. Birdwine cackled to himself.

I gave him a stern look.

"Do you see something about Hana?" Julian asked.

"I don't know yet. Birdwine? Is this about my case? Huh?" Dammit, I should have had him updating me every single day. But I hadn't wanted that. I'd been very busy trying not to think about where Hana might be, what he might be finding. Trying to get square at my firm.

He didn't answer. Stella Martin's profile picture showed an attractive dishwater blonde, somewhere around forty. Her top posts were all from the vacation. I scrolled through lots of pics of Stella with a dorky, freckled man that she'd tagged "The Hubs." They had a slew of children: a teenage boy already towering over his mother and then a herd of little blond girls like stair steps running down from him. I put the oldest girl at ten or eleven—close to Hana's age—but beyond that, I couldn't see any connection.

Then I remembered. Stella was the name of Birdwine's ex-wife. The one who called him Zachary. She'd left him for another man, and now they lived in Florida.

"Are you posting on *your* Stella's wall, Birdwine?" I asked. I meant to say it quietly, and I was surprised to hear how sharp and loud my voice had gone.

"Nah," he said. "Ammustaliner." *Nah, I'm just stalking her.*

"What?" asked Julian. He had found a huge plastic cup with the Hulk on it and was filling it from the tap. "Who is Stella?"

I sat back. This was ex-wife bullshit, which made it instantly Not Julian's Business. Not mine either, truth be told, but I scanned the page anyway, and saw that Birdwine was logged in as someone named Jennifer James.

My loud voice said, "Who's Jennifer James?"

"Me," Birdwine said, and that, at least, was clear. He should hold all his answers to one syllable.

"What are you looking at?" asked Julian, bringing the water over. He handed the Hulk cup to Birdwine, who guzzled at it in a noisy, greedy way that could not possibly have been any less attractive.

"It's not about Hana. I'll search his other files in a sec, okay? But can you . . ." I paused, casting about for a reason, any reason, to get him from the room. I wanted to ask Birdwine why the hell he was stalking his ex-wife. More than that, I needed thirty seconds to get myself in hand. " . . . Go change his sheets? We should put him to bed, and they're probably disgusting."

Julian looked alarmed. "You want me to, like, open all his drawers and look for sheets?"

"The spare set's in the linen closet. It's a narrow door halfway down the hall, beside the bathroom. Then his bedroom is at the very end."

"You know this place real well, huh?" he asked me, his head tilting to the side.

"Julian, please?" I said. "He could pass out any second, and we'll never get him moved."

Julian's mouth scrunched up into a wad that made him look like all those disapproving rabbits on the Internet, but he went.

I looked back at the screen. The former Stella Birdwine, now Martin, was one of those people who said yes to any friend request. She had almost six hundred, making it easy for Birdwine to invent a profile and friend her on the sly. Now he could watch her life like it was television.

"This seems really healthy," I said to him.

Birdwine nodded, drunk-wry, and the movement almost tipped him from the chair. I felt inclined to let him fall. Let him smash himself up a little more. What was another black eye between friends?

Better question—why was I so pissed that he was mooning over Stella? I didn't like the implications. Right before he left to go find Hana, I'd realized that he'd once been in love with me. I hadn't asked myself the natural follow-up. Had I been in love back?

I must have been, at least a little.

I hadn't noticed. But in retrospect, I could see that I'd gone about systematically killing it. I hadn't had to think about it. I knew how. I'd had plenty of practice.

I'd fallen for my best friend, William, back in high school. I'd slept with him once. Hell, I'd slept with him first, but I had never followed up. I'd started screwing college fellows, and I'd helped William land the girl of his dreams. The three of us had ended up best friends. In law school, Nick and I had a thing that could have turned out serious. He'd wanted that, at one point. I made it clear that I was nothing like monogamous, telling him stories of my conquests like we were bar buddies. I started acting as his wingman, both in mock trials and when he noticed a girl. The sex petered out, and we ended up business partners.

Then Birdwine. I looked across the table at him, blood-crusted, smelling like roadkill. Ye gods help me, I hadn't killed whatever was between us. Not all the way. Sure, I'd made him into a colleague and a friend, roles with much longer shelf lives than my lovers got, exactly as I had with William and Nick. But almost without noticing, I'd stopped looking for new men. I'd given up my friendly late-night calls to exes. And I sure as hell hadn't worked to put other women on his radar.

No matter. Son of a bitch had done a fine job tracking his ex-wife all on his own.

Birdwine's eye was swollen almost shut. I got up and checked his freezer. Both ice trays were dead empty. There was a bag of store-brand frozen peas, though. I brought them over.

"Hold these," I told him, smacking the peas against his eye. He grunted, but he managed to get a big paw up and hold them in place. He smelled like old sweat and older bourbon, with the copper tang of blood just under that.

When I tried to turn away, he grabbed my wrist with his free hand. He stared up at me with his one good eye bleary and mumbled out a string of urgent words.

Between the smashed lips and the quarts of liquor, it took me a moment to parse out the meaning, but then I got it:

I don't give two shits about Stella.

He held my gaze, and I didn't think that he was lying.

"Well, what do I care," I said, but my voice had softened, and all ye gods and little fishes, it sure seemed like I did.

Not in my usual take-it-or-leave-it way, either, though he seemed like my type, on the surface: easygoing, fucked up enough to be forgettable. I hadn't forgotten him, though, had I? Funny, I'd always told myself he was an expendable convenience, but looking back, my actions told a different story. I'd even stalked his ass to get him back into my orbit. I'd treated him like he was Nick or William: quality stuff.

Now here I was, smacking him in the face with peas, mad to find him looking at his ex on social media. Almost like love were an open option. Almost like I wanted Birdwine to myself, in my life as well as in my bed.

Well, not in my bed tonight. Not drunk and stinking. Not with my little brother hovering, as uncomfortable here in Birdwine's shithole as he had been in Oakleigh Winkley's Buckhead mansion.

"Paula?" Julian said, back already. He looked at Birdwine's grip on my arm, how close our faces were, and upped his disapproval game; he went from rabbit all the way to prim religious auntie. "I think the extra sheets are dirtier than the ones on there."

I straightened up and shrugged off Birdwine's hand. Changing the sheets had been busywork, anyway. Birdwine was so foul we'd likely need to burn the whole bed in the morning. Even so, I couldn't help remembering that back when Birdwine and I were a thing, he always had clean sheets around. He'd had good motivation, then. So was he sleeping by himself these days? I didn't like how fiercely glad the idea made me.

I started levering Birdwine to his feet. "Give me a hand?"

Julian came and braced his other side, and we walked down the hall, toward the bedroom. It was a familiar path for me with Birdwine. I'd never once thought I would walk down it with an overly protective baby brother along.

Birdwine leaned on us heavily, favoring one leg.

"Birdwine, where's the Hana file?" I asked him.

He slurred out a few words not even I could translate and shifted his arm down, resting his hand companionably on my ass.

"Don't even think about it," I said, and he cackled that weird drunk laugh again.

"Issa dammmmm goodass," Birdwine said.

Julian's mouth set in an even tighter line.

"I know," I said, and left his hand where it was. If Kai's picture could be believed, I'd have this ass for quite a few years yet, but it had been underappreciated of late.

We helped him maneuver through the door, aiming right at the bed.

"Dump him facedown, in case he pukes," I told Julian, who did not react. He might be naive, but he had been to college.

We timbered Birdwine over, and he crashed onto the mattress. He spoke into the pillow, saying the clearest thing he'd said so far. "Get in with me."

Julian looked appalled, but I grinned outright to see there was a living ember down in Birdwine, sparking to me still.

"Not even a little tempted," I told him. "But try me again after you roll around in bleach." I meant it, too, though he might not remember in the morning. On his end, this could all be nothing more than drunk.

I looked at his wrecked eye. The corner of his bloody, swollen mouth. All the damage he had taken, walking his face into some other guy's fist, repeatedly, while his own rough hands were as blameless and unbruised as any baby's. I thought then, *No, he's still in love with me.* When it came to love, I was the walking incarnation of fists, served in a convenient female package with a nice ass. He'd meant it just as much as I had.

I pulled the blanket out from under his feet and draped it over him. Julian waited behind me, his discomfort so thick that I felt it rolling off him in waves.

Birdwine's breathing had changed to deep and stentorian. The sound of it called Looper, who came jingling in to leap up into the bed. He flopped at the foot.

"Oh, now you show, you worthless sack of fur," I said, and gave his ears a rumple.

We backed out, Julian with his head down, peeking at me from under his flop of forehead curls.

"What?" I said.

He blushed and cut his eyes away. All he said was "Did you understand him? Where's the Hana file?"

"We'll have to hunt for it. I'll check the computer, but it could be a real file, made of paper. Birdwine kicks it old school. Why don't you dig around?"

We were back in the den now, and Julian said, "You want me to ransack a huge, crazy, drunk guy's house."

I waved a hand at the shattered chair, the overturned table. "You think he's going to know?"

"Point taken," Julian said.

That made me smile. It was something I would say, and he'd used my inflections. I took him by the shoulders and aimed him at Birdwine's desk in the corner.

"Start there," I said, and headed for the kitchen.

I sat back down with the craptop and swirled the mouse to wake up the screen. Stella Martin's Facebook page reappeared. It was still open to a shot of the whole family, posed on the deck of the beach house. My breath caught. Now that I wasn't focused so wholly on his ex-wife, I saw it instantly.

Which one of these things is not like the other?

Blond Stella held hands with her weedy, ginger-headed hubs. I saw how their features and their colors blended in the three little girls. The boy towered in the middle, dark and barrel-chested.

I clicked back two pics, to one where the boy stood tall and thick and sturdy in the surf, the littlest girl climbing up him like he was her own pet tree. I leaned in, studying his face. He had big brown eyes with heavy lids. His hair was thick and wiry, and his skin was olive. He was tanned, while the rest of the family was in various phases of turning pink and peeling. His teeth were very straight, but the front two had a gap in them.

I knew that gap. I'd always liked it on Zach Birdwine.

I did the math. The boy was big, but he had no hair yet on his chest, barely any on his legs, and he still had a round-cheeked baby softness to his face. As old as fifteen, maybe as young as twelve. Either way, before my time. Either way, his life span overlapped with Birdwine's marriage.

I sat back. It could not be so. I'd worked with Birdwine for almost a decade. We'd been lovers for more than half a year. Now we were supposedly friends. This was a large and toothy chunk of history to leave out.

At a glance, his boy had landed in a good place, with books and beach vacations and a wild pack of adoring little sisters. The Hubs's arm looked both possessive and comfortable, resting on the boy's shoulder. The whole family had good body language in their pictures, actually, leaning in and turning slightly toward each other. They looked like a regulation happy family. On Facebook, at least.

Was this why Birdwine had abandoned him? If so, it was a cop-out. The kid wouldn't see it like that. Kind as Mrs. Mack had been, I hadn't felt relieved or grateful when the state of Georgia spared me from the company of my mother.

Julian appeared in the doorway, his face set in stress lines, holding a manila folder. "It was in his car."

As he brought it to me, I minimized the browser. Pissed as I was, I wouldn't sell out Birdwine by opening up his private life to Julian, who already didn't like him. Also, I didn't want to look at a happy family, posting happy stories that might even be true. I was here with some jagged ends from families that hadn't worked.

There were more of us. The world was full of us, the leftovers and the leavers, the bereaved and the broken.

I said, "Good job," and took the folder. Julian hovered over me, hands twisting.

The top pages were Birdwine's interview notes, scrawled in his dark, side-slanted writing. First up, an interview with Tolliver, Kai's Austin boyfriend. Her sudden disappearance in the dead of night had baffled him. She hadn't even told him she was sick, though by his account they'd been deeply in love. Sure they had.

I glanced up at Julian, but he wasn't reading. He was still twisting his hands, looking at me.

"What's eating you?" I asked.

"I didn't realize you two were a thing. You and Birdwine," Julian said.

"We're not a thing," I said, flipping another page.

"Oh. Okay," he said, with exaggerated disbelief.

"Julian, stop hovering. We're not a thing," I told him, and the last sentence came out raw and angry.

Mostly because bare minutes before I saw Birdwine's cuckoo bird, dropped into some other fellow's nest and left behind, I'd been considering him. Considering us, even.

He moved to sit across from me and folded his hands on the table. "Well, good. Because he's a scary guy. And he clearly has some kind of substance problem."

"Oh, you think," I said, flicking blindly through four more pages. "Drop it. It isn't relevant."

"It will be, though," Julian said. "When we find Hana. That guy, he isn't— He doesn't seem like he'd be good for a kid."

I felt a lightning stab of blue-bright anger. If he'd said it half an hour ago, I would have called him on it, hard. I would've snapped, *Try not to be a privileged little shit.* But between my embarrassing Goodnight-Sweet-Prince tableau at Birdwine's bedside and this moment, I'd gone through a sea change.

One look at Birdwine's son, ditched down in Florida, and my loyalties had shifted, from history to blood. Julian, after all, was desperately trying. He was chock-full of hopeful plans, wanting to make a family for Hana. Birdwine had so thoroughly abandoned his own child that the boy didn't even live in Birdwine's conversation.

Part of me wanted to take the folder right now, walk out, hand the whole damn thing over to a fresh PI. One I'd never met before. Preferably female.

Even so, I couldn't let Julian's starry-eyed statement stand. I spoke as kindly as I could. "You think Birdwine's not our kind. I get it. But, Julian, there is no *our* kind for you and me. Sure, as it turns out, Birdwine is an asshole. But that is my kind. This girl we're looking for? She's going to be my kind, too. You think this"—I waved my hand around, encompassing the wrecked house, the sketchy neighborhood, the feeling of unfriendly eyes on us outside—"would offend her tender sensibilities? Baby, you grew up with Little League and meals made off the food pyramid, but Hana comes from here, where people ditch other people, or use them, or eat them whole."

Julian got redder and redder as I talked, and so I shut up before he lost his temper.

"I know," he said, and he didn't sound angry at all. "But isn't that the point of a rescue? You take somebody out of where it's bad. You bring them someplace better. Not perfect. No place is perfect. You bring them to the best place that you can."

I blinked, knocked off my high horse. Damn, but the truth had such a ring to it.

Julian was right, again. I should take it as given that he had a better handle on the personal than I did. I couldn't resurrect my mother, make her marry Hana's mystery father the day before she was conceived, set them up in a cottage by a balmy sea. But we could find her. We could make sure she was safe and fed and cared for, because it was the least that she deserved. It was the least that any kid deserved.

"All right. I hear you, but you need to hear me, too. Any plan we make assumes too much. You're assuming we will find her. We're assuming Kai is dead, and Hana isn't. Also, she's ten. She may already be embarked on some mad self-rescue of her own, bonding with someone, making herself a place. We can't plan a damn thing from a base of total ignorance." My words rang true enough to match his.

"Okay. That means we have to focus on what we do have." I nodded, thinking he meant the file, just as he added. "You and me. I think we're starting to really be a team." I stopped mid-nod, but he was already beaming at me, glowing like a piece of Muppet-headed living sunshine. This kid! He was so inclined toward nesting—and so sweet in the core of him. I couldn't help but smile back, pleased he understood that I'd been genuinely trying.

I broke eye contact before it turned into a love-in, though, flipping through more pages of interview notes. I skimmed, hoping something would leap out at me that could put us back on Hana's trail. Near the bottom of the stack, I found the map.

Time stopped.

"What?" Julian said. I couldn't answer. I was breathing so hard it was like I had been sprinting. I rummaged through my bag to pull my envelope out again, reread Kai's final note.

I am going on a journey, Kali. I am going back to my beginning.

Tenderhearted Julian instantly came back to stand beside me, one hand on my shoulder, asking me, "Are you okay?"

I wasn't. Birdwine had drawn their route in high-lighters, a bright orange line of color squiggling through the South. I ran my finger along the line, tracing Kai's trajectory. Was every mystic-ass, pretentious line of Kai's note literal? When had Kai ever been literal?

"Look," I said, though it was meaningless to Julian.

"At the map? Why? Do you know where Hana is?" he asked, now with an urgency that matched mine.

I looked up and into those eyes he had, my mother's own.

"She's in my life," I told him. "Hana's somewhere in the middle of my life."

Chapter 9

It's better this way, I think, as the door shuts behind Joya. I'm not crying. What I feel is so far past crying that I can't move, or it will get out of me and be a sound, and I don't know what that sound is. I lie on the bed unmoving, but inside my skin, every atom is seething with a single thought: I want my mother. I want my mother blindly, like a newborn mouse. Inside the quiet shell of me, I churn and shudder. My body so badly wants to root and seek, attach, be warm and full.

I hear Mrs. Mack and Shar, Karice, and Kim talking and banging the door as they get back from dinner. I don't hear Candace, but that's normal. She'll be mincing along behind them, quiet. If she comes in this room right now, if she so much as looks at me with her wet eyes, I am not responsible for what I do to her.

Then come all the happy sounds of Joya's mama arriving. I listen, lying stiff and still, as Joya's things are loaded up. I hear the thump of the bags and the grown-lady voices of Mrs. Mack and Joya's mama talking. If I stand up, I'll be able to see them from the window. Our room faces the drive. But I stay rigid on my bed, even when the car doors close. I don't cry or move as I hear the engine start, when I hear them drive off, when she is gone away with her own mother.

It's long past midnight when I finally crack. Alone in my bed in the darkest part of night, I wake to find I am already weeping. My body bucks and rocks, and I have to smother the loud brays that I feel rising. I turn to the wall and push them down deep into my pillow. I hug my cool pillow to me, and it does not hug me back. I gulp and weep into the cloth anyway, biting at it, pressing close until I'm gagging on it.

I roll away from the wall, sick, and find Candace's bug eyes looking at me, six inches away. She's peeping up over the edge of my bed, alligator style. I jerk back so fast it feels like I left all my skin behind, and a scream bangs its way up my throat. I snap my mouth shut, trapping it behind my teeth. I sit up and glare at her, letting the scream out as a long hiss of breath. I've been startled out of puking.

Candace doesn't move, still crouching on her knees by my bed. I can see the whites of her eyes gleaming in the dim light from our clock.

"You're whoopin' in your pillow so loud that I can't sleep."

She says *can't* so redneck. It sounds like *ain't* with a *c* on the front. I don't speak her brand of English any more than I spoke Joya's. No one here speaks like me and Kai. No one wears colorful scarves or admits to playing the tambourine. Kai's people eat sardines tinned in mustard and talk about *The Tao of Pooh*. They are all art-farts and petty criminals—light-fingered musicians, stoned painters, writers penning novels and bad checks. Even Tick, that racist asshole, was a poet. Kai's tribe owns water pipes and finger bells the way regular Americans own coasters. We are gypsies among other gypsies, shifting in and out of love, towns, names, constantly in flux, reinvented by and for each other.

No one here talks like me or gets my references or knows the songs I know. I don't look like any of them. Even my bond with Joya was based on not belonging here.

I scrub at my face with my hands, and all at once anything is better than being alone. I scoot back, making room for Candace. She rises up enough to rest her pointy chin on the bed's edge, suspicious of the offer. It's unprecedented. She's always had to wheedle or bribe her way in.

I press my back against the wall and say, "I'll sleep better with you taking up seventy percent of my mattress than creeping around on the floor and goggling at me." I try to say it tough like Joya would, but my throat is full of snot and my voice is trembly.

Candace thinks about it, then slithers in under my covers. She lies on her back, looking straight up at the ceiling. "Yesterday, you wouldn't've peed on me if I was on fire. You're just crying over Joya."

"I'm not crying over Joya," I said, and it's true enough to sound true.

"Well, why then?"

I am not going to tell Candace, of all people, that I miss my mother.

"Maybe because I'm going to get my ass kicked in the morning." Candace's eyes gleam, full of questions in the dark. "Shar, Karice, and Kim. They never got Joya. Now that she's gone, they'll come after me." Just to be mean I add, "They'll probably whip the shit out of you, too."

Candace swallows audibly, then whispers, "Do you think they'll come in here and get us while we're sleeping?"

This is the last place they will start it. Mrs. Mack's suite is exactly under our room. But Candace isn't a fighter, and she doesn't think strategically. She is staring at the door, big-eyed. I soften and I add, very exaggerated, so she'll get it, "They could burst in any second and kill us all. If I were you, I'd sleep under the bed."

She makes a tittering sound and relaxes. "They wouldn't mess with me nohow," she says, "excepting Kim."

"Kim's big, but Shar's the one you have to watch for."

I may not be crying about the fight, but it *is* coming. It's nice having a living body, even Candace's, between me and the door. Or maybe, tonight, it's simply nice to have a living body close.

"Are you really scared?" Candace whispers, as if the idea I might feel human things like fear is new to her.

"Who wants to get the shit beat out of 'em?" I ask instead of answering.

"I could help you," Candace says, almost truculent. "If you wanted to make friends with me."

I snort at that. Candace cringes at the sight of any lifted hand. I can't wave at the girl without her shivering and crawling backward like a beaten dog, except a dog is at least a vertebrate. Candace is as spineless as a bag of jam.

"I'd like to see you be my friend in front of Shar," I say.

"You never wanted me to before," she says, sulky. "I can't hardly even come in my own room. All Joya ever said to me was *Get out,* and you let her."

"Well, Joya's a bitch. I don't want to hear her name again," I say, too loud. To my surprise, I start to cry again. "I mean it. I don't want to hear her name." I am crying so hard now that I'm not sure Candace understands me.

She must though, because she says, "Well, you ain't got no one, then, huh?"

I don't answer, and Candace's mouth turns downward, thoughtful. After another minute, she squirms over closer and wraps her weirdly spongy arms around me.

"There, now," she says, patting at me awkwardly, like I'm a tiny baby. "There, now, don't be sad. There, now."

I spin in place, turning my wet face to the wall, and I can't imagine I will ever stop. I will lie here and weep for my mother—my best, first love—until I am a husk, as dry and light as dandelion fluff. The wind will lift me up and blow me away, and Candace can make a wish on me.

She scoots in even closer, spooning, her knees tucked into my knees, her belly pressed against my back. She rocks and coos and squeezes me, saying it over and over. *There, now. There, now.* We stay like that until at last, the crying stops. I stare at the wall, hitching and gulping until I catch my breath. As soon as I am quiet, Candace falls into a boneless sleep, untroubled. Eventually I sleep, too, uneasy. In my dreams, I run down bare and endless hallways, seeking something lost. There are no hiding spots, and none of the empty hallways brings me to it.

I was still looking. Sometimes the lost thing was Kai, sometimes a little girl with a cloud of dark curls and crescent-moon eyes. Sometimes I didn't know what it was. I only knew I had to find it. I ran, my footsteps echoing off the bare walls. Then I thought that it might be above me, in the world that was awake. I found myself rising toward the surface of my sleep. I felt another body, soothing me with breath, easing me with heartbeat. A living warmth, a proof against the darkness. I tried to ask, *Is that you?* and my own voice woke me up.

I jerked my gummy eyes open, disoriented. I smelled ripe dog, and my throat was sour and dry from remembered, ancient crying. It took me a moment to orient. I recognized the ugly wall of plaid in front of me; my face was crammed up against the back of Birdwine's wide sofa. The body pressed against my back was Looper's. I glared at him over my shoulder. He thumped his tail at me, and his giant mouth gaped open in a stretch just inches from my face.

"Ugh, your yawn smells terrible," I told him, and struggled to get myself around him and up. He stretched and rolled onto his back into my warm space. I said, "Honestly, dogs," and gave his belly a scratch.

I was creased and rumpled, covered in golden-brown Looper hair that showed on both my black skirt and my white shell. Great. Julian was dead asleep in the baggy leather Barcalounger. I offered to drive him back to his car last night, but he wouldn't go. He knew I'd drive straight back here.

So we'd both stayed. I'd booted up my own laptop and gone into my cloud account. I cross-referenced my personal files with Birdwine's paper one, drawing new routes, taking notes, cussing at Birdwine's poky Internet connection. Julian alternated between checking my progress and cleaning up. He'd swept up the plaster and other debris and put Birdwine's furniture back in order. He'd even done the dishes. Now he slept like happy babies do, on his back in the Barcalounger with his arms thrown up around his head.

I edged closer and ruffled his hair, softer than I'd scratched at Looper, but the same in spirit. He leaned into the touch in his sleep, the way a flower turns its face unthinking to the sunlight. I stopped before he

woke up, marveling at the way Julian, even uncon-
scious Julian, assumed that any hand on him reached
out in kindness. His eyes moved behind his closed lids,
dreaming easy. I let him sleep on.

I had no more gentleness inside me, not this morning. I'd woken full of thunderstorms, with a strong
desire to aim them all at Birdwine. I could hear water
running in the bathroom down the hall, so he was up.
And bathing, which indicated a certain readiness to
come back to the sober world.

He wasn't ready for me, though. I wanted to barge in
while he was vulnerable, wet and naked, and ask him,
What the hell? He'd never so much as hinted that he had
a boy, even back when we were lovers. The only clue
had been how invested he'd been in the hunt for Hana.
He'd been alarmed and overanxious from the first. In
my office, when I told him Kai had reinvented herself
as a person with no daughter, he had been so cryptic
and emphatic, saying, *A parent can't just do that.*

Well, he had. So how complicated could it be?

And to think last night I'd stood over him all
sweet-mouthed and sugar-hearted, almost yearning.
I remembered how sad he'd seemed, telling me I had
broken his heart. Sure I had. His heart, and probably
some unicorns; I was apparently quite hard on mytho-
logical creatures.

Now I wanted to put my face in his face, let him see how done with him I was. Then I'd show him my notes and the new lines and dots I'd filled in on his map, and tell him to get off his bruised ass and find my sister. After that, he was free to go his merry way. All the way to hell. I'd give him a map for that, too, if he needed it.

Birdwine's file was sitting on the coffee table. I picked it up, and it was shaking too hard for me to read it. It took me a full second to understand the shaking was coming from my hands.

I had to pull myself together. I was furious and rumpled, and I'd woken up missing my mother, or maybe missing the feel of any human body in the bed beside me. Well, that second part was fixable.

The shower was still running, and Julian was out cold, so I had a moment. I went to the kitchen and got some coffee started. My mouth felt like this whole filthy house had crawled inside and died there. Last night, I'd searched the bathroom and come up with a toothbrush I was pretty sure was mine. I'd brought it to the kitchen and washed it with some dish soap, just in case. I used it again, now.

Then I got Birdwine's duct tape from the junk drawer and pulled most of the hair off my skirt and blouse. That felt so much better. More like me. I put my shoes on and shrugged back into my jacket. My blowout was failing, so I slicked my wild hair back and secured it at the nape of my neck. I did the two-minute version of full war paint: matte skin, dark striped eyes, a mean red mouth.

I checked myself in my compact's mirror and was heartened to find a reasonable approximation of my hardest self. Good enough to break a piece off in Birdwine. Even good enough to go straight to work from here. One advantage of my endless sleek black suits was that only Verona would realize I was wearing yesterday's. She had a good eye for cut and label, combined with a twenty-something's interest in other people's walks of shame. She'd be so disappointed in me if she saw the hairy drooler who had shared my sofa. From here on out, I would do better. The best way to get the dregs of Birdwine right out of my system was to get some other body into it.

By then the shower sounds had stopped. His laptop was still open on the kitchen table. I woke it up and turned it toward the doorway, so he'd see it when he came in. As he came up the hall, I poured coffee into two of his random coffee mugs, one plain green and one with happy daisies that said TEACHER OF THE YEAR. If only he'd had a FATHER OF THE YEAR or WORLD'S BEST DAD mug. I was up for a little ugly irony.

He limped around the corner in an old T-shirt and some Levi's that looked even older. His dark hair was wet and brushed back off his face, giving me a good view of his bruises. The swelling had gone down a bit around his eye, thanks to the cold peas, but the colors were coming in: black and violet and a spectacular deep plum. He gave me a wholly fake sheepish look; the real expression in his eyes was wary.

He did not apologize for last night. He'd once told me he never did, for drunk. Sorry implied a promise to stop, and he'd sorry'd about it endlessly at Stella. He could no longer muster the required faith to form the words, lifetime-level tired of watching himself fail to mean it.

Then he saw the picture open on his laptop's screen. I'd left the browser open to the best close-up of his son, standing shoulder to shoulder with the Hubs. The boy's head was already even with the man's.

Birdwine stopped, his eyes gone serious and blank. If I'd had any lingering question that this was his kid, his face was answer enough. Birdwine's good eye met my gaze, and his fingers moved to press against his temple.

I held out the mug with the daisies. After a second, he came over and took it. He leaned on a piece of counter catty-corner to me. He still didn't speak. Neither did I. I used his own old cop trick. I was obvious about it, giving him prizefighter eyes, letting the silence build and charge. He took a sip, considering me over the rim of the cup. He knew what I was doing.

He said, "Okay. Let's start with the kid."

Oh, it was a good opener. His speaking first gave me the win—his way of saying he was sorry, after all. But it begged the question, which damn kid? We had a herd to choose from, he and I: my orphaned brother snoring in his Barcalounger, my missing sister, his abandoned son.

"Why don't we start with yours?" I said. It came out sharp, accusing.

He'd given me the opening, but I could see he was regretting it already. "Really? Because I know where mine is."

"Don't worry, we'll get to Hana when Julian's up. He should be in on that conversation."

"Okay. But I don't want him in on *this* conversation," Birdwine said, like a warning. He would talk about the boy, but he was setting a timer.

"Fine," I said. I tried to sound impersonal, as if I was questioning a witness on the stand. "When did you last see your kid?"

He looked deliberately to the screen, then back to me. "One second ago."

Okay, so it was a hostile witness. "In person."

"When he was three."

"How long ago was that?"

"Ten years."

I had my next question locked and loaded, but his answer paused me. The timing was odd. Ten years ago, Birdwine started going to AA. It felt backward, to get in AA and then stop seeing your son. Most people started twelve-stepping so they *could* see their kid. I changed course.

"Why haven't you seen him?" I asked.

"Wasn't invited."

"So?" I snapped. This was now the least impersonal cross-examination in the history of the justice system. "Do you need an invitation?" I amended.

"Yup."

Birdwine was good at hostile witness. He'd give opposing counsel exactly what they asked for, and no more. But this was not a courtroom. This was the kitchen of a man I'd almost loved. I'd been ready to try at least, last night. Now I felt that sweetness like a bullet I had barely dodged.

"Why?" I asked, and it came out like a donkey's bray, raw and angry. He didn't answer and it only made me angrier. "Why won't you explain yourself?"

He shrugged, impassive. "I don't see the upside, Paula."

"You don't? Well, I do. At least I'd understand your choices, even if—" I stopped myself. The rest of the sentence was stuck in my throat. I'd almost said, *even if I can't forgive them.*

Birdwine gave me a rueful smile, eyebrows raised. I tipped my head to him, acknowledging the hit. He was right. There was no upside.

I dropped the line of questions and said, flat, "You should have told me. Before. When we were a thing."

"Oh, yeah. Because you're taking it so well." That sounded more like him than anything he'd said so far, and as he went on, I finally got why he had ditched me in the first place. "I don't have a good bedtime story for a chick with abandonment issues."

"It was the truth, though," I said. Understanding it did not make me less angry. I didn't want a conversation, anyway. I wanted an apology; it would feel so ugly-good to not accept it. "And you were supposedly in love with me."

"Yeah," he said.

"Then you should have told me, Birdwine, shit. I think I was in love with you, too."

"I know you were," he said, so sad and sure and world-weary all at once that the urge to hurt him, to pick a bruise and press my fingers hard against it or to bite, was almost overwhelming.

I stepped to him, tall enough in my shoes to jam my lips against his swollen mouth, not carefully. Not carefully at all. He hummed the hurt of it against my skin, but his hand went to my hip, automatic, like a reflex. His mouth opened, surprised by pain, and his breath came out. I pulled it in, tasted old bourbon down behind the mint.

I broke the kiss, but stayed close, eye to eye, so angry. "I'm not starting anything."

"I know," he said, even though his hand on my hip had already pulled me closer.

My lips twisted. "You should send that memo to your pants."

He flashed me that gap in his teeth, though the grin had to hurt. "You're so damn romantic." This close, I could smell the faded copper tang of last night's blood.

"You understand that was good-bye." I said it like a window closing.

"Yeah," he said. He dropped his hand and moved away to the coffeemaker for a refill. He didn't speak again until his back was to me. "It's not what I want, but I can't change it."

I wasn't sure if he was talking about the boy or me.

It didn't matter. Either way, the love was breakable. All love was. At my job, I helped dozens of couples who were staggering out of it, shell-shocked or enraged.

Many of them tore their kids in half and shattered that love, too. Even crazy Oakleigh with her murder-kittens had loved Clark Winkley, once. Now he was risking a broken neck to worm across her roof to pee in her compact and scribble out her face in pictures. My clients, every one, had made promises in front of priests and rabbis and judges and all their friends and their relations. Made a home. Made babies. Then happily ever after cracked, and I came to break it open and divvy up its jagged pieces.

There was something left between me and Birdwine, or I wouldn't feel this way. I wouldn't be closer to crying than I had been since—I could not remember, and then I did. Since the last time I saw Candace. Some feeling for him was alive inside me, still, and I would have to break it. Fine. Breaking things was what I did best.

I stepped back, but it wasn't far enough. I backed all the way across the kitchen, and he stayed by the coffeemaker. So Birdwine and I had loved each other. So what. We'd each had a share in wrecking it—he'd been too silent, and I'd been too cynical. Now here we were. He was still silent, and I was still cynical enough to know a hungry body could be fed on anything.

"Are we back to emails titled 'Here is the information'?" I asked. I didn't want him to quit, now. The specific ways his life was wrecked made me want him on this case. It was like me and my pro bono work, getting my mother's little avatars out of prison. No other PI on the planet would be this overinvested.

"That's what I said I wanted, all along," he said, with no inflection. But then he quirked an eyebrow up and added, wry, "How lucky that it's all working out for me."

It was his best and blackest kind of funny, and I would have laughed before. The job aside, Birdwine and I were over enough to have an after. After started now.

"Good morning," said Julian from the doorway. Looper was with him, lolling out a happy tongue. Julian seemed almost as eager, but he drew up short as Birdwine and I turned to him. Looper, oblivious, trotted through to squeeze out of his doggy door into the backyard. My brother's human nose lifted, though, as if he smelled the fury and the pheromones that still charged the air.

I said, "Birdwine, I don't think you've officially met my brother. This is Julian Bouchard."

"Julian," Birdwine said. He moved forward, impassive as a pile of bricks, to put his hand out.

Julian shook it, looking back and forth uneasily between us. "Oh, sorry. I've interrupted something. I should have stomped more, coming in, but Paula said that you two weren't a thing."

Birdwine answered, when I didn't. "I'd say that's a fair assessment."

I'd been too surprised by Julian's directness. He stated the truth so baldly, even when it brought discomfort to the room. It was another way the kid was like me, but we didn't get it from our slippery shared parent. Was it some odd recessive gene? Or had we each gotten it separately, from our fathers? Maybe Kai had had a type, after all.

"Oh, sorry. You look like you might have a—be a thing." Julian was flushed, as pink-cheeked as a maiden auntie who had caught her Pomeranians canoodling.

"You came in at the end of the end of the story. You're seeing credits roll," I said, brisk. "Can we get to business? Show Birdwine the map."

"Map?" Birdwine said, turning to Julian.

"You didn't tell him? How could you not tell him?" Julian asked, then turned excitedly to Birdwine. "We know where Kai was taking Hana. I mean, we know where they'll go next. I mean where they would have—where they went. Or gone."

He'd wound himself around in the verb tenses, but Birdwine picked up on the meaning.

"No, Paula didn't mention that," Birdwine said, shooting me an oblique look. It occurred to me that he was angry back. But with what cause? He could have defended himself, but he had taken a hard pass. He was still talking to Julian, though. "You picked up Hana's trail from my file? How?"

Julian looked to me, but I turned deliberately and went to get more coffee, saying, "Julian, why don't you catch him up?"

"Yeah. Okay. Well, last night, Paula figured out where Kai was going. Sort of," Julian said, looking uncertainly back and forth between us. He got the map out of the file and spread it out on the kitchen table. Birdwine came to stand beside him, casually closing his laptop and moving it back, out of the way. As if it was convenience, and the boy pictured on the screen had nothing to do with it.

Now Julian partially blocked my view, and I hoped the kid would hurry. Cold as the air was now between me and Birdwine, Julian could die of hypothermia if he got wordy.

"You went to Austin, and you traced the car to Dothan, Alabama," Julian said. He pointed at the line of orange highlighter, traveling their route via index finger. "That's where Kai grew up. Paula was born there." He trailed his finger along the line. "Next, they head for Montgomery."

Julian was taking too damn long already. I wanted out of this house, so I chimed in.

"We moved to Montgomery with Eddie. Then we lived in Jackson, Mississippi, with Tick." Julian kept track with his pointing finger as I talked. Kai and I had traveled all over, sometimes gypsy lifing it for weeks between boyfriends. We'd city hop, changing names and modes of transportation, especially if the relationship behind us had ended ugly. But this route she'd taken with Hana ignored our brief pauses, the men who didn't last or matter, all our winding roads. She'd taken Hana only to places where we'd lived a year or so. All the places where we'd had a home address and an approximation of a family. "New Orleans is where we met Anthony. You see?"

"Holy shit," said Birdwine, seeing.

Julian said, "It's her life. She was taking Hana on a tour, the main stops of her life, in order. Birth to— something."

I said, "Next is Asheville with Hervé, and that's where you lost her."

Birdwine was shaking his head. "Dammit. I should have texted you her movements."

I couldn't fault him for this. It was standard to give a PI a list of known associates, but I hadn't a clue about any of Kai's current people or places. I'd been thinking about brain cancer, delusions, heavy meds. I'd imagined some crazy flight from Texas child protective services into a murky future—not into our own ancient history.

"That's my bad. I told you to call me only when you had results," I said, but it was an icy absolution.

Julian shifted his weight from one foot to the other, uncomfortable. "Do you think it's possible she's still alive?" he said into the silence.

Birdwine shook his head, and his gaze on my brother was both sad and very gentle. "The guy who bought the wagon in Dothan said"—he paused, but Julian still had that baby bird look on his face, like he was hoping to be filled with something lovely—"that she looked like the walking dead. He barely recognized her from her picture. He said the Kai he met could have been November Kai's grandma. I'm sorry."

Julian swallowed, looked away.

Birdwine filled the silence. "From Dothan, they went Greyhound. In Asheville, they stopped taking the bus. She got a ride or bought another car. Not at a dealership. I checked all over. She could have found one on Craigslist or passed some junker with a For Sale sign in the window."

"Or stolen one. Or gotten a man to give them one," I said.

"Worst-case scenario, they started hitchhiking. At any rate, I lost them," he said, flipping through the notes I'd printed out last night. Kai was touring Hana through her past, but it had been my past, too. I'd written it all out for him and traced it on the map in blue. "But now, see, I know her destinations."

The search radius had narrowed from "anywhere in the world," to a journey from fixed point to fixed point. She was visiting every city where there had been a different boyfriend, a different Kai, a different me. How expurgated or invented was the tour that Kai gave Hana? So far, the geography matched Kai's real history, which in itself was shocking. The truth was not a story that my mother told.

Julian said, "After Asheville, Kai moved west of Atlanta with Dwayne. Then downstate." He flushed. "That's where I was born. But Paula thinks she might leave that part out. The prison part, and the me part, too. So it was Asheville, to Paulding County—"

"To here," I finished for him. There was no other destination possible. Kai didn't know Ganesh's new name, and she'd never left a lover without burning every bridge behind her. She'd meant to bring Hana here. "To me."

Birdwine was nodding. He remembered Kai's note as well as I did. *Death is not the end. You will be the end.*

She'd meant it literally, exactly as written. She'd had a plan for Hana, after all. To bring my sister to me.

It was a desperate move, but all the gods knew that I owed her. I would have taken Hana in, no questions, had I truly been her journey's end. She'd miscalculated, though. Somewhere on her wobbly path from Asheville to Paulding County to my place in Atlanta, my mother had run out of time.

"I'm on it," Birdwine said.

"Great. Julian, let's go. Your car is still parked by my office."

Julian was looking back and forth between us, bewildered. "But, wait, what happens now? We can't go home. We're so close!"

"We're closer," Birdwine said. "But I've got a crap ton of phone calls and database searches to do now. Every hospital, every police department, every wrecking service along every route that she could have taken. A terminally ill woman traveling with a little girl will have left a footprint, but realistically, it will take days or even weeks of grunt work to find it."

"So you aren't going back to Asheville," Julian said, thoughtful.

"I'll be more effective here. My PI license gives me access to search engines that would blow your mind, kid, and I know how to work a phone. If that fails, then, yeah. I'll run her possible routes in person, with pictures. I'll canvass, asking everyone with eyes. I hope it won't come to that."

I hoped not, too. I'd have to make a much more comprehensive list. Would Kai have taken Hana to the Dandy Mart, shown her the row of pay phones I had used to break our lives? Did places still have pay phones? Maybe they'd been ripped out, and all my mother could show Hana was the hole where they'd once been. That was the journey itself in a nutshell— looking at the holes where we'd once been.

"If it's phone calls and computer stuff, I could stay and help," Julian offered. "It will go faster with two." He looked back and forth between us, eager.

"What about your car?" I asked, buying time to think.

Our shared mother had died indigent, traveling under a name only the gods knew. The narrowed search radius had upped our odds of finding out what had derailed them, but Hana's fate itself was still in play. She was still that famous cat in its closed box, dead and alive at the same time. I wasn't sure that Julian should be the one to open it.

"I'll get it later," Julian said. "Although I need to borrow a charger. My phone is—it's almost out of juice."

"I could use the help, but I can't begin to guess what we're going to find," Birdwine said in cautious tones. He understood that Hana was a coin spinning in the air.

"I'm not stupid. But even if Hana's had a hard time, finding her can't be anything but good news," Julian told him, bristling. "She's alone right now, and we're her family."

I fought the urge to trade a speaking glance with Birdwine. I was off his team. I said gently to Julian, "We know we're her family. But—"

He turned to me, eyes overly bright. "When we find her, she's going to know it, too. Last night, after you fell asleep, do you know what I did? I got on your laptop, and I started filling out a transfer application to Georgia State. I trolled Craigslist, too, looking for roommate ads here in Atlanta. I want her to know that even before I met her, I was changing my life for her. That I wanted be a real big brother to her, before I ever saw her face, or anything."

I recognized the righteous temper. This boy truly shared my blood. Then I did look to Birdwine. It was inadvertent. I found him looking back, thinking the same thing. I turned away, fast. It would be too easy to fall back into our old rhythms, especially as we worked to find my sister. I could feel our connection, tenuous but living, under all my anger. It would take more than simple rage to kill it. I couldn't join up with him for anything, even a simple try at giving Julian an out. The kid wasn't going to take it, anyway.

I'd been trying to feed Julian reality in little sips, but the idea that we could get this close and not retrieve a Hana who was alive and well, one who wanted to be in our family—it was a bitter gulp, and it would not go down. This kid, who had recently lost his parents, was not ready for any more losses. Even imaginary ones. Hell, when he was asking for a charger, he wouldn't even say his phone was dead.

Birdwine tried again. "All I'm saying is, you need to be prepared. This story might not have a happy ending."

"I'm not looking for the end of a story," Julian said, firm. "I'm looking for a little girl."

Whatever Kai-created train wreck was raging toward us, he was bound and determined to stand in the middle of the track with his arms spread wide. No, more than that. I was waiting to get hit by what was worst, and Julian was planning for a best. I was bracing myself for impact, and he was actively preparing for a future.

Maybe I was getting schooled, again.

For the first time, I indulged in Julian's game of *what if.* Best case, Kai had taken Hana to her bio dad, and he was a happy, invested, stable sort. I thought that was about as likely as finding her cheerfully colonizing Mars. Real best case, she was living with some kind-hearted friend or lover Kai had picked up on the road or in the foster care system with a decent placement. Worst case? She'd fallen hand in hand into the black with Kai and Joya; there was no plan needed for that contingency. Next worst case? She was living on the streets, or someone in the range of indifferent to awful had made her into baggage or prey.

In every case but "magic, loving bio dad," if she was alive, then I was going after custody. So why wasn't I making best-case plans, like Julian? There were things I should tack onto my to-do list: Look for a house in a good school district. One with walls, that said *I have room for you.* Call a meeting with my partners, let them know all the ways my life was about to change.

"Fine," I said. "I'm going in to work. I have a difficult negotiation starting up on Monday, and I have to go in prepped. If"—I stopped myself and looked deliberately to Julian—"*when* we find Hana, I'll need some time off, so I need to bank goodwill with my partners now. Julian, can you send me updates, every hour on the hour?"

Julian grinned at me. "Absolutely!"

I spent the day drafting a settlement proposal for *Winkley v. Winkley,* and I was in quite a mood. It was weighted so heavily in Oakleigh's favor that it was not a true proposal. It was the opening salvo in a war, and it promised that the war itself would be long and dark and bloody. When Dean Macon saw it, he might well crap his pants or recuse himself.

Julian kept me in the loop, texting me all day. Perfect. I wanted my fingers on the pulse of the search, but I didn't want to hear from Birdwine. Not even a four-word text. Not even a sorry-faced emoticon. Not until whatever sweetness I had discovered at his bedside was ashes, cold and light, easily blown away by any wind.

I went home and fed Henry. I scratched his belly until he'd had enough and batted at me. Then I got in the shower, set the water hot as I could stand it, and scrubbed the day off myself. I stepped out mother naked, and as I dressed, it felt more like I was readying for a battle than a good night out. Maybe I was.

I left my hair to dry naturally, hanging in long shaggy loops and spirals down my back. I chose jeans cut to frame the good ass my mother gave me, paired with a fitted T-shirt that said LUCKY on the front. I traded my diamond studs for long bangles made of a multitude of delicate, free-swinging chains, each with a tiny garnet near its end. I went easy on the makeup: fresh skin, brown mascara, and a pale, glossy mouth.

The only part of daytime Paula left was my shoes, their red soles now an invitation, not a warning.

I shook out my drying hair. The little garnets swung on their chains to ting and chime like bell song in my ears. I was going out, and if any god who walked above the earth or under it had mercy, I was getting myself laid.

Chapter 10

I have a scoop of eggs, a biscuit, two floppy strips of bacon, a canned peach half with a maraschino cherry resting on it like a nipple, and no place to go. I don't hesitate or look around, though. I walk to the eight-top table nearest the kitchen and take my usual seat on the end. Two of the four Hispanic kids are already there, eating, but there is an empty chair between me and them. Joya's former chair is across from me. There's a third open chair catty-corner to me, so that I am surrounded by absence. The empty spaces are a circle drawn around me, making me the center of a bull's-eye.

Shar, Karice, and Kim saunter through the door before I take my first bite. They pause, scanning the room, and then Shar finds me. She sets the pace, eye-locking me and strolling slow toward the breakfast line. Karice and Kim flank her, one behind each shoulder.

I've settled arguments and ended grudges in the wooded parts of parks or behind the temporary buildings at school. I've done fine, thank you, both by myself and backed by Joya. I'm tall and strong and mean. But this? This is a pack. I have to go in smart or it will end very, very badly. They have hyena faces, chins down, eyes bright with heat over smiles so wide I see their red tongues.

I look back, very serious and calm. If a pack smells fear, they come in faster and harder. I don't even blink, not even when Shar pauses, breaking stride to run her tongue over her bottom lip. She's got a wide mouth with a host of big, white teeth all snaggled in it.

I lean toward her, show her all my teeth in answer. I am not going to be a punching bag for bitches until my mother comes. It isn't in my nature.

I see Candace scuttling with her tray right past me, head ducked down, heading for her regular table. So much for last night's *There, now*s. Once she sits, she gives me the side-eye, folding a tissue-thin strip of bacon into her mouth, accordion style.

After the pack sits down, I'll let them eat most of their food. Then I'll leave, making sure to pass right by their table. If they don't follow, I'll cast some shade to spark them up and after me. I will lead them down into the basement of this building. There's a hallway after the stairs, leading past unfinished storage to the laundry. It's long and narrow, so they can't surround me. I'll retreat down it, try to knock one of them all the way out of the fight before we get to the laundry room. I can make a final stand there, between the shelves and the big machines. Even if I lose, I have to hurt them enough to kill their thirst for repetition.

I know my plan, but I am not prepared for theirs; Shar swerves, bypassing the line to come straight at me. Kim and Karice wheel with her, holding the formation. I feel my spine elongating. I sit tall in my seat. Shar pulls back Joya's old chair and sinks down into it, her two lieutenants standing behind her, one at each shoulder.

"Good morning," I say, to Shar and only Shar, as if this fight is one on one. In some real sense, it is.

"How long you think till Joya's mama go back on that pipe?" Kim says to Karice over Shar's head. She speaks theatrically, like they don't see me there, trading the evil eye with Shar across the table.

"Joya be too busy trickin' herself to worry about that," Karice says.

They don't know Joya and I fell out. Still, I find my temper rising to it. I don't like her name in their mouths any more than I liked hearing it from Candace.

I ignore them, looking for Shar's weak spot. Except for those snaggle teeth, she is pretty. She'll try to protect her face. Behind her, I can see the other two Hispanic kids have come out with their trays. They see us and pause, uncertain, milling by the silverware cart.

"Oh, yeah," Kim agrees, "Joya's mama gonna turn her out."

Shar wears her hair short, in little rings, but not so short that I can't get a good hold on it. Her ears peek out from under, and I can see the places in her lobes where Joya jerked her earrings through. They've healed split, each edge sealing itself, so that her lobes are doubled.

When I don't react to Kim and Karice's bait, Shar reaches fast across the table and snatches the top of my biscuit. She licks it with her tongue, a big, juicy lick, taking half the jam out. Then she sets it back in place. She gives me an eyebrow quirk, like she's asking what I'm going to do about it, luxuriously licking my jam off her fingers.

"I never see you this up close, Shar," I tell her. "I didn't realize how much your earlobes look like butts. It's like you have two old-lady sag-butts hanging off your ears."

Shar stands so abruptly that her chair scrapes back along the floor. Now she's looming over me, and Kim and Karice lean, too. For a single, breathless second

I think it's going down right here, right now. I find my body rising, too, readying to improvise.

In that second of fraught silence, Candace, of all people, sinks into the chair beside me.

"Hey, y'all," she says, and we all boggle at her.

She blushes and ducks her head, drawing her knees up and perching her heels on the chair's edge, wrapping her skinny arms around herself. She holds her biscuit in both hands, like a little mousie with a nut.

It's baffling. When I look back across the table, I am baffled further. Karice is backing up. She's a little behind Shar, so Shar can't see her going. Karice takes two steps away, then three, and then she turns and walks toward the line, as if she needs her peach half with its maraschino nipple, stat. Kim stares after her, then back at Candace. My odds just got crazy better.

Shar is glaring with such hate at Candace now that Candace's spine becomes a curve, as if she's going to fold herself in two. I think she'd keep on folding if she could, into quarters and then eighths, smaller and smaller, until she disappears.

But instead, she peeks up over her knees and says to Shar, "Did you just lick her breakfast?" She sounds genuinely curious.

The two Hispanic kids feel the winds shift as Karice goes past them to the line. The fight they smelled has been deferred, so they file to their end of the table with their trays.

"I think she licked her own breakfast," I say. I push the tray across toward Shar.

Shar is about to speak, but Candace interjects. "In the supply closet?"

Kim's been looking uncertainly from Shar to the hole that used to hold Karice, but now she turns to Candace. "Bitch, no one here cares you exist. Don't make us care."

Shar leans back, oddly silent. She glances behind her, to her right, where Karice should be, and does a double take. She looks around until she spots Karice in the line.

Candace spins her biscuit in her hands, takes a tiny nipping bite.

Now no one is looking at me. I've puffed into a fighting shape, only to find myself invisible. It's disconcerting. I sink back down into my chair.

Candace says to Shar, "That was nice that Paula got you breakfast. Go on, now. Take it to the supply closet." She turns to me and adds, "You know how Shar likes to eat stuff in there."

Shar's mouth closes all the way, and I can see all the spine draining out of her. I'm so interested in understanding the mechanics here. Back in Paulding County, I learned that I pick fight over flight. From Joya, I learned to find the weak spot, then hit it first and hardest, skipping the preliminaries. Now I'm watching Candace turn a fight with implication. It's pretty damn effective; Kim is so unmoored she's taken a literal step back.

"This is not your fight," Shar tells her.

Candace spins the biscuit and nips at it again. This is her standard, enraging way of eating anything shaped like a circle. She takes little bites off the sides, turning it in her hands, making it smaller but retaining the round shape. "I know, right? It's yours and Joya's, but I guess Joya's gone. Oh well." She scootches her chair close to mine, so close we're almost cuddling.

I'm interested enough to abandon my own plans and back her play. I snuggle even closer and tell Shar, "Maybe you should head off to the supply closet, get you a bite of whatever it is you like to eat in there."

Shar's cheeks puff out in a fast exhale, as if a blow has landed.

"What is this?" Kim asks Shar, confused, but Shar shakes her head.

"How do you know abou—" Shar says to Candace, and then stops talking.

It's a shame, because I'm deeply curious about the end of her aborted question. Candace has some dirt on Shar. It's not surprising, considering the way Candace weasels around, eavesdropping. I know this from highly personal experience. What is surprising is her long game—she's held this secret to herself, but now she is deploying it on my behalf.

Candace spins her biscuit, nibble nibble nibble, and Shar shoves her abandoned chair out of her way and walks off. Kim hurries away in her wake, already asking questions.

"What happened in that closet?" I whisper to Candace.

"A lot. You know how Karice goes with that tall boy, Arly? Well, Shar got with him in there when they was broke up," Candace whispers. Her biscuit is barely the size of a silver dollar now. "Karice is back with him and still don't know."

"And what do you have on Karice?" I ask. It has to be big, to make Karice abandon Shar mid-intimidation.

"Nuthin'," she lies. Her eyes go wide and round, telegraphing innocence.

"Yes, you do," I say. It's something worse than boy thieving.

Candace changes the subject. "Did you see Shar's face when I set down?" She snickers and peeps at me again, spinning her tiny biscuit coin. She pops it in her mouth and sucks on it, as if it were a particularly savory lozenge.

"Yeah," I say, smiling. I'm feeling warmly toward her. It's as if we came through an actual fight together, and we won. Not warm enough to see her all rosy. I know Candace doesn't have friends. She has quid pro quos. I say, in my nicest tones, "Is there anyone you don't have dirt on, Candace?"

"Kim, but only 'cause she's boring," Candace says. "People aren't careful, and we all live real close up on one another." She swallows and looks right at me. "People tell each other things, like you would not believe. They get distracted, like, they'll get in a big fight. They won't even think about who might have come on in the building. They'll say all their darkest things out loud."

I feel my stomach drop, dizzy sick. She's looking almost through me with those eyes so light blue they are barely darker than the whites. Cold trickles up my spine.

Did she hear me telling Joya about that 911 call? I think of Candace creeping to kneel by my bed. She can move in such silence. Her big ears seem to pick up sounds from space. Is she bluffing me, the way I bluffed Shar by picking up on her reaction to the word *closet*? I can't tell. She's better at this kind of fight; I'm new to it.

"Want a piece of my bacon?" I ask, sweet as I can.

Candace smiles at me and takes it. She folds the whole thing into her mouth. She drops her gaze, her lashes in demure, pale fans across her cheeks. Every atom in me whirls and clenches. She knows. She knows. She owns me in this moment.

She picks the second piece of bacon off my tray and bites the end off without asking. A bold move, testing the pecking order.

I consider my options, but they are limited. Maybe I should concede? My time here is finite, after all. Kai's release date is set, and if everything goes right, I could be home with her in a couple of months.

Watching Candace chew my bacon like a cud, I realize I will not make it.

"You know what I like about you, Candace?" I ask, reopening negotiations. "You didn't rat out Karice to me just now. That's pretty cool. Not many girls know how to keep their mouth shut, like me and Joya. It's why me and Joya were so tight."

She peeks at me, still in profile, but I can see her eyes gleaming. I have changed the stakes. I am offering my willing friendship for her silence, and my currency is valuable. She can make me be her bodyguard and hold my heartbeat in the bed beside her, but she can't make me like her.

As she thinks, I jerk my bacon out of her hand. She spins toward me, indignant, only to find my face is very close to her face, and my eyes are hard. Friendship is on the table, sure. But I will not be her dog. If she doesn't bend a little in her style of fighting, I will go back to mine and bend her all the way in half.

Her mouth twists. I can practically hear the crafty machinery of her mind spinning and whirring, reworking calculations. Her currency can be spent only once, but I can beat the living shit out of her endlessly. I tell her so with my eyes and the insolent, openmouthed chewing of my own damn meat.

She drops her gaze, demure again. When she speaks, her voice is tentative, almost a whisper. "You want to sit beside me on the bus?"

"Sure I do," I say.

We might as well have spit into our hands and clasped them. There will be border skirmishes and small negotiations, but we have the broad strokes of a deal. One I can live with, for the short time I have left.

Or so I thought then. It was months before I understood how thoroughly I had been played. Candace would have made a hellishly good lawyer. For example, when Candace met dead-eyed Jeremy in the rec hall stairwell, she wasn't trading sex acts for Fun Dip or SweeTarts; she wanted both, the candy and the touch. She liked him, but she made him pay with sugar to kiss her, which she wanted, to touch her budding breasts, which she wanted, so they could put their hands down each other's pants. All things that she wanted.

I learned the rudiments of dark negotiation from Candace. She got the candy *and* a boyfriend. Or her idea of one. Candace didn't come from a world where a boy might like her, sweetly and simply. Love was something furtive to be paid for or extracted; her life had given her a dim view of that animal. But she wanted it. She was starving for it, though she wouldn't have recognized it if it had run at her and slapped her—which, of course, it would. I'd see to that.

But was I any better, even now? Deep into my thirties and still one cracked heart away from walking to a pool hall in my fuck-me pumps, looking to pull a strange. And over Birdwine—a long-botched love that should already be scar tissue. Even so, last night, this morning, now, I was feeling it. It was an itch lodged deep inside my chest, too far below my skin to scratch or soothe. I had to shut it up. Shut it down.

Some kindly reminiscence with an old friend wouldn't do it. Removing Birdwine required something ugly and immediate, spiced with the danger that came only with the unknown.

I was going to McGwiggen's, an old-school midtown dive that had survived gentrification with its steeze intact. It was an easy walk, even in heels, especially if I didn't mind a cut-through between buildings. I didn't. I put my hand inside my bag, wrapped around my mace with a finger on the trigger, and took the turn. Walking down this dim road, narrow, lined with back doors and trash cans, was like walking back into my past.

My past had no Hana, her fate hovering out of view, secreted beyond a dark horizon. The only lost girl here was me, eager for something that felt more like a fight than straight-up sex. I walked into an old, familiar darkness, into a former Paula, one reincarnated by the staccato beat of my heels against hard concrete, the faint smell of decay. I remembered this hunger. It had lived in me before William, before Nick, and definitely long before damn Birdwine. I learned it at thirteen, in love with a dead-eyed mother who smelled like an ashtray and cried when she drank wine. It deepened as Kai and all her last names, all her incarnations, died. I was left with Karen Vauss, a parolee who kept her eyes focused faintly to the right of me. She pawned her mandolin, traded her bright silk skirts and bare feet for a waitress uniform and ugly orthopedic shoes. Karen Vauss did not tell stories often, and so she didn't tell me who to be. She could barely stand to look at me.

But boys would look. I learned that, fast. Boys would follow me and beg and yearn, and I could push them down and own them, for an hour or two. I could invent a new self under each new gaze, could be unhungry, powerful, alone.

I wanted that again. Right now. I could feel the ghosts of all the girls I'd been behind me in the alleyway, creeping in my wake. I could almost hear my own past footsteps as an echo. For a moment it was so real that I spooked myself. I stopped and turned to look. There was only silence and darkness. I walked on.

I'd had boys in the back rooms at parties, in garden sheds, in gas station bathrooms, on rooftops with their parents sleeping soundly below. I'd had one up against a wall on a dark road much like this one, his back to the bricks, his knees bent so I could get my legs around him.

Now I needed a new male body with a different shape, a different smell, to push myself against. If I pushed hard enough, I could shove myself all the way past Birdwine. I wanted a new mouth to reinvent my tastes, to scrape fresh mint over bourbon off my tongue.

The front entrance to McGwiggen's was around the corner, but there was a smoked glass door here in the alley. It let into the hallway by the restrooms. Wes, the bartender, must have seen me come in on the security camera, because he'd already pulled a tray of balls and was popping the cap off a Corona as I came into the center room. I claimed a table by the back wall, though I knew it had dead rails and a five-inch tear in the felt near the foot spot; it gave me a good view of the bar and the front door.

My only concession to the present was my cell phone. I dug it out and jammed it in my back pocket. If Julian buzzed me, I would feel it. Then I put all thoughts of siblings from my head. I scoped the local talent while I racked for nine ball. Slim pickings, but it was early yet.

The old white guy on the end had a healthy overinterest in my solo game, but he either was twice my age or had lived hard enough to look it. He was as welcome to the view as any tourist, but I wasn't going to take him home. Four stools down was a real prospect, a black guy, maybe forty, broad through the shoulders with his head shaved down to dark stubble. He was looking, so I looked back. Then he smiled, showing me the gap between his two front teeth. That blew it for me.

I kept one eye on the front door as I played against myself. I was overstriking, but it felt good, especially when I sank my shots. I liked that rebounding clatter, the balls landing in the pocket with a gunfire smack of sound. A regular I knew came in; we nodded to each other, but I wasn't interested. He was someone I would likely see again. A young man came in the back. Cute, but clearly a fetus. Wes took his fake ID and sent him home to mother.

I was racking for my second game when a man with some potential walked in the front door. He was a white guy, very fair-skinned, with dark blond hair. He was maybe five ten in his boots, built slim and elegant. My age or close to it. He paused to scan the bar, and when he got to me, he smiled. A good smile. Like I was exactly what he'd been looking for.

He had a pretty-boy face I didn't mind at all: narrow jaw, sculpted nose, high cheekbones. Add the rangy build, the fair skin, and the light eyes, and he was the opposite of all things Birdwinian. That alone put him ahead on points. I smiled back.

I lost sight of him while I broke, but when I lined up for a bank shot on the one ball, there he was. He'd taken a stool directly opposite my table. His back was to the bar so he could face me. He was giving me the sex eye, and I gave it back as I walked around the table for my next shot.

He wore a generic navy blazer over a plaid shirt with that yoke-shaped piping at the top that made it read vaguely western. He had on western-style boots as well, but he didn't read to me like an outdoorsy kind of fellow. His pale hair was short enough to be corporate, worn brushed back from his temples.

I blew the angle, and the two ball went wandering off to sit behind the nine. He lifted his beer to me in a rueful little toast. I toasted back, and he took it as permission to come over. I liked the way he did it, too, a slow, unhurried stroll, directly to me.

"Kin I buy you a drank," he said, his drawl so exaggerated that I laughed.

"That's the worst fake southern accent I've ever heard," I told him.

He grinned, and his teeth were perfect. Straight and even.

"Well, when in Georgia," he said with no accent at all. He could be from anyplace, and I liked that, too. "How about it?"

"I have a drink," I said. I nodded toward my beer, half-full, sitting on the bar rail behind me. "Want to play?"

"Sure," he said, and reached for my cue. His hands were so well kept they looked almost manicured, nothing like Birdwine's callused bear paws. He didn't bother to rerack or restart, just looked to make the shot I'd bungled. I took it as a tacit understanding that neither of us gave a crap about winning at nine ball tonight. "What's your name?"

"Lady at the Bar, right now," I said. "But it could be Fond Memory."

"I like that second option," he said, flashing those white teeth again. He walked away around the table, talking soft to make me follow. "Would it hurt my chances if I said my name was"—he paused, sizing me up—"Cowboy Passing Through?"

"Nope. I didn't come to find myself a husband." I liked the honesty inherent in his chosen pseudonym. It said plainly that he was looking for a ships-in-the-night scenario, which made up for the costume feel of that shirt, those boots; I'd never seen a more unlikely cowboy. Accountant passing through, maybe. His ring finger was bare, but I checked anyway, saying, "I'm not looking for someone else's husband, either."

"I'm not married," he said, but then amended it. "Well. Not anymore."

Good enough. He shot, and I picked my beer up and drank deep, swallowing, feeling the cold of it warming as it came to my center. I watched the lean and sway of his chosen angles. He sank two before he whiffed and passed the cue back. As I bent to shoot, his gaze slid frankly up and down my body, a balm against the burn inside my chest.

We had begun an old dance, and a familiar one. I'd learned it the way a future deb learns to two-step at cotillion. I didn't ask any more questions; I didn't care. He could be a banker or a busboy, from Austin or Albuquerque. His clothes were nondescript, excepting that slight faux-western flair, but he had fresh-cut hair, and some serious cash had gone into his teeth. I liked that he'd put more care into the body than the packaging. His forearms were corded with lean muscle, and I suspected I would find a gym body, complete with skinny-guy six-pack, when I peeled the blazer off and yanked open his shirt.

My little garnets, swinging from the chains, chimed in my ears as I bent and shifted, my body swaying toward him, then away around the table. We played the game, and sometimes I was chasing, sometimes letting him chase me. It was so familiar that the man himself began to seem like someone I remembered. In his movements, he became the avatar of every Kappa pledge that I'd seen once, then never seen again.

I'd done this dance with football boys, built thick like human walls. With basketball boys, long and delicious. A shy chess player approached me at a mixer, on a dare. I liked the way he rocked with nerves; there was an instinctive understanding in the sway of hip and thigh. I'd gone back to his dorm room, and there I'd made him king of all the dorks. I remembered a culinary arts major who cooked for me, and this same dance was in his deft hands, working the knife. I'd let him suck the butter off my fingers. And now this cowboy. Yes, I knew him. I knew a thousand of him, seemed like. He was a deep bell, tolling low down in my memory as we moved.

No one had sunk the nine ball, but I straightened up and slotted my cue into the wall rack. I had already decided. He would do.

He grinned, and his gaze got sharper and more eager.

He came around the table toward me, and I heard another bell, a real one: the ding and buzz of a text landing. I stepped back, reaching for the phone in my back pocket.

"One sec, I have to check this," I said. "My little brother's having a day."

He eased back into a waiting slouch. We both knew we were done with the preliminaries; I was tempted to drop the phone in my bag and check on Julian later. Real life was not what I wanted buzzing and pinging in my pants just now.

But the last time we'd talked, he'd been acting as Birdwine's hand puppet. Birdwine's voice had rumbled in the background, and Julian parroted and paraphrased the details of their slow search as it crept toward Georgia. They had to check every route for any hint of Kai and Hana. It was painstaking and meticulous work, and my little brother sounded frustrated. He hadn't wanted to stop, because the next lead might pay off, or the next one. Birdwine and I, more realistic, knew this kind of inquiry could take weeks.

"I'm going to call in sick again tomorrow and come back here," Julian had told me at the end.

"Do you need me to get you and bring you back to your car?"

"No. Birdwine's giving me a lift."

It was the first time he'd called Birdwine by his name, and I didn't half like the admiring tone. They'd apparently spent all day bro-bonding as they worked. Just what I needed—for disapproving Julian to join a pro-Birdwine faction the very day that I'd gone full and angry anti. Worse, Julian's car was parked in my office lot. I hadn't wanted to be anywhere nearby when they showed up.

I'd saved my file and said, "Good, because I'm going to McGwiggen's."

"Oh, what's McGwiggen's?" my guileless brother had asked.

"A pool hall," I'd told him, but Birdwine knew that it was more than that. McGwiggen's had a rep for getting its patrons laid efficiently; Birdwine wasn't the only one who knew how to work a phone puppet.

I hadn't talked to Julian since, and it had been a stressful day for him, no doubt. So I pressed the pause button on the cowboy, and I swiped my phone to life.

The text was not from Julian, though. It was from Birdwine. Directly.

Shoot me Julian's cell number? Forgot to get it.

Just words. Nothing of consequence. But it was as if my naked foot had touched his chest, as if I'd felt his big heart beat against my instep.

I stopped. The whole world stopped. The air fell still around me, and I was still, too, unmoving inside silence. The buzzing of my body faded. The jukebox sounded like a distant, faded chiming.

I'd come here to wipe away my history with Birdwine, but in the moment of this simple contact, I fully understood that my foot was poised on something live. All I had to do was press down, stamp, and I *would* kill it.

I tried to remember the last time I'd gone to bed with a stranger. By the time I passed the bar, I'd had my dating life in hand. My last one-off had been—law school, when Nick started calling me sweetheart during sex. Love could be broken, in spite of what poetry and chick flicks said. I'd broken it much like this with William, then with Nick; it was what I did.

I couldn't take this back, once it was done. I thought of Birdwine's bruised face, silent and unforthcoming in his kitchen. He had a kid out there. A kid he never saw, that he had never mentioned. It was a bad bedtime story for a chick with abandonment issues, as he'd said, and maybe I could not forgive it. Perhaps forgiveness wasn't in my nature.

I wouldn't know. I hadn't tried.

"You ready to get out of here?" Cowboy asked.

I blinked, reorienting. The world restarted. Now I could hear Guns N' Roses blaring from the jukebox, but my internal song had stopped. I was done dancing. I gave him a rueful smile, and waved my phone at him.

"Yeah, I'm going to have to cut out. This isn't going to happen."

"I'm sorry?" Cowboy said, his voice gone higher than he had been speaking. A little edge of pissed-off had come into it. "Are you serious?"

"Stand down," I said, uninterested in temper tantrums. I was thinking of Candace again. Not her skill set or her propensity for misdirection, but her hungers. At least she'd known what she wanted. "I've burned less than thirty minutes of your evening, and the pool table is going on my tab. Have a nice life."

I walked to the rail and finished off my beer, picked up my bag.

"Wait, hold up," he said. He'd seen that the pissed-off-baby thing wasn't working. He tried another tack, walking around the table toward me, leading from the hip. "We're having a good time, yeah? Let's not stop. I'll get us some shots, or, hell, we can move this back to your place."

I think I blanched, and I knew I'd made the right call. I'd imagined our bodies intersecting, but I hadn't pictured it in my loft. I couldn't picture it, not in any setting where I lived my life. If by some miracle we found Hana soon, the last thing I wanted was this traveling man's CK One lingering on my sheets.

"Gotta go," I said.

I walked away, already thumbing at the call button under Birdwine's name.

"Are you kidding me?" he called after me, back to pissy. "Hey! Are you fucking kidding me?"

I kept walking, disappearing into the hallway that led to the bathrooms and the back way out. It was quiet enough here for me to hear the phone, ringing and ringing. Damn Birdwine, he let me go to voicemail. I waited for the beep.

"So I'm at McGwiggen's," I said, with no preamble. "I met this guy. Could've left with him, but no. I blew him off. I wasn't even nice about it, and you have no idea how bad I want to lie to you." I was talking loud, making myself be heard over the music. I slipped out the back door into the quiet alley. "I want to say, 'Hey

Birdwine, I'm calling from the top of reverse cowgirl.' Then I'd get to hurt you without the risk of bad sex or chlamydia." Ye gods, but it felt good to yell at him, though. Crazy good. If I had only thought to call Kai like this, back in the day, I could have saved so much money on birth control, maybe skipped a solid third of all that therapy. There was no one to hear me except the row of old-school silver trash cans where McGwiggen's unfinished wing platters came to die. It smelled sour, like hot sauce and bones, with the nasty tang of ranch dip going wrong. "I ditched him like I owed it to you. Why is that? Why do I still feel like I owe it to you, when you are so patently an asshole? When you are—"

Light spilled into the alleyway around me, and I whirled to see that Cowboy had followed me. I stepped back as the door swung shut behind him.

"Are you running off on me," he said, but it didn't lilt up on the end into a question. It was a statement, both proprietary and weirdly emphatic.

I hit the button to close my call and slipped my phone back in my bag, instantly wary enough that I wanted both hands free. I wished I'd thought to palm my mace when I stepped out, but I couldn't very well go digging for it now. I straightened up, tall enough in my high shoes to have an inch or two on him.

I made my voice cold as I could, which was pretty close to arctic. "I told you, it's not on. Go back inside."

"You don't want to piss me off," he said, as if something was at stake here.

Very intense, considering we weren't even the cost of a drink to each other. Adrenaline began leaking into my bloodstream. I could feel myself swelling with it. The air around us had charged, and it was charging still.

He took one step toward me, not quite into my space, but closer. He was between me and the door, and I'd be giving him an opening if I tried to duck around him. If he knew how to fight, if he leveraged his much greater upper-body strength, I didn't stand much chance. But a guy like this—gym-made muscles, capped teeth, and a fresh, expensive haircut—he might start soft, a testing slap or grab. I could go after his soft bits, immediate and hard. Disable him long enough to get inside.

He took another step into me. I held my ground, because prey retreats, and hunger follows anything that runs. The lights above the door made his hair a yellow nimbus. A shadow fell across his eyes, so I could see them only as a gleaming. The light bounced off his sculpted nose, his narrow jawline. Elegant. Familiar.

I recognized him then.

He wasn't pinging in my memory against every one-off frat boy I'd ever taken off behind some trees. He'd seemed familiar because he was familiar. I'd seen him before. Just once, in a picture. I hadn't recognized him without the demon horns, the red eyes, and the Hitler mustache.

My pickup wannabe was Oakleigh's husband.

"Clark?" I said, so shocked that I stepped back, banging into the row of silver trash cans. I reached behind me, put one hand on the edge to steady myself. "Clark Winkley?"

"Shit," he said, angry to be recognized, but he did not back off.

He took another step in, shifting how the light fell, and I could see his eyes again, shining with something purely ugly. I thought he'd make his move, and my body coiled in on itself. I couldn't allow him to get a solid grip on me. I had to hurt him bad enough to get away.

But he stayed where he was. Instead of reaching for me, he slipped his hand into the pocket of his jacket, where he balled it in a fist, grabbing something. Then I realized why he hadn't done the cliché move tried by every man on earth who'd ever shot pool with a woman: the lean-over from behind to help line up a shot that didn't need relining. It wasn't because he hadn't been happy to see me. He hadn't wanted me to feel the gun.

"Clark, this is not about me," I said, as cool as I could with my mouth gone suddenly so dry.

"You should have gone to bed with me. But no, you had to be a bitch about it," Clark said. His pretty-boy face was twisted, sculptured nostrils flared. Oakleigh had picked out that nose at the plastic surgeon's, I remembered. The sides of his mouth were wet, spit leaking out, and he didn't even notice. "Jesus, everyone who's ever met you says that you're a whore. You should have gone ahead and been a whore."

So I had his lawyer, Macon, to thank for this. That sackless piece of crap must have talked about our past. Ye gods, how small men hated to be beaten by a woman. Especially a woman they were sleeping with. So his lawyer had called me a slut, and Clark had come up with a plan to get the easy lawyer into bed. And if I had brought him home with me?

Of course. I'd show up for the meet on Monday to find last week's nameless cowboy was the opposition. I'd have to recuse myself.

"Clark," I said. "Nothing has happened. Not yet. Right now there's no big story here. We played some pool. I realized you were my client's husband, you realized I was Oakleigh's lawyer. We walked away."

It was an error, saying Oakleigh's name.

"No. No, no, dammit," he said, and that spittle leaking out around his lips hit my face in pinprick sprinkles. "You're bitches, and neither of you gets to walk away."

Why had I plugged his rat hole? He'd been perfectly happy to stalk Oakleigh, to risk death climbing trees, creeping along her roofline, peeing in her makeup case. I'd claimed his attention for myself when I'd locked him out. All of his attention. He'd come into McGwiggen's not half an hour after I did. He'd known right where I was, the same way he'd known whenever Oakleigh left the house. He'd been following me.

For days now, I'd felt watched and followed. Even Julian had felt it, back at Birdwine's place. Tonight had been the first real opening he'd had, and he had taken it. I put one hand up, propitiating, my other hand still braced on the trash can's greasy edge, holding me steady and upright.

"Clark, let's take a breath, okay?" I said, almost lilting, the way I'd talk to a dangerous dog who had backed me in a corner. "I know you're really angry."

"Bitch, you don't know a damn thing, yet."

He took his hand out of his pocket.

Then all I could see was the snub-nose pistol.

It didn't look real. I felt an absurd bubble of laughter rising up. He was holding a lady gun, bright silver with mother-of-pearl glinting at the handle. It was a silly little thing, too slight a weight to make his jacket hang wrong, crafted to rest between a compact and a purse dog. It was exactly the sort of gun a girl like Oakleigh would find darling. And yet this shiny bit of nonsense was pointed at my middle. It could put a hole in me. It could kill me.

"Wait," I said, though other words were crowding in my throat. Useless ones. I wanted to tell him that I couldn't die right now, not with so many things unfinished.

Hana unfound. Kai's fate unknown. My best friend's new baby, named Paul after me, would never know my face. My new brother would be hit with yet another loss. The last words I'd ever say to Birdwine would be the ones I'd just recorded, angry, unforgiving, calling him an asshole.

Clark laughed then, a hoarse and breaking sound. He swept the gun up until it was pointing directly in my face. It gleamed like a bright toy in his elegant hand.

The small, dark hole at the end of it looked into my left eye, promising oblivion. I looked back, and time slowed. Stopped. I saw my end inside that pinprick darkness, saw it as if it had already happened. As if it had happened a long time ago, and was still happening now.

Chapter 11

This is the dangerous time.

Outside, the sun is shining, and yellow light streams in the window. Outside, Kai is on her way to me. This morning we have our first visit in the flesh since her release, and I feel like I am filled with butter-colored sunshine, too. Inside my body, I am bright with it, barely able to stay inside my skin. Even so, I keep my face blank and lie still. I am beside a bomb.

My mattress is shaped like a long, narrow valley. Candace lies in the center trench, staring up at the ceiling. The depression in the middle is the weight of history, shaped over time by every kid who ever slept here. Candace's slight weight has not changed it in any way that I can feel on those rare moments when I have my bed to myself. She doesn't seem like a bomb right now.

She seems like a girl who is about to fall back asleep in the choicest spot.

I lie along the raised edge on my side, my back to the wall. Even now, I can feel the two depressions in the ridge that Joya and I made, back when we used to sit here every day. It is a solid proof that we were here, as personal as a graffiti sign or a fingerprint. The last time Joya fit herself into her space here, she was readying to leave me, and we burned each other to the ground.

"What's she look like? Your mama?" Candace asks.

Candace has gone spelunking in my private lockbox often enough to see my mother in pictures from every angle. I answer anyway, to placate her.

"She's tall and pale," I say, offhand. I don't say how beautiful she is. I don't say, *I used to put my bare feet on top of her bare feet, and she would spin while I yelled, "Dance me, dance me."* "She has long hair. Or used to have."

It's Saturday morning, and Mrs. Mack has sent the other girls to watch the TV in the center building's rec hall, so Kai and I can have the common room. Candace wanted to wait with me, and I didn't fight her. I will not fight Candace on anything. Not now.

My mother and I have made plans during our court-mandated phone calls. I know she is already job hunting, apartment hunting, working to meet every requirement to regain me. Soon, I will be going home with her. Every step I take between now and my departure, I am walking on a knife edge with this crazy girl who knows enough to ruin me.

"I think it's weird your mama is a white lady," Candace says.

"Yeah," I say.

"I can't imagine what all your daddy was, huh?" Candace tells the ceiling.

I feel a lightning flash of temper, but I let it pass and fade.

"I don't know."

That puts us on more common ground. Candace only ever had a stepdad, and he was bad news. He's one reason that her mama has lost parental rights forever and Candace is available to be adopted. She's white, but she's also an adolescent who's been broken in ways that make people uncomfortable. Outlook not good on adoption.

"Here's a weird thing about cats," Candace says, abruptly. She shifts in the bed, rolling on her side to face me and scootching back. Now she teeters on the opposite edge of the mattress. The trench is between us, tipping us in toward each other. We both have to brace. "A mama cat is whatever kind of cat she is. Maybe she's a calico. But she can have a litter with three kittens and one will be black, and one yellow, and one stripy, because they all have a different daddy."

"Yeah. So?" I say, not following.

"Maybe you're like that," Candace says. "Maybe you're all three kittens."

I can feel my face flush. I'm pretty sure that in her crazy way, she's called Kai a whore and me some kind of mutant. But all I say is, "That could be kinda cool, if I got three child supports. I'd be so rich. I could go to Disney World and stay all summer."

Candace was hoping for a rise, and my attempt at humor agitates her. She blinks rapidly, then slithers in closer. Her breath is sweet, milky and butterscotchy, as if she's been eating pudding.

"I had a secret dream," she whispers. "In the nighttime, I was dreaming that your mama took us both. We both went home to live with her, and you let me pick out the color to paint your room. Isn't that weird?"

Trick question. I deflect. "Depends. What color did you pick?"

Her brows knit. "I think green?"

"Then that's not weird," I say.

"Well, but, I had to sleep inside a drawer under your bed."

That makes me smile. Sometimes Candace can be funny. "Okay, that is weird."

"I wish, though, I wish it could be true," she whispers, even lower, and her eyes on me are so intense. We are not talking about her dream now. "Do you think your mama would ever be a foster?"

"I don't think they let people who went to jail be fosters, is the only thing," I say.

It is far from the only thing. But it is the only thing that it feels safe to say.

"But they'll let her have you back, so she can't be dangerous to kids," Candace argues.

But I am Kai's, by right, I want to say. *I was born to her, and we share blood and history. We got a judge who made exceptions and bent rules based purely on the force of the bond he saw between us. And who the hell are you?*

It's true, but it's a truth that would burn and blister if I let it touch Candace. I don't want to remind her of all the ways that we are different. Chief among them, I belong to somebody. I say nothing, until Candace answers herself.

"Anyways, I was mostly wondering if she would like it, not if they would let her. Like if she was that kind of person who would want more kids."

This subject is too dangerous. I change the conversation. "You know we'll still see each other, you and me." I am feeding Candace the same spoonful of crap

Joya tried to serve up sweet to me. Still, I have to try. Candace owns a weapon that can only be used once, but if she's losing everything anyway, what's to stop her?

Kai must never know I am the one who made the 911 call, that I cost her her freedom. And Dwayne, too, whatever that was worth. He mattered enough for her to ask me if I had gotten any letters from old friends, three calls in a row after I sent the poem. He never wrote me back at all. The fourth call, she didn't bring it up, so I asked, *What happened, with, you know, that poem about Rama and Sita?* There was a long silence, and then she said, *Rama who? I don't remember any Rama in our story.* She never mentioned Dwayne again.

"But what if you live far though?" Candace asks, plaintive.

"Kai will get a car, or a boyfriend who has one. She always did before."

Candace leans in even closer and talks fast, low, her words a nervous tumble.

"I was thinking, though, what if I ran away. There'd be a fuss right at first, but no one would stay bothered about it. They'd be looking for me at my mama's anyhow, and after a while, they wouldn't look at all."

I see where this is going, and I talk fast to nip it down before it sprouts. "You're a kid, Candace. People freak out about missing kids."

Candace and I both know this isn't wholly true. Kids like Candace don't get the kind of press the missing children of middle-class or rich folks get. On the other hand, Candace is blond and big-eyed and thin—all the things TV likes. There could well be a little stir.

She says, "I won't cut out right away. I'd make Shar and Karice be my friends, until everyone forgets about you and me being tight. Then I'll run away and hide until they quit looking. Then I'll come to where you are."

I have to work so hard to make my face stay bland and kind. Inside, I recoil from the intensity of pleading in those lamp-like golem eyes. I want to pinch some sense into her skin. Her plan is impossible, a fantasy, but Candace is not very connected to how the world works when it doesn't line up with her wishes.

"We'll have to think about that, Candace. Kai's parole officer will be coming by our place. Parole officers can show up anytime, and you have to let them in. If they see you, they'll send her back to prison, and then you're back here, anyway."

Candace pulls her bottom lip in and munches at it. After a little thought, she says, "Yeah. But so are you. Maybe forever. She wouldn't want you back, after that. If they took her to jail again, and it was your fault, I bet she wouldn't even come back for you. She'd be so mad."

Oh damn, she is crafty. She is pressing on the blackest bruise I have inside me. I make myself smile. "I'm not saying no. I'm saying we need to think it through. Be slow. And anyway, I bet we can work it out for you to visit, for sure."

"How long of visits?" Candace asks. "How soon?"

Just then, from downstairs, I hear the sounds of Kai's arrival. The knock. The clap of Mrs. Mack's old-lady shoes on the linoleum as she goes to answer the door.

I should stay here, at least another minute. I should reassure Candace, soothe her. But I hear Kai's voice, her present voice, not crackling through a bad connection while I press the old phone against my ear. I hear her living voice lighting up the room below me. I can't help it. I scramble over Candace, my knee jamming into her stomach so that all her air puffs out. I launch off her as if she is an object. I run. I don't even look back, bounding down the stairs to see my mother.

She stands at the bottom, a brightness in the common room. She makes the gray slab walls, the deflating beanbags, and the sagging navy couches fade away. There is only my mother wearing sunshine-colored paisley: orange, yellow, gold. Her hair has grown out longer, falling way past her collarbones and over her small breasts. Her face is tipped up to mine and smiling.

I leap at her from the last two stairs, right into her arms.

She says, "Oof," and she is laughing.

She spins me and her dark hair swings around us, her skirt wraps my legs.

It doesn't matter that her body feels different, softer and spongier around her middle. It doesn't matter that she smells different, too, the acrid stench of cigarettes over cheap shampoo. Her arms are still her arms. Her crying eyes on me are still her eyes, even spilling tears.

"You're so pretty! You're so pretty!" she keeps saying. "You're so tall!"

There is nothing that can touch me in this moment. Nothing. Mrs. Mack leaves without me noticing, like she's been teleported from the room.

Kai's brought a Tupperware with her, and it's banging me in the back as we hug and clasp and almost dance together. It's the pancakes, the ones with orange rind in the batter. They are cold, and the syrup has soaked through and made them soggy. The butter has congealed. We sit side by side on the navy loveseat and eat them with our fingers anyway. Kai can't stop touching me. Can't keep her syrup-sticky fingers off my face, my hair. She's quiet, but I whisper and plan for both of us, talking with my mouth full. Not about the past, or even much the now. Today I only talk about our brightest nexts, and she leans in, rapt. I am the storyteller now, telling her a future that is half pretend, half hope, certain and glorious. Kai can't stop crying and smiling. Tears leak the whole time, but it is sweet, for all that. The sweetest hours that I have known in literally years.

Time has never moved so fast. I want to slow it, make it stop, stay here in the common room with some old cartoon running silent on the shared TV and Kai's long leg pressed against my own.

"I'll be back for dinner Monday night, remember," Kai says, feeling it, too. "And then again on Wednesday, and again, and again, until one day very soon, I'll take you home."

I beam at her, and past her, I spot Candace. She has crept out to crouch at the top of the stairs with her shoulders in a hunch. Her chin rests on her knees, and she peers down at us. Her eyes shine as pale and blue as any bitter winter. In that glance, I feel joy teeter on the cusp of ruin. I see the end of everything.

It was perhaps three seconds of my life, that look. Then Candace crab-walked backward, out of sight, and I turned back to Kai. But that moment when our eyes met, it stayed with me.

I learned in that span how certain time is. It marched forward always, with me in it. Sometimes it dragged, sometimes it flew far too fast, but it was always moving. It would always move, inexorable, until it brought me to the word, the bullet, the breath that ended it.

It brought me to this alleyway. To Oakleigh's husband.

I stared into that small black hole, and Clark's pupils behind it were two more small black holes, exactly the same. All three held the promise of a crazy blankness. His hand shook and tightened, time so slow that I could see the flex of every tiny muscle in his fingers. The light glinted off the blond hairs on his hand. They were like live filaments, electric, and so beautiful.

All I could say was "Wait, wait," in that futile way that people do. Wanting one more second.

He waited.

Clark was a gym body, with civilized white teeth. He'd been pushed beyond his edge, but he was new to violence. He hesitated, and I had time for one more thing.

In this brief stay, I could say *Wait* again, or *Please*, or *No*, but it wouldn't stop him. I could see this wasn't personal. He didn't care that I would not find Hana. That I would not be there to watch over Julian. That I'd never tell Birdwine that here, inside the gun's dark eye, I saw his flaws and all his failures clearly, and knew they did not change how dear he was to me, how necessary, good, and worthy.

Clark had fallen over some edge or another. He was tumbling, and I could not call him back with the concerns of my inconsequential life, or make him see the fine web of connections he was cutting. I wasn't real to him. Another debt I owed to Candace, this clarity: his acts against me had nothing to do with me, and any sentence of my story was only that—a story. So in the small space of his hesitation, I forgot myself, and told a piece of his: "Oakleigh's got something on you."

His chin dipped down, and I had bought another breath, though the tension in his finger on the trigger did not abate. The gun's black eye looked into my left eye, exactly. I tried to see past it, see him, but it was so hard. So hard to look at anything but that silly, silvery gun.

"What?" he said, as if he hadn't heard me right.

"She has something that will ruin you."

The tension in the finger eased. His neck elongated. I had his interest.

"Tell me," he said, "or I am going to shoot you."

He was going to shoot me anyway. I could see it in the lines of him.

I said, "Footage. You're right outside a bar. You're giving Oakleigh footage of yourself, shooting her lawyer."

It was so hard to look away from the gun's black eye. But I made myself. I made my eyes cut away over his shoulder, to the kinder gaze of the tiny security camera stationed over the door into McGwiggen's.

He glanced back, reflexively, a half turn of his head to look where I was looking. As he moved, I moved with him, ducking down and stepping forward. I felt so slow, like I was trying to sink into concrete, trying to get under the gun's trajectory.

His hand jerked, and I heard a huge roar, so close it deafened me. I was dazzled with the muzzle flash. I didn't know if I was hit. I couldn't tell. I didn't even know if I was living, until I felt the bone-deep jarring when I slammed my heel into his instep.

He screamed, and I heard the champagne pop of a second shot, muffled by the endless echo of the first shot in my ears. Already my knee was coming up. Already my hands were reaching for his eyes.

I heard the clatter of the gun falling away, and then his hands were scrabbling at my throat, grasping for purchase, and we were animals. Animals each trying to be the living one when it was over. My knee connected hard with his balls, and he bent to it. My nails dug into the meat of his pale face. Someone was bellowing, a tearing scream of sound, and I could feel the way the noise ripped at my throat from the inside, so it was me.

His grip released, his body choosing flight for him, his nature rising as surely as mine had. I could feel wetness and skin jammed in my nail beds, and I dug and ripped. He shoved me, his fists double hammers that banged into my chest. I felt my hands tear from his face. I was thrown backward, airborne, into the trash cans. I slammed into them and two of them tipped over and spilled in a great clatter of metal. I fell between them.

I heard my voice still blaring, and when I got my head up, he was scrambling away in a slow staggering run, crouched over his balls. I kept screaming, a banshee's wail, a howling. I didn't see how the people inside hadn't heard me. I should be bouncing back off satellites in space.

Even as I thought it, the smoked glass door burst open, and it was Wes, with his eyes bugging in his broad, young face. Grace was right behind him, too, another bartender. She was a tough girl with almost as much ink as she had skin space. I had to make the unearthly sound coming out of me stop, on purpose, like I was turning off a bad song on the radio. Wes stared wildly around, then took off down the alley after Clark. Clark saw him coming and sped up, still hunched over his balls, running away.

I sprawled between the overturned cans, and my feet were bare. He'd thrown me right out of my shoes. My hands started running up and down my body of their own volition, trying to find out if I had holes in me. I touched my face, my hair, my neck, my chest. Down the alley, I heard a clatter and another scream. Wes had tackled Clark.

My throat hurt inside from the rasping yell, and my chest hurt where his fists had hit me. My whole body hurt where I had smashed into the cans and then the ground. I sat up anyway. The gun was lying near me, shiny as a toy. I saw my shoes there, too, one on its side, one upright. Grace was kneeling by me now, though I hadn't seen her move.

She said, "Oh my God, Paula, we saw you on the feed. Billy called the cops." Billy was the bar back.

"Am I bleeding?" I croaked at Grace. "Do I look shot or bleeding?"

"No," she said. "No, but God, your hair is so fucked up."

I was in shock, I realized then, because I started laughing.

Grace said, "Who is that? Are you dating him?"

I shook my head, and the world swung all around me. "That was the thousand and first guy."

Down the alley I could hear Wes yelling, "Stay *down*, asshole!"

Grace helped me up, and we peered down into the dim light. Wes was sitting on Clark's back, grinding his bleeding face into the pavement. Clark flopped like an angry flounder under Wes's bulk. Standing deepened the throb in my left hip, but the pain seemed distant and unimportant. An interesting fact that I was noting. Inside me, my blood rushed in circles, every vein part of a racetrack, all my red cells jostling to be first and fastest.

"Are you okay?" Grace asked.

I was better than okay. There were no holes in my good body. I had won. I had seen him running. I was seeing him held down now, right now, the blood in streaks of red all down his face, and oh ye gods and little fishes, it was good.

Billy came out the glass door then, eyes wide, mouth panting. He took in the scene, then ran to help Wes.

"Come inside," Grace said, and tugged me toward the door.

I took one sideways step, a lurch almost, away. I realized I was heading down the alleyway to kick Clark in the head. But Grace put her arm around me, catching me and stopping me. I clutched her, weaving, and my hand left red smears on her shirt. His blood had painted the tips of my fingers.

She took me in and made me sit in the office. A few minutes later, I heard sirens coming, and that sounded good to me as well. It sounded like order, like my old good friend, the law, wailing on a righteous pathway to me, through my city.

McGwiggen's back office was a white-walled, windowless hole that I suspected had begun life as a closet. I was waiting there when Birdwine burst in, wild-eyed and panting. He took in the scene, me sitting in the only chair, a wheeled black cheapo thing in front of an IKEA desk that housed an old computer.

"Hi," I said, hoarse from that weird bellowing. I'd never been so glad to see him.

"Oh, hi," Birdwine said, drawing up short. He wavered there, uncertain, then shoved one catcher's mitt of a hand through his wild hair as he tried to get himself in hand. When he spoke next, it came out elaborately casual. "So, you know, I'm here to rescue you. Ta-da."

That made me grin, but as soon as I could make myself look serious, I told him, "I'm sorry I called you an asshole." I wanted to take it back before the building collapsed in on us, or the sun went nova, or some final, tenacious chunk of Skylab fell out of space and killed me. That message I'd left, angry and unforgiving, could not be the last words I ever said to him.

He looked puzzled, so I added, "On your voicemail? I called you an asshole."

"Oh, right. *De nada.* I got your message, maybe fifteen minutes ago. I heard that man talking as you hung up, and there was something in the tone. I knew it had gone all kinds of wrong. I called you back, four times, and it kept going to voicemail. So I came down here, already wound up, and the lot was full of cop cars. People were saying your name, talking about gunshots, an attack. You calling me an asshole has fallen pretty far down on my list." He looked sick, in fact, recounting it. "Grace told me you were back here, gave me the twenty-second version. Are you really okay?"

"You should see the other guy," I said.

"I'd like that very much," Birdwine said darkly.

I slid my feet into the neon-orange Crocs Grace had loaned me from her locker. The cops had bagged my shoes. Then I stood up, wincing, and we looked awkwardly across the small space at each other. "Do your rescuing services extend to an escort home?"

That set him back. He looked at me, eyebrows beetling suspiciously, trying to get a read on me. All at once, he was so wary that it broke my heart for him. But all he said was "You can leave?"

"Yeah, I was waiting for a uniform to drive me," I said.

An EMT had cleaned my scrapes and looked me over, but I didn't let him get too handsy. I was fine, barring a spectacular set of deepening bruises from landing in the trash cans. A tech had collected samples from under my nails, while a detective named Martinez took an abbreviated statement, probably because I had been drinking. He wanted me to come down to the station tomorrow to give a longer one, and so they could get more pictures. They had a better witness in the tapes anyway. The hallway's camera showed Clark following me out. The alley camera got most of the fight, and they'd retrieved the gun, too.

By then I'd calmed down a bit, and my lawyer brain was parsing all the ways I was going to screw Clark Winkley to the wall. Try to shoot me dead, would he? That opening salvo of a settlement agreement I had written earlier was looking like a kindness. I could fix that. Ye gods, how a jury would love this, though I doubted his lawyer would let this stinker go before a judge, much less a jury. They'd settle, fast, so Clark could focus on his criminal case, and my inevitable civil suit against him.

Birdwine said, "My car is in the deck across the road."

"I'd rather walk," I told him. "Work the kinks out."

That made him draw back even farther, not sure how literal I was being.

We had to exit through the big front room, since the back alley was blocked off as a crime scene. I thanked Grace, Wes, and Billy, and I let Martinez know I didn't need the ride after all.

Then Birdwine and I walked out into the night together. My adrenaline rush had long faded, but I hadn't crashed. I felt only peaceful. I liked the feel of walking toward home as if I owned this night, as if I'd already run off everything in it that could hurt me. The sidewalk was cracked and jagged in spots, but so bright with yellow streetlights that it wasn't hard to navigate. Traffic zoomed past, busy and impersonal, setting the hot air of late summer into gusty motion.

We walked from pool to pool of warm light. We had eight inches between us, and I couldn't breach it. Julian, direct and sweet, would have already reached across it, and I wished then that I was more like him. I could feel that Birdwine was full of a sharp energy. Too much to contain, it leaked from his big body, prickling in the space that separated us. His feet banged down as if the earth itself had done something to piss him off. He was silent, and I wasn't good at this. I didn't know how to tell Birdwine how little knowing the worst of him had mattered in the face of a real ending.

Finally he spoke, and his voice was calmer, more under control, than his body language. "I *am* an asshole. But I'm not bad at my job."

"I don't think you're bad at y—"

"Yeah, you do," he said. "You must. You've seen my house. You know I'm always strapped. But I work my program, and when I'm on it, I'm very good. People hire me, Paula. People who don't even want to sleep with me hire me."

"Okay, okay," I said, laughing a little. "You're good at a lot of things."

He got serious again. "I'm broke all the time because about a third of my income goes into a trust fund. For the kid. My son. For college or an emergency—whatever he might need. Not because of a court order. I decided I would do it, and I've stuck with it, ten years now. I'm not a shitty person." He gave me a sideways glance and then amended, "I'm kind of a shitty person. But I'm not as thoroughly shitty as you think I am."

We turned right, and we were walking toward my building now. When that gun was pointed into my left eye, I'd forgiven his past choices and accepted all his deep-scarred imperfections, whole. But him putting aside that money laid bare all I knew that was best in him. Some people might not have been touched by this, the sacrifice of money, but they had likely always had enough—and they definitely had not seen his house. I knew what it was to want. Kai and I had lived next door to homeless when I was little. I'd waitressed my way through junior college until I could get some scholarships. It mattered to me, that he'd done this.

"I don't think you're shitty," I said. "You don't owe me an explanation. You don't owe me anything. Whatever happened with your kid, however that played out, it's terrible and sad. You don't live easy with it, though. That's obvious. You did the best you could, at the time. You're still doing the best you can with it. I know that without you saying, because I know you."

He wouldn't look at me then. Not at all. He reached across the space between us, though. He grabbed my hand, squeezing until my bones compressed, just shy of pain.

I had spent my whole life hungry for forgiveness. It had not come, so I didn't know firsthand what he was feeling. But I had imagined it, over and over. I'd wanted it so bad. I'd wanted Kai—or anyone, anyone who knew the worst in me—to say that I was still dear, and good, and worthy.

I gave him this thing that I had always wanted, and it made him turn his face away from me. I saw his reflection in the glass wall of the building we were passing. The shadows made his eyes into black pits, and his mouth was twisting down. Then he put his head down, silent, and we walked on, our hands clasped tight together, for almost a block.

"His name is Caleb. He doesn't know I exist," Birdwine finally said, picking his way along the broken concrete in the streetlight's yellow glow. "I didn't know about him until he was three. I mean, I did. I knew she was pregnant when she left me. She told me, straight up, that it wasn't mine. I even let her hurry the divorce, so she could marry that Martin guy before the baby came. It's his name on the birth certificate."

That rocked me. Martin was the legal father then; in Georgia, his rights hugely outweighed Birdwine's.

I swallowed, and said quietly, "Well, she lied. You pretty much cloned yourself. The guy she married, he knows?"

"Unless he's stupid. He knows what I look like. I met him a couple of times back when he was screwing my wife." To his credit, it was only slightly bitter.

Had Martin married Stella blind, knowing the baby might not be his? Not a gamble so much as a decision; he would love, no matter how the coin fell. Maybe that's what true love looked like, at its best. It looked like this to Julian, an adopted kid who talked to me of teams and rescues. He was already on an apartment hunt, putting in transfer applications, changing his life for the sake of a lost girl who was a coin spinning in midair. Tonight, I wanted to be a little more like him. I didn't mean to blind myself to how hard and hateful the world was; sweetness was hard to find and harder still to keep. I only meant to reach for it, anyway.

"How did you find out?" I asked Birdwine. He wanted to talk, and he had carried this by himself so long. I needed him to know we could talk, after all.

"Some asshole friend of Stella's who knew us both back in the day. Bridesmaid in our wedding. She sent me a letter, saying she'd waffled and prayed, and she'd decided that I had the right to know. That was about ten years ago," he said, and now he did sound bitter, a thousand times blacker and more caffeinated than when he spoke of his wife's affair.

The timeline made sense to me, though. Ten years ago, Birdwine had walked into his first AA meeting. "And that's when you saw Caleb?"

"Yeah. They'd moved to Florida by then. I drove down and staked them out. For more than a week, but they never saw me. You know how I am. Damn, Paula, they looked good. They looked happy. I would know, because I didn't want them to be happy. I was hoping for a reason to storm in. But their first girl had just started toddling, and my kid, Caleb, I heard him telling the ice cream booth guy that he was a big brother. He couldn't say *th*'s. He said it like, *brudder,* and he sounded so proud. Every other word he said was *Daddy.* 'Daddy, look at me.' 'Daddy, pick me up.' And Martin would pick him up. Stella carried the baby, while Martin rode my son around on his shoulders."

"Shit," I said. The bridesmaid had taken her sweet time growing a conscience. She'd waited three years after Stella'd made a judgment call, choosing Martin before the birth, when biology would give its testimony. There was no clearer way to tell a man you didn't think that he was good enough for your kid, but I asked anyway, because he had to know that I would listen, and that the story would change nothing. "When Stella told you she was pregnant, you didn't wonder? You didn't do the math?"

His shook his head, a huge, shaking no that started in his shoulders and reverberated down through our clasped hands. It was a lie he told with his whole body, or maybe it was just denial, because the words that he spoke next were true:

"I wanted to believe her. I guess I decided to believe her. I was really, really busy drinking. It was a relief, when she said she was sure."

Birdwine lifted his free hand in a *whatcha gonna do* gesture that said he didn't blame her.

Maybe I couldn't, either. I imagined Stella, pregnant thirteen years ago. Married to the ruin I'd seen when he was bingeing. He'd been drinking every day back then, hanging on to his job by a thread. She'd met another man, reliable and sober. She'd cared enough about Martin to break her marriage vows. When she realized she was pregnant, she'd had the luxury of choosing. I'd seen Birdwine at his worst, so I got it. And really, what would I have done in her shoes?

It was the wrong question. I knew my stupid answer: I'd have chucked the steady ginger and rolled my dice with this one.

"Do you think you'll ever meet him? Caleb. Maybe when he's grown?" I asked. I wasn't sure if that was right, but I didn't see a clear right. We were deep into the grays, here. Perhaps this wasn't all that different from what Kai had done for Julian. For the first time I wondered if Julian had grown up knowing he was adopted. I thought so, from the way he'd talked about his family. Birdwine's boy hadn't. Had Caleb been abandoned or stolen, saved or released? It didn't matter, because Birdwine was shaking his head no.

"Not unless he needs bone marrow or a kidney," Birdwine said.

"Well, the gods be with him if he ever needs some liver," I said, and Birdwine winced. "Yeah, low blow. But you know it's true."

We had reached my building now, and I let go of his hand and turned to face him. My back was to the wall. He faced into the gold light that streamed out from the lobby doors.

Birdwine said, "When I started AA, I made a promise to myself. I thought, if I could stay sober for a year, get my chip, then I'd go and meet Caleb. I told myself that, then, I'd be worth meeting. I started the trust fund, so he'd know he mattered the whole time, right? If I could just get that year chip, I kept saying."

I shook my head. "That's a lot of pressure to put on a recovery."

"Yeah. I got to ten months once. When he was nine. Even started planning out what I would say to him, how to approach Stella . . . Woke up two weeks later, down in Mexico." He shrugged, a rueful gesture, and then said, "I'll tell you one good thing that came out of our breakup, if that's what I can call it. Whatever that was in my kitchen, when you saw his picture. I gave it up. The whole idea. Meeting him is a fantasy. I could get ten years sober, and I still won't go and see him. I'd have to tell the kid his mother's a cheat and a liar and his dad's a thief. If I wasn't going to blow his life up like that when he was three, I don't see how I can do it now, when he's a teenager. When it's time for college, or before, if something happens and he needs it, I'll turn the fund over to Stella. She can explain it however she wants." He bent to look at me. He put his eyes so close to mine it became hard to focus. "I'm not telling you this because of us. I'm not now going to try to get a year chip with you as some kind of messed-up prize at the end of it. I'm done with that kind of deal, and I'm done with drinking. For what that's worth. I've said it before, but this time there's no conditions. I'm just done. I hope—I believe—I mean it this time."

"I hope so, too." Even if he failed again, he would not stop trying. I knew he wouldn't, because I knew him.

He threw up his hands and said, "And you know I fucking love you. So?"

I looked into his right eye, then his left, back and forth.

"Why do you love me?" I knew what I wanted, but on his side, I didn't want it to be because I could be so bad for him. I didn't want to be a pretty fist that he could bang himself into. I leaned against the wall, my head right by the keypad. "If we're going to take a run at this, it has to be more than good sex and your masochism."

I wasn't sure he was going to answer. I wasn't sure he had a reason, and he could be so hard to read. But then he smiled.

"Because everyone on this shithole planet says a lot of pretty words to make themselves look good while they do awful things," he said. "You're the opposite."

It was a good answer. A good thing to say. I peered from one eye to the other, back and forth, harder than I had looked into Clark's eyes, or the gun's. Birdwine's left one was rimmed in black and violet, still swollen. I watched his pupils expand as I leaned up. There was a fair amount of crazy present, sure, but in the darkness of his eyes I saw myself reflected clearly. I was real to him. He saw me all the way down to the bottom and knew every awful thing I'd done. More—he knew all that I was capable of doing, and yet he looked at me like I was something worthy and good.

"Come upstairs," I said. There was a promise in the words that spoke to more than sex. I thought it was implicit. But he only waited, silent. He didn't even blink, until my own eyes felt dry and itchy on his behalf. Finally I added, "Yes. Okay. Yes. I fucking love you."

"Oh yeah," he said, and punched the entry code in for my door. I didn't think I'd ever given it to him, so he must have watched me key it in and remembered, damn the man.

We were silent and untouching in the elevator. We waited, and it felt right to wait until we were in my place. There we had a door to close behind us, and no walls. We went up the stairs to the loft, and we had each other there with Henry dozing on the dresser, purring to himself.

We were so careful with each other. We had to be. We touched softly in deference to all the ways that we were wounded, working around each other's bruises and ruined places. This was not our usual sex. It was a delicate, new thing, and as we moved together, I could see Atlanta's skyline spread out before us in an electric dazzle, as if the city had set itself alight inside the blackness strictly for our pleasure.

He stayed put after. I never wanted anyone to stay, but I did not want him to leave me. Not tonight. He folded himself around me, dozing, but I didn't sleep. I was thinking of my mother. I was thinking that she had looked down the barrel of her own gun, in those medical scans. When the doctor told her, *Weeks, if you are lucky.*

She'd started bringing Hana to me, but she'd come the long way, trying to find a way into a future through our past. She had *counted* on being lucky.

In the darkness, with Birdwine's arms around me, I knew that Kai was dead. Nothing else would have stopped her from delivering my sister. I'd known her death was probable; I'd assumed it was imminent and inevitable the day I got my check back, and Birdwine's find at her Austin apartment had confirmed it. But now I knew it in the bones of me.

Kai's time had already run out, and she would never reach my door, never take my hand, never say some asshole mystic shit like, *Look here, Kali Jai, you have a little sister. I named her after Hanuman, the monkey god, because she is much stronger than she knows.* I was crying quietly, but Birdwine must have felt the shaking in my body. He pulled me closer and I felt his face press into my hair.

Was this what forgiveness looked like on the other end? It was too hard for her to forgive my part in our unraveling because so much of it was her fault. Her whole life was like a loaded gun, left cocked with the safety off in the middle of the table. As a child I had picked it up, and played with it, and cost her Julian. His absence had wrecked us.

She hadn't changed, though. As soon as she got off parole, she was on the move again, trusting fate to back her plays, no safety nets in place. Even when she learned that she was dying. She should have brought Hana straight to me.

Maybe it was the only way she could bring herself to come, traveling my little sister through the best parts of our shared past. Perhaps she'd needed to remember who we'd been to one another, back when she'd spin me on her feet, and I'd yell, *Dance me, dance me.* When the smell of orange peel and campfire smoke in her dark hair was my greatest comfort. When the two of us were all that was unchanging in the world.

That's the Kai I wept for, and released.

When I woke up, Henry was smack dab in the middle of Birdwine's abandoned pillow, floppy and dense with sleep. I could smell coffee brewing downstairs, and I heard the soft clatter of hands on a keyboard, so Birdwine had not gone far. His shirt was still on the floor, a dark green T from a local brewery. It was size XL and soft with age. I pulled it over my head and went to the railing.

Birdwine, barefoot, in only his jeans, was dwarfing my office chair, peering deep into my laptop with a steaming mug beside him on the desk.

"Bring me a cup of that?" I called down.

He looked up at me, and I'd never seen his olive face so pale.

"What?" I said, instantly tense. "I mean for shit's sake, what now?"

"I think I found her." He turned to the screen and touched it, then looked back to me. "It's a police report from four months ago. I think this might be Hana."

"What?" I said. "How?"

"I wanted to work, but I didn't want to leave with you asleep. I couldn't pick up where Julian and I left off, not without my notes from home. I might create a gap and miss something. So I started at the other end. Paula, I think I found her."

"Where is she?" I asked, my hands so tight on the railing that my nail beds had gone pale.

"Here," he said, and he waved one hand out at the cityscape. The sun was coming up, drenching the skyline with new light. "I think she's right here in Atlanta."

Chapter 12

Candace is sitting on the hood of an ancient, low-slung Chrysler that is parked in front of our place. Mine and Kai's. I am walking home in air so humid it feels thick with moisture, fresh off the school bus, when I see the shape of her from a long way down the block. Her shape does not belong here. She's leaning back, braced on her hands, swinging her feet off the front edge of the car to kick the bumper. She's so foreign, so invasive, that she stands out in brighter colors than any other object in my view. She's as comfortable as if she had been born right here on this road. As if it were hers, and she belonged here, my ruin on skinny legs.

I am running, now, my body pounding toward her of its own volition. My heavy backpack bangs against my spine. I feel cold terror in my long bones, and violence is uncoiling as I come close and closer. She has a round sucker in her mouth. I see the stick poking out, see how it makes one cheek bulge.

The driver's-side window scrolls down, and Jeremy, her dead-eyed boyfriend, leans his head out. He calls something to her, pointing down the road at me. She looks at me, and she stops swinging her hand-me-down tennis shoes with all the laces frayed, untied and hanging down in scraggles. She doesn't try to get up or run or even back away. She waits for me, boneless and accepting.

That's how I know it's all already done.

Somewhere a chipmunk is yelling his staccato love song, and the sun is warm on my back. I run at Candace because I cannot go inside. I don't know how I'll ever go inside.

Candace looks at me with her bland, blank Candace eyes as I skid to a halt in front of her, dropping my backpack off in a shrug. I'm already slapping her before I hear it thunk onto the asphalt. I keep flailing at her face and head, palms open, but so intense and furious it's like I have a hundred hands.

Her shoulders hunch, her legs curl up and in, her hands cover her face, but she doesn't roll away. She bunches up like a hood ornament and waits for me to finish. She doesn't understand; I'll never finish.

"Hey, now! Stop, now!" Jeremy is yelling. He scrambles out of the car, but I ignore him and keep whaling away at her. I am crying and she is crying out. Her sucker drops onto the hood and rolls away. I see it as a splash of orange falling away in my peripheral vision. Then Jeremy wraps his arms around me from behind, pinning me to his chest. He pulls me back and off her.

"Stupid—stupid—" I hiss at Candace, too squeezed and clamped by Jeremy to scream it. She shouldn't be here. They are not allowed to be here. I lash out with my feet, trying to kick her in the face as he drags me backward.

"Don't hurt her!" Candace calls to him, uncoiling, worried.

We are frozen there for a timeless span, Candace watching with her flossy hair in a muss, her eyes stinging with tears. Jeremy holding me, my breath heaving against his restraining arms. He doesn't let go until he feels the need to beat her leave my body.

What's the point? It's done.

Kai and I have been here less than a month. She came back from prison different, but hasn't this always been her way? New location, new Kai. Always before, I changed myself to fit the narrative, the yang to her selected, shifting yin. But we are living under our real names now; her parole ties us to our true history. Karen

Vauss sings less, tells fewer stories, drinks more wine than any Kai that I have ever known. Karen Vauss is too broken and world-weary to ditch parole and run.

I slacken in Jeremy's arms, and I think, *I can do that with her.* I can be silent on the sofa and not deviate until Kai does. I can, and I will, because my ever-changing mother is the only presence in my life that has been constant. I wrecked it, sent us both to separate institutions, but I have her back now. I have to let her know that I can stare like a sad-eyed orphan at Marvin, if that's what she wants. He owns the diner where Kai works. He's started sending home bacon-stuffed biscuits for me at the end of her shifts, and one morning, soon, I know I'll wake up and find him in pajamas and bare feet, eating them at our small dining table. I can back her play, if only she forgives me.

I swear this to myself, though I'm scared to see the Kai who's waiting for me inside. The truth she knows now may have already changed her. Fine. I am making promises to every god who ever walked: I'll be her match no matter what it is, when she forgives me.

Jeremy steps back from me, and I stand trying to stop crying in the road in front of the car. Candace clambers down off the hood and gets her sucker off the curb, inspecting it. She picks away a piece of grass, a bit of leaf. I can see my handprints all on her pale face.

"You should of took me with you," she says, as if I could have, even if I'd wanted to. She puts the dirty candy in her mouth. Her eyes are wary and unsorry and something else. Something I can't read.

"You should get off of my street," I say, scrubbing my last tears away.

"You don't own it," she says, but not like it's a dig. She's stating a fact. "You don't own nothin' here."

She's right. We are renters. Kai and I have the dim basement apartment of a three-unit house that is the biggest eyesore in the neighborhood. The rent is low, especially for Morningside, which is not our kind of place. It's full of blond people who buy name-brand dogs and care about their lawns. But it's safe, and the schools are good.

"We got to go," Jeremy tells Candace, shifting uneasily from foot to foot.

He speaks only to her, as if the second I stopped hurting her, I stopped being relevant. I look only at Candace, too, as if he stopped existing when he took his arms away.

"I was going to call," I tell her. It's not true.

I'd hoped that once I was gone, Candace would forget me. She's such a creature of immediacy, she might well busy herself blackmailing Shar and Karice to be her replacement friends, or swapping Jeremy for someone who had pot as well as candy. If that failed, I'd hope she wouldn't be able to find me. I told Mrs. Mack and my caseworker and my guardian ad litem that I didn't want them passing on my contact info, and they said I had that right. But Candace is so good at weaseling and snooping, one big ear pressed to any closed door she comes across, sugar-sticky fingers creeping through other people's private things. She found me, and she had Jeremy get a car someplace, so she could get to me and ruin me.

I have myself in hand now. I'm done crying in front of her. I don't even want to hit her more. Candace is a well with no bottom. I can throw endless sorrow or violence at her. I could even throw in love, if I had any to spare. She would take it all, disappear it down her blank, black mouth hole, as if it were the same. None of it would ever fill her. It would hurtle down and down forever, falling through her endless, hungry depths.

"Why are you still here?" I ask her.

Candace gives Jeremy a look, and he walks over and folds himself back into the driver's seat. He closes the door and sits inside the car, dead eyes front. I watch the window scrolling up, his arm pumping as he works the crank.

Candace says, "We ran away. Jeremy's driving me to California."

I peer at him through the windshield, not sure what story this boy thinks he's in. Romeo and Juliet? Bonnie and Clyde? Maybe slouchy boys like him don't read, so he can't see how bad it's bound to end. Does Jeremy even have a license? I think he might still be fifteen, but I'm not sure. Even if he's legal to drive, there's no way he bought this car.

I thump the hood and say, "This is going to land you both in juvie."

Candace shakes her head. "We stoled it off some Mexicans. Illegals don't report."

"I report, Candace," I remind her, frustrated. It's been her leverage, so how can she not see the irony? "I dial 911, and I report shit."

In the wake of this threat, she only sidles closer. "You didn't take me, but I'd still take you."

"Take me where?" I ask, uncomprehending. "You mean to California?"

She nods, and I realize she is serious. She's done her level best to trash my life, and her left ear is bright red from where I boxed it. Now she's inviting me along on her road trip?

"I hope you die in California," I say, so cold it barely has inflection. "No, I hope you die on the way and never get there."

I grab my backpack and sling it back up on my shoulders. I step out of the road, walking away toward the house.

She calls after me, "You should've seen your mama when I told her. She slapped me, too." That stops me. Kai in every incarnation is nonviolent. A word person. A charmer who'll kiss puppies on the mouth. Candace follows me onto the patchy grass of the rental house's lawn. "They got sea lions out there, did you know that? They sit up on the same beach as where the people go. I saw it on a video in science class. You can walk right up to them, and they don't mind it. Don't you want to see that? Don't you want to get up close?"

I understand her then. She didn't tell Kai for revenge or even out of meanness. She did it because I am a Got-mama, and she can never join my tribe. She's done this thing to move me into hers. I am floored at how much ugliness can be alive inside simple pragmatism.

"I hate sea lions," I lie. The Kai who lives in this house—Karen Vauss—is sour and insular, so I will be, too, and she will forgive me. I can't see this new us on a beach.

Candace says, "Well, where I'm going, I'll see lots of things."

"I hate seeing lots of things," I lie. Karen Vauss rarely leaves the house, so I won't, either.

I walk away, heading around to the side door that leads down into our apartment.

"Hey, you want me to wait?" Candace calls after me, and there is a desperate edge now to her voice. "In case of you need that ride?"

I don't turn back. I barely hear her, because I will not need that ride. I am thinking to myself, *My mother knows*, and so the worst already happened.

I open the door and look down our dark stairwell.

I could put my game face on and lie. Right now, it is my word against Candace's. Kai won't want it to be true, and nothing helps a lie float like a hopeful listener.

I hear the shit car starting with a huge chugging noise. Its muffler is dead or dying. It is the roar of another lost girl on the move, hoping to go far enough to get up close to sea lions. Or past that, into the ocean. Or past that, right off the edge of the world.

I'm so relieved to hear her going that I know I won't lie. Lies and California are not real. The only real way out is through the truth.

So the unthinkable has happened—Kai knows I broke our lives. Now I have to go downstairs uninvented and see what happens next.

I walk down with a changed future only a few steps before me. It is a wall of white without Kai's handwriting on it. What if Kai hits me? She's never hit me. She's never let a boyfriend hit me, either. If she does, I'll take it, like Candace did. I have earned it. I've earned any acts of penance that she might require, and at the end, I will be forgiven.

I want to be punished, actually. It would feel good to bow to it and say, *This is what should happen now.* When the awful part is done, she will fold me in her arms. She will say, *Baby, baby, we will be okay.* Not today, but one day, when I am fully punished and forgiven, she will say these words to me. I know she will, because us, together, is the driving repetition of our incarnations.

The stairwell is dark, and it is even darker in the large room beyond. It's a combination den and dining room with a kitchen running in a strip along the back wall. It only has windows on one side. They run in a narrow horizontal line up by the ceiling, and it's been raining on and off all day. The sun is behind a thick blanket of clouds. I peer into the dim light, seeking her.

I have been mostly happy here, in this small span of time.

She is sitting on the sofa. She's been drinking wine, the purple Kool-Aid-colored kind that comes in a big jug with a round ring for a handle. I can smell its thin, acidic tang. A juice glass sits on the coffee table, a few bright dregs staining the base of it. She's holding a cigarette that has burned down to the filter and died without her noticing, a tube of untouched ash perched between her fingers.

I set my backpack down by the front door, and Kai starts at the sound. She sits up straight, and the long ash breaks and crumbles. The big pieces fall and scatter down her front, while some dusty bits drift slower in a gray and weightless haze. Her eyes seek me and find me, tearstained and sweaty from the exertion of beating Candace. Her eyes meet mine.

I think she tried hard not to believe Candace. Maybe she succeeded, but not all the way. She reads the confirmation on my face. The truth has such a power to it, and it's already been spoken in this room.

There is a beat, a single breath that lasts a century, and then there is nothing for me in her expression. No thought, no feeling. Her eyes roll slowly in their sockets, past me, to look into the darkness of the stairs behind me.

The world's very tilt changes. I feel it. The whole planet shifts under my feet. The ground is water, and the ocean is the sky. Everything that was once moored now floats. I am drifting, too, helpless in a sea of stories with no current and no wind.

"Mama," I begin, but she talks over me.

"Oh, hello, baby," she says. Her eyes have become ·chips of green rock. Her pale face shines, expressionless, like carved marble glowing in the darkness. "Do you want a piece of fruit?"

"Mama," I start again. "I'm—"

"There's bananas, or I think there's still an apple," she says, cutting me off again.

She notices the filter in her hand and sets it in the ashtray, which is already bursting with a hundred stubbed-out Camels. When we first moved in, there was a dank green basement smell, mossy and thick. Now, the whole place reeks of stale smoke. She brushes at the scattered ash that's graying out the colors of her skirt, then gets a new cigarette from the pack and lights up. Her gaze slides over me again, and this time it settles on the kitchen.

"Kai," I say, urgent.

I want for her to come at me. I need her to. She could slap me, hard and openhanded, as many times as I slapped Candace. More. She could squeeze me tight enough to shove the breath from me. I want her to scream and flail, to be a raging storm. I want her to be anything that has a chance of being over.

I step into her line of vision, but it is as if I am a moving spot of Teflon. Her gaze slides away, unable to pause or stick. She gets up, weaves her way to the stripe of kitchen on the back wall, and starts cutting up the apple for me.

I don't remember my mother ever looking straight at me again.

I'm sure she must have. There had to be times when, by sheer chance, her gaze and my body intersected. It was not a large apartment. But in my memory, her eyes wore out the air around me, year after relentless year. To an outside observer, I doubt that much would have changed, but I knew. I'd been locked outside her story, and the longer I stayed out, the more guilt and fury worked their way under my skin like backward shrapnel, slow-digging their way deep into the meat of me.

So I remade myself into a creature built to plague her. Paula the slut, the scrapper, the petty criminal, the rebel. I'd come home at four A.M., stinking of boy and beer, and still she looked just past me. She never told me to be any different, the jagged scrape of a thousand guilt and fury slivers rasping on my bones became background music, an ever-present hum. Once I moved to Indiana, I remade myself again: the woman who made good to spite her mother. I let my checks tell that tale for me. The amount on them growing larger with the years, but asking the same angry question. Six months ago, she finally answered: *I am going on a journey, Kali. I am going back to my beginning; death is not the end. You will be the end. We will meet again, and there will be new stories.*

Classic, cryptic Kai, speaking just off point, her words sliding over me and past me like her gaze. Why couldn't she say, *Hey, sorry, but I'm dying, and I'm coming to Atlanta. Do you want your little sister?*

Now the only new story I had was the four-month-old police report that pinged on Birdwine's radar. In it, an ancient eyesore of a Buick with a crumpled hood and a long scraped side came driving in wild loops through Morningside. One good wife of the neighborhood saw the sketchy car pass by, out of place on her street. She also clocked a kid in the backseat, and noted how erratically the female driver wove from curb to curb. She did nothing. Not until the second time it passed, and she worried that her neighborhood was being cased. *Then* she called the cops.

A cruiser was dispatched, but by the time it arrived, the Buick had already wibbled off the road and banged into an evergreen in some upstanding citizen's front yard. The accident happened two blocks down from the lot where our old apartment used to be. If Kai was looking for it as the last stop on her Past Lives Tour, she was out of luck. The whole house had been torn down, and a faux craftsman with three thousand square feet of living space had been crammed onto the lot.

The driver—Karen Porter from New Orleans, according to her ID—was groggy and disoriented. She'd whanged her head against the steering wheel. She and her child were taken by ambulance to Grady Hospital, where they ascertained that the concussion was the least of her problems. She was in the end stages of lung cancer that had spread all through her—brain, bones, and beyond. The child was treated for a sprained wrist and released to DFCS. The woman remained, drifting in and out of consciousness with limited lucidity. She died six days later.

I'd accepted that Kai was dead. I'd wept and wept in Birdwine's arms as we stared out at my city's skyline. But if this woman was Kai, then my mother had already been cremated; Adult Protective Services, unable to locate a living relative, had done it at the end of May.

That info came from Birdwine; he'd followed up on the woman while I tried to get a bead on the kid. He thought DFCS would be more open to inquiries about a ten-year-old girl-child from me. I was a female blood relative and upstanding member of the bar, while he was a fired former policeman, emphasis on *man*, with less than a week sober. Fair enough.

I spent the better part of two business days poking my way through endless automated menus, only to get a person who would transfer me to another person, who inevitably sent me back into the menu or, if I lucked out, into a voicemail. I recorded a honey-throated message whenever I got the option, building up a solid legion of inquiries.

Julian, new to red tape, got frustrated fast. He'd quit at the suburban Mellow Mushroom and was both interning for me and looking for another job in midtown. He'd completed his transfer application to Georgia State and was sending me endless links to real estate listings in good school zones that had yards and at least two bedrooms. They all had carriage houses or basement apartments, too. The implication was I'd have a brotherly built-in renter, close enough to help with after-school care. He wanted the both of us to storm DFCS in person, locked and loaded.

I told him to stand down. I stayed sugar-sweet and patient, even when I got disconnected after a solid half hour spent on hold. I was casting a wide but very gentle net. If this was Hana—and I hoped it was—I wanted her caseworker already thinking well of us, predisposed to see us as an asset. I promised him if no one got back to us by Monday morning, I'd take the afternoon off. We'd go to the DFCS offices and run a good cop/ bad cop, pitching tents and hissy fits as needed, hurling lawsuit threats and bribes around, whatever it took, but to let me try the sweet road first.

It was almost lunchtime on Friday when Verona poked her head into my office. She looked spooked.

"It's a woman from Social Services," she said, eyes wide.

She knew how important this call was—the whole firm did. I'd invited Nick out for a drink on Wednesday, and I'd leveled with him about all that had gone down with my family situation in the last half year. Nick was more than forgiving; he was downright supportive. As well he should be. We went way back, and I'd literally taken a beating—almost a bullet—for the firm. It didn't hurt that *Winkley v. Winkley* was unfolding beautifully, both in terms of the settlement itself and the good publicity. Oakleigh adored my sorry ass; I'd turned her life into a big fat bowl of roses. She was an asshole, sure, but she was *my* asshole, and Nick all but glowed, rhapsodizing about the referrals she'd give her spoiled, rich friends when it came time for their inevitable divorces.

As a bonus, Nick was an incorrigible gossip, so I'd only had to plop my fresh and steaming guts out on a table once. The tremble in Verona's voice as she told me who was on the phone was testament to how fast and thoroughly he'd spread the word.

I hit Save on the motion I was writing and set my laptop aside, saying, "Super, put the call through."

"No, not on the phone," Verona told me in a hushed, dramatic whisper. "There's a woman here. Right here. In the lobby. Now."

I felt the little hairs on the back of my neck rise up. I knew enough about government agencies to guess this wasn't usual. I kept my face neutral, though, and said, "Super, send her back," with the same inflection I'd used when I'd thought it was a call. I didn't want to encourage Verona, who was acting as if this were reality TV and she'd bagged a juicy cameo. Ye gods, these millennials.

"She doesn't have an appointment," Verona said. "I offered her some coffee, and I ran to tell you."

"It's fine," I said. "Just bring her here, then go push back my conference call."

I came out from behind my desk while I was waiting and took a quick peek in the outsize mirror hung behind the sofa. My hair was sleek, and I hadn't eaten off my lipstick. I looked professional, and by the time Verona returned, I also looked pleasant and calm. Relaxed mouth, eyebrows down, easy in the shoulders.

"Sharon Watson here to see you," Verona said, ushering in an attractive black woman, heavyset and tall, about my age.

I hadn't left anyone of that name a voicemail. Curiouser and curiouser. Ms. Watson wore an inexpensive navy suit and a string of pearls that were too large to be anything but costume. She had on pearlized earrings, too, flat and wide like silver dollars. Her navy pumps were sensible but flattering, much like her short haircut.

"Thanks, Verona," I said, dismissively enough to be definitive. She backed out, slowly. I waited until my door closed all the way before I stepped toward the woman with my hand out. "Hello, I'm Paula Vauss."

She took it, saying, "Oh, I know who you are. And you know me."

I didn't, though. Not until she smiled at me. Her mouth stretched wide in her pretty face, showing me a huge wall of slightly overlapping teeth. Then I knew her.

"Hello, Shar," I said, cool as I could manage it. Twenty years older, with a different last name, but it was Shar. She was my past, rising around me, and she was also impossibly here and now. She was exactly herself, but taller, stouter, and wearing braces on her big teeth, the transparent kind. They hadn't quite finished their job yet, but that didn't stop her from grinning wide, enjoying my shock. I had to work hard to make my voice not tremble as I asked, "You're with DFCS?"

"Yes. A lot of us end up doing social work," she said. I wasn't sure who *us* was. She must have seen it on my face because she clarified. "Former foster kids. When the system works, we tend to want to pay it back." She gave me a long, scraping look, from my blowout to my bitch heels, and then cast another, even louder speaking glance around my office. She put those big teeth back on full display and added, "Not you, though, huh."

I felt my own smile starting to go sharky. I hadn't seen Shar since she was thirteen years old, but she was still an instigator.

I resisted her bait. I wasn't going to throw down with my pro bono work, metaphorically unzipping and then calling for a ruler so we could measure our respective virtues. Not only because I would surely lose against a woman whose life's work was in Social Services. It was more important to understand why she had come here; I thought she'd taken the potshot to get a rise or a feel for me, so her visit had to do with Hana. This could not be a simple case of auld lang syne. Not with this timing, and the Shar I remembered had not been remotely sentimental.

I kept my voice sweet and said, "Apparently not. Please, sit down." I waved her to the sofa instead of the client chairs, and I took a seat on it beside her. I didn't want the desk between us, which could read as adversarial or patronizing. She sat very straight, but I thought that was due to good posture, not a fighting stance. I was having trouble reading her. Hell, I was having a little trouble processing, period. "Your last name is changed. It used to be . . ."

"Roberson," she said.

"That's right. So you got married?"

"I sure did." Shar had a satchel purse with her, large enough to double as a briefcase. She'd dropped it by her feet when she sat down. Now she fished her phone out of a side pocket and pulled up a picture to show me. In it she stood arm in arm with a tall, broad-faced black man with a mustache and a comfortable belly. Three boys of varying sizes clustered around them. "You married, Paula?"

"Nope. Never married, no kids," I said. I couldn't tell if this was another gauntlet, but it was not an arena where I'd ever felt competitive.

"Well, looks like you're doing all right, in your own way," she said, chuckling.

That threw me. It sounded good-humored—almost kind—and I was still looking for her angle. The last time our paths had crossed, we had been mortal enemies. Of course, we had also been children.

"Are you here about my phone calls?" I asked. But that was too indirect. "Are you here about my sister, I mean. I don't remember leaving you a message."

"Well, I'm about the only one in Fulton County who hasn't heard from you. You left a lot of messages," she said. "I'm a supervisor now, not a caseworker, but you're a former foster kid, trying to find a younger sibling in the system. You know that's going to rate high as watercooler talk. Once I heard your name, I had to see if you were the same Paula I remembered, even though the case isn't under my jurisdiction. I found your picture on your firm's website. I knew it was you like that." She snapped her fingers. "You got even taller, but your face is exactly the same. I thought, Look at that! Another one of Mrs. Mack's girlies, making good."

She was chatting at me as if this were a social call. Perhaps this was the necessary small talk people did before they got down to it? Nick was so much better at this part. It was not my bailiwick, but I gave it my best try.

"I remember that. Mrs. Mack calling us her girlies," I said.

"She was good to me," Shar said. "I don't think you knew her like I did. You had a mama coming for you, and she didn't try to get in between that. She was different with us on the adoption track. Especially the ones like me—I'd been suspended three times for fighting. Not like I had sets of perfect parents lining up to bid.

She kept up with me even after I aged out. She was my oldest son's godmother, before she passed."

"Oh. I'm sorry for your loss. It sounds like she was lovely to you," I said, awkward and formal. Shar still looked expectant, maybe wanting the nutshelled version of my life in return, post–foster care. Instead I asked another question. "You keep up with anybody else, from back in those old days?" As I spoke I heard how far I'd sunk into the rhythms of her speech. *You keep up*, without the word *do* at the front. That wasn't how I talked now.

I wondered if my presence was pushing her diction back in time as well. Her accent was on the spectrum common to professional women of any race here in Atlanta, similar to mine, but this was a matter of sentence structure. The rhythm of her story was a song straight out of the time we'd spent together. Back when we were Mrs. Mack's girlies, as Shar had styled us.

"Me and Kim stayed tight," Shar said. "She had a kid when she was young. A girl. Twelve now, and a pistol. Kim got married to a good man, though, a couple years back. They have a baby boy. He's the fattest little thing. So cute. Looks like he's made out of pudding. Got all those little knee fats and elbow fats. Makes me miss those baby days. Not enough to go back to them, mind you."

I was interested in spite of myself and all the context in the room. "What about Karice? Did you keep up with her?"

Shar's expression sobered. She shrugged in a way that didn't mean she didn't know. She knew all right, but she wasn't going to talk about it. I could fill in the blanks: Karice was dead or missing or some known flavor of ruined. She, too, had fallen off the world.

"Yeah, okay. Same with Joya," I said. I repeated her own shrugging gesture back to her.

In the wake of this exchange, I felt an understanding between us. The last time our histories had intersected, we'd been standing on the world's cusp. We all had been. Gotmamas and adoption trackers, boys and girls, black, white, brown, and all colors in between. We'd all been abandoned, lost, or rescued, and therefore of one tribe, although we hadn't known it. Shar and I had been among the Children of the Edge, too young to feel ourselves teetering. I hadn't liked Kim, but I was glad to hear that she was well. I'd had no fondness for Karice, and Shar had hated Joya, but it didn't stop the common ground from rising around us in the here and now. Shar and me? We'd both lost people we loved over the edge, and neither one of us had fallen.

Although, considering that history, I couldn't help it; my gaze twitched to those outsize pearl earrings. It was a fast look, barely a blink's worth, but she busted me and laughed.

"Oh, you want to see?"

I did. I couldn't help it. "Bet your ass," I said.

She slid the earrings off; they were clip-ons. The fissures were gone, but I could see a faint, neat scar in the center of each lobe, pointing straight down.

"Plastic surgery," she confided. "They had to excise the old wounds, and that hurt about as much as it sounds like it would. Expensive? Lord, yes. But I saved up and had it done when I was twenty. I never forgot you saying my earlobes looked like old-lady bottoms."

I looked down at my hands in my lap, rueful. "Well, I was kind of a turd."

"You and me and every twelve-year-old female ever born. It's going to be a miracle if Kim doesn't flat eat her daughter. I'm glad I had boys," Shar said, still smiling. "I'm sorry about Joya, but at least your other friend landed on her feet."

It took me a second to realize who she had to mean.

"Candace?" I asked. "I did not keep up with Candace."

Shar's eyes widened with surprise. "You two were peas inside a pod."

I had no response that was both true and suitable for polite company, so I only said, "Last I heard, she ran away."

"Yes. She ran away a bunch of times, but she always came back. Candace and I aged out together. Well, it's a long story, and I have afternoon appointments. But sometime, you should Google *her*. She goes by Candace Cherries now. She's a little bit famous."

"In porn?" I said. I didn't know what else it could be, with that name. It wouldn't have surprised me, either, but "porn star" didn't fit with Shar's pleased tone.

"Just Google her sometime," Shar said, closing the subject, but she made no move to leave. Small talk was over, then. I felt my spine get a little straighter.

"So this *is* about Hana," I said.

"'Course it is," Shar said. "Once I realized it was you, I got what's called a little overinterested. So tell me. Why do you think this girl is your sister? She's a quiet type. Doesn't say three words if one will do, but she told me she has no siblings, same as she said when she was interviewed at intake."

"Told you?" I said, leaning forward. "You've met her?"

"I came here straight from meeting her," Shar said, and instantly I was on my feet, going to my desk to get my laptop. "I didn't tell her about you. I said I was a supervisor, checking on a few things. No sense in riling the child if she isn't the girl you're looking for. But if she—" She stopped talking abruptly because

I'd brought the laptop back to her, open to one of the scanned pics of Hana feeding fat ducks on the riverside with Kai. There was a long pause, and then Shar said, "Well, I'll be damned," with wonderment in her voice, "that's her."

"Are you sure?" I said. My voice was shaking now, in spite of my best efforts.

"'Course I'm sure. I left that girl's foster home at about eleven thirty," Shar said.

"So you're really sure," I said.

My hands went numb. My face, too, as Shar nodded. This was Hana, so Karen Porter was Kai. And Karen Porter was ashes. I'd known that Kai was dead, down to my bones, but this was so specific. Not just dead, but small, reduced to only that which would not burn. Ashes in a box. How Kai would hate that.

At the same time, this was Hana, alive, and maybe even safe, and—I needed to go see her. Now. No, I needed to call Julian. Or— I didn't know what to do next.

I stared at Shar, suddenly helpless in the real and simple presence of a woman who had seen my missing sister not an hour ago.

Shar reached out a hand and touched Kai's face on the screen. "I remember her."

I blinked. "You saw Kai? But the mother in this case was—" I faltered.

"Oh, God, no, I'm sorry," Shar said, overloud, almost horrified. "No, no, Karen Porter passed. Months ago. I'm so sorry. I meant, I remember seeing her at Mrs. Mack's. Years ago. When she came to visit you."

It was the second shock I'd had in as many minutes, but of course she would remember Kai. My mother had visited me four times a week while she worked on finding a job and getting us an apartment. That would stick hard in the memory of a girl like Shar. I couldn't think about Kai now. Not with Hana found, living and so close.

"So now what do I do?" I said.

I didn't mean the process, necessarily. I meant it more existentially, but Shar gave her shoulders a little shake and let her hand drop away from the screen. She dug in her oversize bag, pulling out a legal pad and a manila file. The tab said *Hannah Porter,* and she opened it up onto the coffee table. She got a notebook with a pen stuck through the spirals, too, and bent over the coffee table to write.

"First, I'm going to give you some direct contact information," Shar said, copying names and numbers and email addresses as she spoke. "I'll talk to Hannah's caseworker myself, get her to contact you ASAP. You're going to want to call the guardian ad litem. This is him, Roger Delany. I don't know him well. He's new. But her therapist, Dr. Patel, is very good. I've worked with her for several years. She specializes in trauma, which considering Hannah has lost her mother—"

"Her name is Hana," I interrupted, not wanting to hear the end of that sentence. I knew what Hana had lost. I'd lost my mother, too, years ago, but also four months back, and again a few days past, weeping in bed with Birdwine. It had happened a long time ago; it was still happening now.

"Yes, that's what I said."

"No, you're saying *Hannah,* and it's *Hana.*" My sister had been named for a god in my own pantheon, and her name would rhyme with Ghana, not banana. Shar stared at me as if I'd grown a second head, and I realized I had no idea what my face was doing. I'd lost control of it entirely.

Shar said, dismayed, "Oh, hey, now! This is good news."

"How's her placement?" I asked. My voice sounded thick, like I was choking.

"Excellent!" Shar assured me. "I know Mrs. Beale. She's a former schoolteacher, retired. Hannah is her seventh foster, and her only one right now." I still couldn't seem to stop the awful shapes my face was making, and Shar petered out. Her voice got cooler, a little more reserved. "It's not permanent. Hannah is going on the adoption track. It was my impression that you were looking for this girl because you wanted her."

"I want her," I said, immediate and raw. I think we were both relieved to hear the truth, ringing in those simple words as clear as bell song. "It's just a lot. It's very fast." Damn Julian, the kid had been right all along, and I was not prepared. "I only have one bed. She'll need a bed. And sheets. Sheets with whatever ten-year-old girls like on them, and I don't know what ten-year-old girls like."

Now Shar was the one with an odd look on her face. I could not read it.

She said, "It's always like this, when a kid comes into your life. You're not going to be a hundred percent ready. But we're going to get you ready enough."

"When can I have her?" I said, changing lanes again, raw and abrupt.

"Have?" Shar said, eyebrows rising. "That's going to take a while. We'll need to do the standard background checks, inspect your house, and give her time to work on the transition with her therapist. Most importantly, you two need to get to know each other. So *have* is going to take a little time. But visitation? If you call this lawyer, Delany, and you and I conference with the caseworker today, they can get you shoehorned into family court Monday or Tuesday. You could start visitation next week." She looked at me, hard, and said, "If that's what you want."

"Yes. I want her," I said again, and damn, but the truth had such a ring to it. Then I amended, "We both want her—I have a brother. She has a brother, too."

"Yes, you said so in your fifteen thousand messages," Shar said, and that look was back again. I placed it this time. It was pride.

Now my smile felt as wide as hers had ever been, and my eyes felt hot, although I didn't cry. I thought I'd likely pull my own eyes out and throw them in a fire before I cried in front of Shar Roberson. But ye gods, I was so grateful to have her here to help me.

I think she knew it even before I told her, "Thank you. You don't know what this means." But that was crap. She did.

"Now, let's get this to-do list going," she said briskly. "I really do have to get back to my office this afternoon."

I bent over the legal pad, and together we laid out a plan to get the wheels of DFCS spinning. Government wheels, so they would spin slow, but we were headed in the right direction. Top of my list was to make contact with her lawyer and her therapist, while Shar set up a conference call with the caseworker.

After Shar left, I sat on the sofa, feeling shell-shocked. I was going to meet my little sister. Next week. She had no idea that I existed, and Kai, the bridge between us, was ashes. In a box. Somewhere.

I imagined her on a shelf inside some ugly government storehouse, like the warehouse at the end of that Indiana Jones film. I saw her lost, anonymous, her box filed in rows and rows of plain white boxes, all the same, full of the ashes of unclaimed people. I knew then that I would not leave her there. I would find her, and I would claim her. But not today. I had to see to Hana, who was whole and living, first.

What if Hana didn't like me, I wondered, and then laughed. I never gave two shits if anybody liked me. It was a foreign feeling. I didn't care for it. Damn Kai and her long way home.

I took my laptop back to my desk, along with the sheet of contact information and my to-do list. I had calls to make before five P.M., and once those were done, I had some housing problems. What if Hana was a dog person? We would need a yard. Great schools. I wasn't even sure what grade a ten-year-old was in. Fifth? I needed to find a Realtor and go look at some of Julian's damn listings.

I stared off into space, thinking I should keep the loft regardless. Most people in my income bracket had two houses. I'd hold on to it for noontime meets with Birdwine. After all, I couldn't very well have a strange man with a drinking problem doing overnights. Not with DFCS looming in the background. More than that—I'd have a kid in the house.

I couldn't swallow. And I sure as hell could not pick up the phone and make all this begin. Hana didn't know me. She didn't even know that I existed.

Then I realized I had to call Julian, first of all. He was still in suspense, and also, he would be so useful. He would drop everything and rush into town to help me out. I needed him to come clot up the air with rosy chatter, bright-siding, and believing all would work out for the best. But I still couldn't reach for the phone.

I'd said the truth to Shar. I wanted this. I wanted Hana. But I couldn't start.

Finally, I pulled the laptop over and I typed *Candace Cherries* into Google.

The first link at the top was Candacecherries.com. I clicked it.

The splash page was a high-res picture of a piece of mixed-media art. I wasn't sure if it was rightfully a sculpture or a painting. It hung on a wall, but it was definitely done in three dimensions. It showed a human figure, the right half of its face cut out from one of those

1970s velvet paintings of big-eyed, weeping orphans. The left half was a wooden tribal mask, broken so that it had a savage, jagged edge. From that side, a coarse pigtail made of what looked like real hair jutted out, tied up in a tatty bit of pink ribbon. The body was composed of rusted bits of metal: springs and pipes and chains and old watchbands. It had been dressed in ragged patchwork.

Doves on stiff wire bobbled in the air above the person, affixed to a huge blue sky made of what looked like painted driftwood. The doves had stolen the figure's hands and a red, fleshy rag that could have been its heart, its tongue, or some other key internal organ. The feathery little fuckers looked quite smug about it, too. It was primitive and visceral and disturbing. It was also really, really good.

The menu bar above gave me a lot of choices: Methodology, Reviews, Show Schedule, Online Gallery, Biography. I clicked the last link, and there was Candace.

She was so skinny she looked like a bobblehead doll, and the emaciation emphasized the crow's feet etched deep around her watery blue eyes. She was wearing jeans with an aggressively ugly serape draped across her shoulders like a blanket. The bio said that she was living in Wyoming on a horse farm with her partner of nine years. It talked about where her work had been shown and the awards and fellowships she'd won. Near the end, it quoted a review that praised, among other things, her innovation with found items. I snorted. So Candace was still digging through other people's things. There were more pictures of her below the bio, several with her partner, a very tall Native American with coppery skin and a wealth of black hair tumbling down her back. She looked like all kinds of an ass-kicker, looming protectively over Candace in most shots.

So, Candace had a type. It was a little disconcerting.

I started clicking through the galleries, looking at all of Candace's crazy pieces. Animals and people made of bits and broken ends. Interesting stuff.

Okay, so I was scared to meet my sister. Scared of who she'd be, and how we'd manage, when we were face to face. Scared her life had been preruined.

But if Candace, of all people, could dock someplace . . . I clicked back to the bio to look at her face.

Sure, it looked like she had some kind of serious eating disorder, but she was still alive. She was doing work that mattered to her. It mattered to other people, as well; there were a lot of SOLD tabs on the pieces in the gallery. She loved someone, and she'd been loved back, for almost a decade now. She'd even found a form of faith, judging by the red string tied on her left wrist in every picture.

Who would have thought it? Fucking Candace.

I closed the website, and I reached for the phone to dial Julian.

Chapter 13

I am nineteen years old when Kai tells me the last story of hers that I will ever hear. I am almost asleep in my room in our basement apartment in Morningside. My door bangs open, and I jerk awake to see Kai framed in the doorway, backlit by dim lamplight from the den. Her face is a dark oval with a glowing red beauty mark: the ember of her Camel.

"What?" I say, groggy with near-sleep.

She takes a long tug off her cigarette, then lets smoke out into a backlit cloud around her head before she speaks.

This happened a long time ago, and it's still happening now. Ganesha and his mother are playing by the river when a wealthy nobleman rides by.

Parvati is quite beautiful, cooling her feet among the stones. Baby Ganesha paddles in the shallows by her, spraying water with his little elephant's trunk. The droplets sparkle in her dark hair like jewels as she sets out fruit and crackers for their lunch.

The nobleman, Kubato, scoops her simple repast back into her basket, inviting the pair of them to dine in his home instead.

I sit up, scrubbing at my eyes. I am in no mood for stories, especially not this one. I don't want to hear this mother-love tale with my army duffel bag already packed. It sits beside my footlocker and some cardboard boxes by the door. I am moving to Indiana with my friend William. We are leaving in the morning, early. Long before she's usually up.

Wishing to impress her, Kubato orders a feast and calls all the nobles of the land to attend. They sit in rows at his fine tables, but Kubato seats Parvati and her son on a cushion beside him, on the dais. He hands Parvati a glass of fragrant wine.

"This wine," Kubato says, "has waited for your lips for a hundred years in a gold casket lined with sweet wood. Every cup is worth a year's wages."

Parvati takes the goblet, but she does not drink. "I think it is too rich for me."

So Ganesha reaches for the cup, and then he gulps the wine all down, greedy, with red droplets running down his cheeks. He smacks his lips, and he sends his long trunk all around the room, dipping into every goblet and pitcher. He sucks the wine into his trunk, then brings it to his mouth and has it all in one long swallow.

He looks up to his mother, and he says, "But I'm still hungry."

Kai has been drinking wine herself all night. She is very, very drunk. If I didn't know this story down to its last syllable, I might not follow, that's how bad she's slurring. I've heard "Baby Ganesha at the Feast" since I was a baby myself, though. I have no concrete memory of the first time, that's how long this tale has been alive between us.

Kubato calls for his servants to bring out the feast platters, heaped with roasted lamb and vegetables. The rice is soft with new oil, yellow and fragrant with costly saffron.

The servants bring the platters to Parvati first, but she says, "Oh no, thank you. It's too rich for me."

412 • JOSHILYN JACKSON

Ganesha reaches for the platters, though, and takes them, every one. He tips them into his mouth, swallowing lamb shanks, bones and all, and bushels of roasted apples, and a hundred thousand turnips and onions, enough yellow rice to feed an army for a year. He even licks the grease from every platter until the bare silver shines.

Then he looks up at his mother, and he says, "But I'm still hungry."

All afternoon, Kai has seen me packing in her peripheral vision. She told my left ear where to find the boxes. She offered her heavy thrift-store coat to the spot just past my shoulder. She asked my hairline to bring her the open jug of Burgundy from the cabinet under the sink. What she hasn't done is look at me. What she hasn't done is tell me not to go. I'm in no mood for a scoop of mystic bullshit from her now.

So the rich man, growing angry, is even more determined to impress her. He sends his other guests away, and then he brings, with his own hands, a single silver dish. Inside it, layers of delicate pastry are stuffed with nuts and honey.

He says, "This is the honey of the dark bees, who are striped in blue and have human hair. Their

sting is instant death. A thousand men died to collect a jarful, drop by drop. Here. I've had it all
made into this sweet for you."

Parvati smiles and says, "I thank you, but this is
too rich for me."

Ganesha's trunk curls round his mother, and he
plucks the sweet from Kubato. He stuffs the whole
thing in his mouth, pan and all, and swallows.

"Still hungry!" he cries. "Oh! I am so hungry!"

I sit in a resentful hunch in the bedclothes. I let her
tell it to the headboard. I let her tell it to my packed
underpants and her own coat.

The rich noble takes them through the kitchens,
outside, to the silos behind his house, and he says,
"Here are my storehouses, built to feed my kin
when famine comes. I have enough grain and oil to
feed my whole household for seven years. No matter
how poor the harvest, those I love will be fat
and fed."

Ganesha rushes into it, wild, stuffing all the bags
and jars and crates into his mouth, swallowing all
that he sees, until there is not so much as a grain of
rice left on the dirt floor.

"Still hungry!" Ganesha bellows.

Kubato is beginning to feel desperate, but his pride is so great, he says, "See this fertile field? I own it. I own every field, in all directions, all the rice and the grasslands where the lambs are grazing, and the forests full of game, and every river. I even own the sea and all the fish in it."

So Ganesha opens his wide mouth—

"That's not how it goes," I tell my mother. She is stretching it out, adding another layer. Before Ganesha eats up all the storehouse grain, Kubato is supposed to cry and quail and beg Parvati to help him, lest he be forever ruined. Then Parvati takes the fruit and crackers from her basket, and feeds Ganesha a bite from her own hand. He is sated at once, and curls up in her arms and goes to sleep.

"Shh, I'm telling it," Kai says, weaving in the doorway.

"I know this story," I tell her. "Give Ganesha the cracker and let me go to bed."

"He doesn't get the cracker," Kai says. Belligerent. "You don't know every end of every story."

So Ganesha opens his wide mouth, and begins to swallow up the farmlands and the forests, slurping up all the lakes and rivers, and when they are dry he begins to suck the salty brine out of the ocean, washing down all the fish and squid and kelp.

Even as he eats, he's moaning, "Oh, I'm hungry. Oh, I'm hungry!"

"Give him the fucking cracker, Kai," I tell her, throwing back the sheet and climbing out of bed. I stand before her, furious, in my camisole and underpants.

"Ganesha ate the whole world up, and all the people, up, he ate them," Kai says. She's lost the rhythm of it. "The rich man was all naked in space, floating, and he said, 'You see that sun? That sun is my own mango. I could bite it open if I wanted to.'"

"That's not even the same story," I say, almost yelling now. "Hanuman tries to eat the sun like a mango, not Ganesha!" But she is talking over me.

"So Ganesha bit the sun in half and ate all halves, and still he's hungry, and he ate Saturn."

Now she's just making shit up.

Tomorrow's clothes are draped over my footboard. I grab the jeans. "Where's Parvati, huh? She hasn't even said the world was too rich, and Ganesha already ate it." I sit on the edge of my single bed just long enough to yank my jeans on. "She didn't even turn down a bite of the sun. Maybe the sun's too buttery for her, huh? You skipped that. You're drunk, and you lost Parvati."

"Ganesha ate her ass already," Kai says, and then laughs. A slurry, drunk laugh, while I root under the bed to find my clogs. She takes a fast, mad drag, then talks through smoke. "He ate up his own mother, and the rich guy says, 'I don't even care about that sun. Space is fulla planets, I'll pick me out another.'"

I have my clogs on, and I shove past her, heading for the door.

"That's not how it goes," I mutter as I stomp out.

"Then Ganesha farted Saturn out, but he just re-ate it," Kai says. She's followed me into the den, and I hear her sloshing wine into a glass behind me.

I slam the door and walk off into the darkness. Out in the night, there's bound to be a boy who's waiting for me. There is always a boy waiting for me. Lots of them, actually, and all I have to do is choose. And be back by sunrise, so I can leave with William.

Kai is asleep when I get home. Or at least, her door is closed. Inside her room, it stays quiet. She sleeps through my leave-taking. She never got to give Ganesha that bite of fruit and cracker that sated him, that let him sleep. Now, she never will.

She will never say, *You didn't know,* or *You were just a kid,* much less own up to her part in our downfall. I will never say, *If you live a life shaped like a loaded gun, your kid is going to come along and shoot it,* and then forgive her anyway. She will never get to yell or cry or hit me or beg for mercy.

Like all true stories, my mother's ends midbeat. It has no moral, and no epilogue, and I don't believe in reincarnation. Any bird that shits on me or sings outside my window now is only that: a bird.

Time runs in only one direction, and I run with it, driving toward my little sister.

The foster mother, Mrs. Beale, lives on a narrow road clustered with tiny 1950s ranch homes. They are square and evenly placed, like rows of teeth. I look for the house that holds Hana. I am not a coward, but I'd pay my own hourly rate to have Birdwine here to back my play—double that for Julian. He is a people person and a natural smiler. Ye gods and little fishes, how he's worn me down and won me over. He's bounced and wept and hugged his way into the middle of my life, until his physical proximity is a pleasure as invisible as Henry's. He will do the same with Hana, I have little doubt. But not today. Today, I am going alone, into a situation that does not play to my strengths.

Hana's therapist thinks that this is how we should begin, given that Hana thought she was an only child a week ago. Julian and I can empathize with that; we do not want to overwhelm her. It's me instead of Julian because I knew the mother she lost. Also, her first decade on the earth looked a lot like my own freewheeling, Kai-centric childhood. Dr. Patel says Hana is open to meeting us. She's only been with Mrs. Beale for a few months, and she's been grieving. She's not deeply embedded where she is.

I am to be warm but not pushy, Dr. Patel told me on the phone. Be polite. Be interested. Don't initiate physical contact. Engage the kid, and let her come to me.

This is my preferred approach in any case; I'm a cat person. But it's good to have my instincts confirmed, and it was good for Julian to hear all this. He may yet need an intensive ten-steps-leading-up-to-hugging workshop before we phase him in.

I see the house, number 115, ahead on the right. This redbrick saltine box with black shutters and white trim is the closest thing Hana has to home territory. She has a room here, at any rate. She has a door, and the right to close it behind her. There's a bright coat of fresh paint working hard to spruce up the sagging porch.

Three people are sitting on the porch swing, Hana between two adults. She doesn't look much different from the picture taken back in the winter. I've never met the other two, but age and ethnicity tell me Dr. Patel is to Hana's left, and Mrs. Beale is on the right.

Hana is slumped in a podgy little hunch. Her hands are clasped in her lap, and her legs are crossed at the ankles. Her feet do not touch the ground.

Her expression is blank and demure, but this girl and I, we have the same shape mouth. I recognize the way she's set it, like she's got a ball of mutiny in there, and she is rolling it around to get a thorough taste. She's not half as placid as she looks. My spine prickles.

She glances at the car and then back at her hands, fast. I can feel my own mouth reshaping itself to match hers. This expression feels familiar. I know this face. I wore it exclusively for weeks, when I first arrived at the group home. I was half girl, half crustacean, impenetrable. It doesn't bode well.

Early days, I tell myself. No one has said this will be easy.

My hands are hot and sweaty on the wheel. I turn the car off, and I blow on my palms to cool them. I've faced down rabid lawyers, angry judges, juries predisposed to hate me, and stayed as bland and warm as fresh boiled custard. Hell, I've faced down crazy-ass Clark Winkley and a gun. Yet now my hands are wringing wet and shaking. I rub them fast down my jeans; no spooky black suits today. I'm wearing flats and my favorite shirt, a pumpkin-colored knit thing that is pilled and soft with age. My hair is tethered in a loose braid, and I've painted on a friendly rose-pink mouth.

Dr. Patel stands up when my engine cuts out. She's younger than I would have guessed based on the calm, low voice. She has a long, earnest ponytail, and her body language says she isn't anxious. That's going to be useful. Mrs. Beale looks like central casting sent over a white gramma type. She is generically kindly looking, from her soft gray bun to her brown orthopedic shoes. She puts a bracing hand on Hana's shoulder as I get out, and I like her for it.

Hana stays seated, staring intensely at her hands, which have begun to twist and squeeze each other as I come up the walk.

Mrs. Beale stands, pulling Hana with her. Hana scowls, her gaze still down. She's in a yellow dress, sprigged with flowers, and the color's not doing her olive complexion any favors. She slouches, poking out her rounded tummy. She's close to outgrowing this dress. The skirt is well above the knee, and her legs are skinny with knobby knees.

As I reach the stairs, Mrs. Beale steps forward with a hand out, about to speak, but as she focuses on my face she stops. She looks puzzled for half a heartbeat, then she visibly blanches and recoils.

"Holy shit!" she says.

Shocking, coming out of that mouth. It is a sweet and elderly little mouth, crumpling in on itself, with her coral lipstick leaking into the wrinkles. The therapist and I both do a double take.

Hana stares up at Mrs. Beale, too, then follows her stunned line of sight to me.

"Hello," I say. Hana's eyes, very like my mother's, are as disconcerting in her rounded face as they were in Julian's the first time that I saw him. Now they widen and go blank with shock. Her mouth falls open. "I'm Paula Vauss."

Hana's Kai-style eyes have welled with tears.

"No, you're not," she says. Her voice is soft and scratchy, as if she had a cold last week and is not quite recovered. But then two fat tears spill out, tumbling down both cheeks in tandem, and I realize her voice is breaking because she's crying. "You're Kali," she tells me. "You're Kali, and you're real."

Then she is bounding toward me, and I barely have time to get my arms out of the way as she hurtles down the porch stairs and slams into my body. Her face smashes into my sternum, her arms wind tight around me, and my own arms enfold her of their own volition.

"Excuse me," her foster mother says, blushing deep crimson. "It's just—you really are real."

The therapist looks from Mrs. Beale to me, and then she says, "Holy shit," too, very softly.

I can't answer at all. Something is happening to me. Or no, maybe it has already happened. It started when Hana's body came so violently to mine. It's animal and strange, how I can feel the shape, my own shape from long ago, her shape right now, imprinting itself on my legs and belly.

I feel wetness, her tears and snot leaking through the knit to coat my skin, and it is as if I am holding a piece of me. It *is* me, and yet it is external, and itself. It has its own breath and heartbeat, but her biology is so entwined with mine in this endless moment, I cannot tell where she ends and I start, where my history leaves off and hers begins.

"You're real," she says, a little muffled because her face is pressed against me. "Mama said. Mama told me you were real."

"Bet your ass I'm real," I whisper, trying to understand this thing she's done to me. She's stepped right in and owned me, and yet, it does not feel like surrender. There is choice inside surrender. This is something much more basic.

Over her dark head, I lock eyes with Mrs. Beale first, and then the therapist, still wearing their matching dumbfounded expressions.

"Come in and see," Mrs. Beale says. "You have to see this."

Hana releases me, but somehow my hand has found hers. We are separate, yet not. Our clasped hands are a cord running between us as she half pulls, half leads me inside. We pass through a den that died and got embalmed way back in 1987, down a dingy hallway, past a pink-tiled bathroom.

Then Hana throws a door open, and we are in a small room at the back of the house. She finally lets my hand go, almost embarrassed now, and my hand feels cold and oddly naked. I can still feel the shape of her hand in mine, but we are separated now, into our own selves.

"This is where I sleep," she says.

She isn't crying anymore. So this is her room, and her sheets have simple flowers on them. This is her room, and I am all over it. My face papers the walls. I see at least fifty of me, me from every angle, my face atop my long, tall body. I am taped and thumbtacked from floor to ceiling, framing the bed and dresser, covering the closet door.

I see myself on horseback, on cloudback, dressed in bones, dressed in a sari. I see all my expressions—I am enraged and in love and sad and joyful and forty more things in between. I am flying and fighting and laughing and dancing. In some pictures, I am my copper-colored self, and in some I am cerulean or navy. Sometimes I have two arms, sometimes four or six, and in one, I have an uncountable suggestion of a thousand arms, lined up one behind the other.

Kai has drawn me for Hana, over and over. Not recently, either. Or at least, not only recently. Some of the pictures of me are so old, the paper is yellowed and cracking at the edges. The colors are faded or smudged.

"Mama said that we were traveling to find you," Hana whispers. She is looking at all the mes on the wall. "But she was sick . . ."

I'm still spinning round, now recognizing that Ganesha is all over, too: round belly, elephant head, since Kai couldn't know what Julian would look like. I touch a picture of him on his mouse, the saddle fading red in colored pencil, and I tell Hana, "He is real, too." Kai is here as well. As Sita, as Parvati, as her own self, dancing in a long silk skirt of sunshine colors.

Near the headboard, I see one of the newer pictures. My face on a Kali dressed in bells. I sit on a white hilltop, dandelion spores caught in my dark hair. Beside me sits a little monkey. A little monkey with my sister's face.

"'Kali Fights the Red Seed,'" I say, and I hear Hana's breath come out in a sigh.

"You know that story?"

I turn to her. "I do. I know a lot of Kali stories, and Ganesha tales, and even a few of Hanuman's stories. I bet you know some I don't, though. I bet I know some that will be new to you." Hana's eyes are wide and bright, her nose red from crying. I realize Mrs. Beale has moved down the hallway, out of sight. Dr. Patel has backed up as well. She is leaning in the doorway, giving us a little room. "You want me to tell you one?"

Hana shrugs, but she sits down on the bed, and her knees are angled toward me.

I sit down, too, far at the other end. She is recontained inside herself, but the set of her mouth has softened, and something has begun. It happened in that moment when her weight landed on my belly and her tears wet my skin. I can't see the future, but it has already started.

In a few weeks, we will drive Kai's reclaimed ashes up to Clay Creek in north Georgia, all three of us, and release her to the falls. Julian will want her interred, but Hana and I convince him better. Kai will never rest if she's not moving.

In a few months, I will for the first time in my life put up a Christmas tree, because Julian wants it so badly, and because Hana will be curious; she's never had one. In two years I will see her side-eyeing my

426 · JOSHILYN JACKSON

body, running her hands worriedly across her own, and I will tell her, *Oh, that's just your puppy tummy, pretty girl. You'll use it later on to make some boobies,* and she will blush and tell me to shut up.

In five years I will hear her crying in her bed, very late, and I will leave my husband's warm and sleeping body to curl myself around her, and she will sob and ask why Jamie doesn't like her anymore. Ten months later, I'll pull her drunk ass out of the middle of a party and ground her for the rest of her life. *I hate you,* she will scream, and I'll scream back, *You're welcome.* Then I'll hold her hair while she throws up.

In eight years, Julian will help her write her college essays. In a brief sixteen, I will still have the ass to pull off pegged tuxedo pants; I'll wear them to walk her down the aisle of that little Boho church she's so attached to, and I should have seen that coming when I let in Christmas.

When the preacher asks, *Who gives this woman?* I will dutifully say my line:

Her brother and I do.

It will be a lie. I will never give her away, not to anyone. She will always have the center of my heart.

But I can't see that from here. I only feel that something has already started, as we sit at opposite ends of a twin bed, our knees untouching but angled toward each other. All around us are the shared stories that have formed our lives.

"A story. Let me think. Do you want one you know? Or a new one?" I ask her. I look from picture to picture. I know most of these. I heard them or I lived them.

Hana peeks at me and then away. She shrugs, like she doesn't care one way or another. But then she says, "Maybe one I don't know."

I think about it. "How about one from when I was little?"

"How little?" she asks.

"Very. Much littler than you, so it's a story that happened a long time ago, but it's still happening now." She sparks to the words, the cadence of a ritual we both know. These words remind us that we have budded from the same strange vine. She leans in toward me, a little closer, without even realizing she's doing it. "It's the story of how I got my name. If I tell you, will you tell me how you got yours?"

She considers the offer, and then she says, "Tell me."

A long time ago, right now, I was born, I say to my little sister.

I was born blue.

Acknowledgments

I want to thank you, first, Person Who Bought This Book. Because of you, I have a job I love. Because of you, the people in my head get to live outside of it. When I meet you, you talk about my characters as if they are old friends (or enemies) we have in common; I cannot explain how miraculous this feels. If you are one of those people who have put my books into the hands of other readers—either professionally as a god-called lunatic who loves books so much you hand-sell them or as a reader who picked one for book club or gave it to your best friend for a birthday—well. This book exists because of you. I hope you are happy about this. I am—happy and grateful and a little bit in love with you.

A wise, keen-eyed editor is a gift, so I owe my wonderful agent, Jacques de Spoelberch, an extra thank-you note for connecting me with Carolyn Marino. She is a Book Person down to the bone. I am lucky, lucky, lucky to be with her at William Morrow, where amazing folks like Liate Stehlik, Lynn Grady, Jennifer Hart, Emily Krump, Tavia Kowalchuk, Mary Beth Thomas, Carla Parker, Rachel Levenberg, Tobly McSmith, Kelly Rudolph, Chloe Moffett, and Ashley Marudas have this book's back.

Three years ago, I started taking classes at Decatur Hot Yoga from the beautiful and excessively bendy Astrid Santana. She often begins class by retelling a classic Hindu god pantheon story, but her sentence structure and word choices and even some images come out of southern oral tradition. It is an odd and compelling blend. Because of Astrid, I started dreaming the stories, and then I began reading them. Paula and Kali intersected in my head, and the novel took a sharp turn east. I gave Astrid's waterfall of long, dark hair and her smiling, crescent-shaped eyes to the character of Kai—if only Kai were half as kind and generous!

"I AM NEVER WRITING ABOUT YOU PEOPLE AGAIN! And by *you people*, I mean lawyers," I wailed to litigator Sally Fox as I struggled with the threads of legal tangle in this book. She combed them out with endless patience over cocktails at Paper Plane, and I came to admire her as a person as well as a professional. She is a doe-eyed redhead, pretty and petite, and she will eat your liver raw on behalf of her clients. She hooked me up with Constancia Davis and Markeith Wilson, a pair of criminal lawyers who helped me plan my characters' various crimes. Anyone eavesdropping on us at lunch is probably in therapy now.

Social worker Sarah Smith has been working with foster kids for years, and she came through the system when she was a minor. She was an invaluable source of information and ideas; I am grateful for her time and expertise, and I sleep a little better, knowing that some of the foster kids here in Atlanta have such a loving, warmhearted, courageous advocate on their side.

Sarah and all three lawyers know their stuff—any stupid mistakes are mine.

My community of writers makes me better and braver. I love them, even when they viciously make me cut a thousand precious, special-snowflake words. Especially then, actually. I list them in the order that I met them: Lydia "Knit, Ride, Dog" Netzer, Jill "the Medicine" James, Anna Schachner, either Sara Gruen and Karen Abbott or Karen Abbott and Sara Gruen (depending on who is telling that story), Caryn Karmatz Rudy, Reid Jensen, Alison Law, and the Reverend Doctor Jake Myers.

Thank you, beautiful family, for supporting me. If I am wings, you get all windsy; if I am a broken sorrow-puddle, you are gentle mops. I love you, Scott, Sam, Maisy Jane, Bob, Betty, Bobby, Julie, Daniel, Erin Virginia, Jane, and Allison.

Endless gratitude for the support and acceptance and grace I find at my big tent faith community at First Baptist Church Decatur. I would be a sadder, colder, meaner, scareder person and writer without it, and without the small communities that have formed me over the last decade and a half: Slanted Sidewalk, small group, STK, and the Fringe. Shalom, y'all.

HARPER LUXE

THE NEW LUXURY IN READING

We hope you enjoyed reading
our new, comfortable print size and found it
an experience you would like to repeat.

Well — you're in luck!

HarperLuxe offers the finest in fiction and
nonfiction books in this same larger print size and
paperback format. Light and easy to read, HarperLuxe
paperbacks are for book lovers who want to see
what they are reading without the strain.

For a full listing of titles and
new releases to come, please visit our website:

www.HarperLuxe.com